Date Due

JE 16 '92			
MY 29 '97			
MY 2			
JE 6 07			

CHELSEA HOUSE PUBLISHERS
Modern Critical Views

HENRY ADAMS
EDWARD ALBEE
A. R. AMMONS
MATTHEW ARNOLD
JOHN ASHBERY
W. H. AUDEN
JANE AUSTEN
JAMES BALDWIN
CHARLES BAUDELAIRE
SAMUEL BECKETT
SAUL BELLOW
THE BIBLE
ELIZABETH BISHOP
WILLIAM BLAKE
JORGE LUIS BORGES
ELIZABETH BOWEN
BERTOLT BRECHT
THE BRONTËS
ROBERT BROWNING
ANTHONY BURGESS
GEORGE GORDON, LORD BYRON
THOMAS CARLYLE
LEWIS CARROLL
WILLA CATHER
CERVANTES
GEOFFREY CHAUCER
KATE CHOPIN
SAMUEL TAYLOR COLERIDGE
JOSEPH CONRAD
CONTEMPORARY POETS
HART CRANE
STEPHEN CRANE
DANTE
CHARLES DICKENS
EMILY DICKINSON
JOHN DONNE & THE
   17th-CENTURY POETS
ELIZABETHAN DRAMATISTS
THEODORE DREISER
JOHN DRYDEN
GEORGE ELIOT
T. S. ELIOT
RALPH ELLISON
RALPH WALDO EMERSON
WILLIAM FAULKNER
HENRY FIELDING
F. SCOTT FITZGERALD
GUSTAVE FLAUBERT
E. M. FORSTER
SIGMUND FREUD
ROBERT FROST

ROBERT GRAVES
GRAHAM GREENE
THOMAS HARDY
NATHANIEL HAWTHORNE
WILLIAM HAZLITT
SEAMUS HEANEY
ERNEST HEMINGWAY
GEOFFREY HILL
FRIEDRICH HÖLDERLIN
HOMER
GERARD MANLEY HOPKINS
WILLIAM DEAN HOWELLS
ZORA NEALE HURSTON
HENRY JAMES
SAMUEL JOHNSON
BEN JONSON
JAMES JOYCE
FRANZ KAFKA
JOHN KEATS
RUDYARD KIPLING
D. H. LAWRENCE
JOHN LE CARRÉ
URSULA K. LE GUIN
DORIS LESSING
SINCLAIR LEWIS
ROBERT LOWELL
NORMAN MAILER
BERNARD MALAMUD
THOMAS MANN
CHRISTOPHER MARLOWE
CARSON MCCULLERS
HERMAN MELVILLE
JAMES MERRILL
ARTHUR MILLER
JOHN MILTON
EUGENIO MONTALE
MARIANNE MOORE
IRIS MURDOCH
VLADIMIR NABOKOV
JOYCE CAROL OATES
SEAN O'CASEY
FLANNERY O'CONNOR
EUGENE O'NEILL
GEORGE ORWELL
CYNTHIA OZICK
WALTER PATER
WALKER PERCY
HAROLD PINTER
PLATO
EDGAR ALLAN POE

POETS OF SENSIBILITY &
   THE SUBLIME
ALEXANDER POPE
KATHERINE ANNE PORTER
EZRA POUND
PRE-RAPHAELITE POETS
MARCEL PROUST
THOMAS PYNCHON
ARTHUR RIMBAUD
THEODORE ROETHKE
PHILIP ROTH
JOHN RUSKIN
J. D. SALINGER
GERSHOM SCHOLEM
WILLIAM SHAKESPEARE (3 vols.)
   HISTORIES & POEMS
   COMEDIES
   TRAGEDIES
GEORGE BERNARD SHAW
MARY WOLLSTONECRAFT SHELLEY
PERCY BYSSHE SHELLEY
EDMUND SPENSER
GERTRUDE STEIN
JOHN STEINBECK
LAURENCE STERNE
WALLACE STEVENS
TOM STOPPARD
JONATHAN SWIFT
ALFRED LORD TENNYSON
WILLIAM MAKEPEACE THACKERAY
HENRY DAVID THOREAU
LEO TOLSTOI
ANTHONY TROLLOPE
MARK TWAIN
JOHN UPDIKE
GORE VIDAL
VIRGIL
ROBERT PENN WARREN
EVELYN WAUGH
EUDORA WELTY
NATHANAEL WEST
EDITH WHARTON
WALT WHITMAN
OSCAR WILDE
TENNESSEE WILLIAMS
WILLIAM CARLOS WILLIAMS
THOMAS WOLFE
VIRGINIA WOOLF
WILLIAM WORDSWORTH
RICHARD WRIGHT
WILLIAM BUTLER YEATS

Further titles in preparation.

Modern Critical Views

BERNARD MALAMUD

Modern Critical Views

BERNARD MALAMUD

Edited with an introduction by

Harold Bloom

Sterling Professor of the Humanities
Yale University

1986
CHELSEA HOUSE PUBLISHERS
New York
New Haven   Philadelphia

PROJECT EDITORS: Emily Bestler, James Uebbing
ASSOCIATE EDITOR: Maria Behan
EDITORIAL COORDINATOR: Karyn Gullen Browne
EDITORIAL STAFF: Perry King, Bert Yaeger
DESIGN: Susan Lusk

Cover by Robin Peterson

Printed and bound in the United States of America

Library of Congress Cataloging in Publication Data

Bernard Malamud.
    (Modern critical views)
    Bibliography: p.
    Includes index.
    Summary: A collection of critical essays on Malamud
and his works. Also includes a chronology of events
in his life.
    1. Malamud, Bernard—Criticism and interpretation—
Addresses, essays, lectures. [1. Malamud, Bernard—
Criticism and interpretations—Addresses, essays,
lectures. 2. American literature—History and
criticism]   I. Bloom, Harold.   II. Series.
PS3563.A4Z55   1986   813'.54   85–26893
ISBN 0–87754–674–6

Chelsea House Publishers
Harold Steinberg, Chairman and Publisher
Susan Lusk, Vice President
A Division of Chelsea House Educational Communications, Inc.
133 Christopher Street, New York, NY 10014

Contents

Editor's Note

This volume brings together what, in its editor's judgment, is the best criticism available, up to this time, of the fiction of Bernard Malamud. It is arranged here according to the chronological order of its publication.

The editor's "Introduction" centers upon the vexed question of the Jewishness of Malamud's fiction, with particular attention to *The Fixer* and *The Tenants*. Ihab Hassan's early commentary on *The Assistant* begins the chronological sequence of the criticism, and helps to provide a matrix for distinctions drawn by later readers. John Hollander, another early apprehender, reviews *A New Life* with a prophetic sense of what was to come in Malamud. A third pioneering view is expressed in Alfred Kazin's review of *The Magic Barrel* (1958), with its shrewd suggestion that Dostoevsky is both close and distant as an aura in Malamud's work.

With Jonathan Baumbach's essay on "the economy of love" in Malamud, we are given a first synoptic overview, with the three initial novels surveyed: *The Natural* (1952), *The Assistant* (1957) and *A New Life* (1961). A review by Herbert Leibowitz of *Idiots First* (1963) introduces Fidelman, whom I would suppose to be Malamud's central man. F. W. Dupee, observing Malamud through *Idiots First*, pays Malamud the compliment of applying to his work the great Jamesian trope "the madness of art."

The next essay, by the noted Romantic scholar Earl R. Wasserman, though it deals with the first novel, *The Natural*, can be regarded as the single best and most influential critique that Malamud has received down to the present moment. Wasserman demonstrates that *The Natural* is "the broad formulation of Malamud's world of meaning," the basis for all the subsequent books. In some sense, whether they have read him or not, critics after Wasserman write about Malamud in Wasserman's wake and tradition.

V. S. Pritchett's review of *The Fixer* (1966) commends the book as fable, "unexpected, inventive, and compelling." The focus moves next to the stories (which may be Malamud's strongest achievement), with Sidney Richman's comprehensive survey, and then back to the first four novels, read here as four versions of pastoral by James M. Mellard. In Alan Warren Friedman's full-scale analysis of *The Fixer*, the trope of the scapegoat prominently reappears, confirming Wasserman's general version of Malamud. A different emphasis appears in Tony Tanner's brilliant reading of the design of Malamud's fables, a design Tanner persuasively insists is essentially comic. Yet another perspective is manifested in Allen Guttmann's suggestion that Malamud's true argument is on behalf of Jewish peoplehood, a suggestion closely related to the way in which Ruth R. Wisse reads Fidelman as a waning version of the Jewish schlemiel tradition.

A very different kind of criticism is represented by Robert Ducharme on Fidelman, whom he sees as the artist in hell, not the Jew in limbo. Mark Shechner, reviewing *Dubin's Lives* (1979), tries to reach a wholly new concept of just what the Jewish element in Malamud's work might be. Confronting the disaster of *God's Grace* (1982), Robert Alter gracefully but strongly relates the book to the most dubious elements in *The Tenants*, (1971), a book which becomes the object of Alvin B. Kernan's subtle analysis of how Malamud deliberately chooses to batter that highly vulnerable object, the literary text. In this volume's final essay, Sam B. Girgus provides us with a provisional valediction that implicitly praises Malamud, for all his psychic rendings and undoings, as a firm moral guide to Gentiles and Jews alike who are in search of the real America.

Introduction

Malamud is perhaps the purest story teller since Leskov. I read on always to learn what will come next, and usually in at least faint dread of what may happen. The dreadful in Malamud is *not* what already has happened, not at least until the horrible final page of *The Tenants*. Perhaps the sense of impending dread, even in the comic mode, is one of the genuinely negative Jewish qualities that Malamud's work possesses. "Every Jew is a meteorologist" says the Israeli humorist Kishon, and certainly Malamud's creatures live in their sense that lightning bolts will need to be dodged.

The Jewishness of Malamud's fiction has been a puzzle from the start, as his better critics always indicated. Malamud's vision is personal, original, and almost wholly unrelated to the most characteristic or normative Jewish thought and tradition. As for Malamud's style, it too is a peculiar (and dazzling) invention. It may give off the aura of Yiddish to readers who do not know the language, but to anyone who spoke and studied Yiddish as a child, the accents of memory emerge from the pages of *Herzog* but not of *The Fixer*. Malamud's idiom, like his stance, is a beautiful and usurping achievement of the imagination. His triumph is to have given us Malamud, and somehow then compelled us to think, as we read, how Jewish it all seems. I can summon up no contemporary writer who suffers less from the anxiety-of-influence, whose books are less concerned to answer the self-crippling question: "Is there anything left to be done?" Like his own first hero, he is a Natural.

Yet having said this, I become uneasy, for the truth here must be more complex. When I think back over Malamud, I remember first stories like "The Jewbird" and "The Magic Barrel," and it seems ridiculous to call such stories anything but Jewish. Malamud's most impressive novel remains *The Fixer*, which is essentially a premonitory vision of a time that the Russian Jews might all too easily enter again. Perhaps in reading Malamud as an extravagantly vivid expressionist whose art seduces us into a redefinition of Jewishness, we in fact are misreading him. A pure enough storyteller, in Jewish tradition, ultimately tells not a story but the truth, and the burden of *The Fixer* and *The Tenants* may yet prove to be the burden of the valley of vision. It may be time to read Malamud as a modest but genuine version of prophecy.

Critical accounts of Malamud tend to diverge widely. Thus Harold Fisch, in his *The Dual Image*, a brief but packed survey on the figure of the Jew as both noble and ignoble in English and American literature, sees the theme of *The Fixer* as "the experience of victimization in general." But to Allen Guttmann the theme is the very different one of "the responsibilities of peoplehood." Robert Alter finds the probable balance: "Though to be a Jew in this novel does involve a general moral stance, it also means being involved in the fate of a particular people, actively identifying with its history." The most hopeful view is that of Ruth R. Wisse, in a fine monograph on *The Schlemiel As Modern Hero*, which sees Bok's acceptance of his imprisonment as "the crucial moment of initiation" and can even speak of "the liberating effects of imprisonment."

But Yakov Bok is recalcitrant to all these views, which might be summed up best in Alter's notion that in Malamud the fundamental metaphor for Jewishness is imprisonment, imprisonment being "a general image for the moral life with all its imponderable obstacles to spontaneous self-fulfillment." If I understand Alter, imprisonment in this wide sense equals civilization and its discontents, and all sublimation thus becomes a kind of incarceration. This is ingenious, but threatens a diffusion of meaning that few storytellers could survive.

Malamud-on-Malamud has been more than a touch misleading, and his critics have suffered by following him. If being Jewish were simply the right combination of suffering and moralism, and nothing more, then all people indeed would be Jews, when their lives were considered under those aspects alone. *The Assistant* encourages such a reading, but is a very unformed book compared to *The Fixer* and *The Tenants*. Though Yakov Bok's covenant is ostensibly only with himself, it is with himself as representative of all other Jews, and so might as well be with God. And where there is covenant, and trust in covenant, which is what sustains Bok at the end, there is the Jewish as opposed to any Christian idea of faith. Bok is, as all the critics have seen, a terribly ordinary man, yet his endurance becomes extraordinary in his refusal to implicate all Jews in the "crime" of ritual murder. Though the process of hardening his will is what makes Bok a Jew, and only *initially* despite himself, I cannot agree with Alter that Bok becomes a Jew in Malamud's special sense, rather than in the traditional sense. Alter may be right in discerning Malamud's intentions, but the storyteller's power breaks through those intentions and joins Bok to a strength greater than his own simplicity could hope to give him. If part of Bok's birthright as a Jew is being vulnerable to history's worst errors, there is another part, a tempering of the will that turns Bok against time's injustices, and makes of this simple man a rebel against history, like so many of his people:

> As for history, Yakov thought, there are ways to reverse it. What the Tsar deserves is a bullet in the gut. Better him than us. . . . Death to the anti-Semites! Long live revolution! Long live liberty!

In context, as the end of Bok's evolution from a solitary fixer, scarcely Jewish, wholly without a sense of community, this has considerable force, of a kind previously unsuspected in Malamud. With the grim strength of *The Tenants* now known to us, it is possible to see retrospectively that Malamud underwent a change in *The Fixer*. His private vision of Jewishness was absorbed by a more historical understanding of a phenomenon too large to be affected by individual invention. Added to this, I suspect, came a more historicized dread than had been operative in the earlier Malamud.

Coming together in *The Tenants* are elements from the story "Black is My Favorite Color" and a number of themes from the Fidelman saga, including the destroyed manuscript. Lesser, the obsessed Jewish writer, desperate to finish his book, which is about love, is swept up into a dance-of-death with the black writer Willie Spearmint. The dance takes place in a tenement ready for demolition, from which Lesser declines to move. For Lesser writes only by rewriting, a revisionary constantly swerving away from himself, and he cannot bear to leave the scene of his book's birth until he is willing to call it complete. But an end is more than he can stand. It will be, if ever done, his third novel, but Lesser has worked on it for nine and a half years, and is now thirty-six and still unmarried. Lesser's deepest obsession is that he has never really told the truth, but in fact he is addicted to truth-telling

Spearmint, archetypal Black Writer, wishing to be "the best Soul Writer," but balked in creation, persuades Lesser to read his manuscript. The rest is disaster, or as Lesser says towards the end: "Who's hiring Willie Spearmint to be my dybbuk?" But each becomes the other's dybbuk. Intending only the truth of art, Lesser destroys Spearmint's self-confidence in his writing, and compounds the destruction by falling in love with Spearmint's Jewish girl friend, and taking her away from her black lover. Spearmint retaliates by destroying the manuscript of Lesser's nearly complete novel. Tied to one another by a hatred transcending everything else, the two writers stalk one another in the ruined tenement, Spearmint with a saber, Lesser with an ax, like the hideous death-duel in the Hall of Spiders between Swelter and Flay in Mervyn Peake's *Titus Groan*. The title of Lesser's destroyed novel about love was *The Promised End,* with the epigraph, also from *King Lear:* "Who is it that can tell me who I am?" The Fool's reply to Lear's bitter question is: "Lear's shadow," and Spearmint is Lesser's shadow, his cabalistic Other Side. When Lear, at the close, enters with the dead Cordelia in his arms, Kent says: "Is this the promised end?" and Edgar adds: "Or image of that horror?" I suppose Malamud wants us to ask the same as his novel ends:

> Neither of them could see the other but sensed where he stood. Each heard himself scarcely breathing.
> "Bloodsuckin Jew Niggerhater."
> "Anti-Semitic Ape."
> Their metal glinted in hidden light. . . . They aimed at each other accurate blows. Lesser felt his jagged ax sink through bone and brain as the groaning black's razor-sharp saber, in a single boiling stabbing slash, cut the white's balls from the rest of him.
> Each, thought the writer, feels the anguish of the other.

Whether as parable or as prophecy, *The Tenants* holds together, all one thing, a unity dependent upon Lesser's love of the truth (which for him is the novelist's art) over love itself. Ultimately, Lesser loves only the Book, and when Levenspiel, the landlord who wants him out, sarcastically asks, ". . . what are you writing, the Holy Bible?" Lesser comes back with, "Who can say? Who really knows?" In the parallel obsession of Spearmint, which the black writer is at last unable to sustain, a troubling reflection of Lesser's zeal is meant to haunt us. *The Tenants,* like Bellow's *Mr. Sammler's Planet,* is Jewish wisdom literature, and perhaps both books lose as fictions what they gain as parables.

IHAB HASSAN

The Qualified Encounter

In Bernard Malamud we find further testimony that the urban Jewish writer, like the Southern novelist, has emerged from the tragic underground of culture as a true spokesman of mid-century America. It may be difficult to classify Malamud in the scheme which Fiedler devised for Jewish authors of the last two decades: Bellow (highbrow), Salinger (upper middlebrow), Shaw (middle middlebrow), and Wouk (low middlebrow). If Malamud does not possess the intellectual vitality of Bellow, his finest work shows an order of excellence no critic—however beetling or elevated his brow—can justly deny. The first and most obvious quality of his fiction is its "goodness." This is a complex quality, compounded of irony, trust, and craft—a touch of Dostoyevsky and Chagall, someone observed. It is the product of a sensitive yet enduring heart, vulnerable where it counts, and deeply responsible to its feeling of what transforms a man into *mensch*. Behind it is a wry vision of pain, and also of hope. We are not surprised, therefore, to hear Malamud say that "Jews are absolutely the very *stuff* of drama," or that the purpose of the writer is "to keep civilization from destroying itself"; or that much of current fiction is "underselling Man." But these pronouncements, which may express the natural bent of a man reared virtuously among immigrants in Brooklyn, do not explain the subtleties of his craft. Malamud's vision is preeminently moral, yet his form is sly. It owes something to the wile of Yiddish folklore, the ambiguous irony of the Jewish joke. Pain twisted into humor twists humor back into pain. The starkness of suffering, the leaden weight of ignorance or poverty, the alienation of the Jew in a land of jostling

From *Radical Innocence: Studies in the Contemporary Novel.* Copyright © 1961 by Princeton University Press.

Gentiles—all these become transmuted, in luminous metaphors and strange rhythms, into forms a little quaint or ludicrous, a bittersweet irony of life, into something, finally, elusive.

His first novel, *The Natural*, 1952, is a bizarre, authentic, troubled work about a thirty-three-year-old baseball player who suddenly emerges from painful oblivion into the crazy light of fame and big league corruption. The snappy slang of sport and gloomy language of the soul are fused in an allegorical tale which probes deep into the meaning of personal integrity but fails ultimately to make itself comprehensible. His collection of short stories, *The Magic Barrel*, 1958, includes some of his worst and best fiction. The poorer pieces are usually set broad; the best deal with native Jewish material and have in common with his second novel, *The Assistant*, 1957, a blazing poetic insight into the daily aches and indignities of man which add up, somehow, to a kind of nobility, a form of aspiration.

The Assistant, presumably, is a love story, a domestic romance, a grocery store idyll of unwarranted poverty and harsh spiritual deprivation. It is a tale of loneliness, of lifelong frustrations and delicate, budding hopes. It is a "human" story albeit deeply ironic. For irony is indeed the key to Malamud's attitude toward man, to his estimate of him. The irony is not "dry," not scathing; it is best described by Earl Rovit when he says, "The affectionate insult and the wry self-depreciation are parts of the same ironic vision which values one's self and mankind as both less and more than they seem to be worth, at one and the same time." This is the ambivalence of vision which qualifies, sometimes even undercuts, the affirmative power of Malamud's fiction.

The world revealed by *The Assistant* is, materially speaking, bleak; morally, it glows with a faint, constant light. Morris Bober and his wife, Ida, toil sixteen hours a day in a grocery store, barely eking out a living. They are well past middle age, and have given up their lives, their illusions, even the promise of a richer future which comes with education for their single daughter, Helen. The store, as we are told many times, is an open tomb. Twenty-one years are spent in it, and in the end Bober dies of double pneumonia, leaving his family penniless; he has to be buried in one of those huge anonymous cemeteries in Queens. America! "He had hoped for much in America and got little. And because of him Helen and Ida had less. He had defrauded them, he and the blood-sucking store." This is what Bober thinks as one of two men who hold up his store slugs him on the head, because he is a Jew, and Bober falls to the ground without a cry. An appropriate ending to his weary, profitless day. Others may have luck, like the affluent Karp who owns a liquor store across the street, or the Earls whose son, Nat, attends law school—and takes Helen's virginity. But the

Bobers live on stolidly, honestly, in squalor and sickening destitution. They are, like the grocery "assistant," Frank Alpine, victims of circumstance. What, then, gives these characters the measure of spiritual freedom they still possess?

The nature of the characters themselves holds the answer. Morris Bober, to be sure, is another example of the *eiron*, the humble man. He is more. He has endurance, the power to accept suffering without yielding to the hebetude which years of pain induce. He is acquainted with the tragic qualities of life—"The word suffer. *He* felt every schmerz"—and he defines the Jew as a suffering man with a good heart, one who reconciles himself to agony, not because he wants to be agonized, as Frank suggests, but for the sake of the Law—the Hebraic ideal of virtue. Yet this is only one source of Bober's strength. His other source is charity, which in his case becomes nearly quixotic. Bober, though close to starvation himself, extends credit to his poor customers. He wakes up every day before dawn so that he may sell a three-cent roll to a Polish woman on her way to work. He takes in Frank Alpine, feeds him, and gives him an opportunity to redeem himself, though Frank begins by stealing the grocer's bread and milk. Nor can he bring himself, in the extremity of despair, to burn down his property in order to collect insurance. Inured to failure, Bober still strives to give suffering the dignity of men who may trust one another in their common woe. But Karp calls him a "schlimozel."

The central action of the novel, however, develops from Bober's relation to Frank Alpine, and from the latter's relation to Helen. Frank, as the title suggests, is probably the hero of the book. He, too, is an *eiron*, a collector of injustices—with a difference. The regeneration of Frank— his literal and symbolic conversion to the Jewish faith—is the true theme of the book. His regeneration, at best, is a strange and mixed thing. When Frank first appears, he is a wanderer, an anti-Semite, even a thief. Yet one of his idols is St. Francis, and his hardened face conceals a hungry soul. "With me one wrong thing leads to another and it ends in a trap. I want the moon so all I get is cheese," he tells Bober. The grocery store, which is Bober's grave, becomes a cave or haven for Alpine. It also becomes the dreary locus of his painful rebirth. Impelled by his gratitude to the grocer, and motivated by his guilt at having robbed him, with the aid of tough Ward Minogue, Frank puts all his energies into the store and ends by pumping some of his own obstinate life into the dying business. Meanwhile, he falls in love with Helen Bober.

From here on, ambiguities prevail. The racial prejudices of Frank are matched by those of Ida Bober, and to some extent, of her daughter Helen, against Gentiles. (The store improves, it is suggested, precisely because Frank is not a Jew.) Frank's gratitude to Morris does not prevent him from continuing to steal petty cash from the register—which he keeps account of and intends to return. Yet when Bober is incapacitated by sickness, Frank takes a night job, in addition to his grocery chores, and secretly puts his pay in the cash box. And his gnawing love for Helen, which she is slow to return, finally ends, ironically, with an act of near-rape as he rescues her from the clutches of Ward Minogue, only to force her himself, right there and then in the park, at the very moment in their relationship when she is at last ready to surrender herself freely to him. "Dog," she cries "—uncircumcised dog!" Guilt, gratitude, love—perhaps even the hope of a life he could glimpse but never attain—combined to sustain Frank Alpine, Bober's strange, saintly, pilfering assistant, in his impossible struggle against poverty, against hopelessness itself.

> He wanted her but the facts made a terrible construction. They were Jews and he was not. If he started going out with Helen her mother would throw a double fit and Morris another. And Helen made him feel, from the way she carried herself, even when she seemed most lonely, that she had plans for something big in her life—nobody like F. Alpine. He had nothing, a backbreaking past, had committed a crime against her old man, and in spite of his touchy conscience, was stealing from him too. How complicated could impossible get?

> He saw only one way of squeezing through the stone knot; start by shoveling out the load he was carrying around in his mind. . . .

> So the confession had to come first. . . . He felt he had known this, in some frightful way, a long time before he went into the store, before he had met Minogue, or even come east; that he had really known all his life he would sometime, through throat blistered with shame, his eyes in the dirt, have to tell some poor son of a bitch that he was the one who had hurt or betrayed him. This thought had lived in him with claws; or like a thirst he could never spit out, a repulsive need to get out of his system all that had happened—for whatever had happened had happened wrong; to clean it out of his self and bring in a little peace, a little order; to change the beginning, beginning with the past that always stupendously stank up the now—to change his life before the smell of it suffocated him.

Purgation in humility, rebirth through love—this is Frank's inchoate purpose, the reason for his willing acceptance of a backbreaking burden others—Minogue, Karp—find easy to reject. Yet it is in consonance with the character of the novel that purgation and rebirth both should appear ironic, awkward, and inconclusive. Frank tells Bober about his complicity in the robbery only to discover that the latter already knows. Bober catches his assistant rifling his till just when Frank had resolved never to steal again. And Frank's attempt to make a clean breast of it all to Helen merely serves to confirm her revulsion. His dogged and desperate love expresses itself in the form of a physical outrage. The Savior of the Bobers is, in a sense, their archenemy. (The symbolic inversion of this relation may be discovered in the burial scene in which Frank topples accidentally into Bober's open grave.) But enemies suffer too, according to their conscience. Frank Alpine, it seems, can only expend the last vestige of his money, energy, or hope in agonized silence, a prey to the ironies which rip and twist his purpose. In the end, the value of confession is to the soul that makes it. And even love is a kind of realized solitude. Like Frank, Helen goes her lonely way, carrying the broken dreams of the Bobers to some distant and uncompromising end.

It is obvious that if the world of *The Assistant* is not drained of values, it is nevertheless saturated with pain, flooded with contradictions. Its two major characters find their identity in humiliation, an extreme and quixotic sense of obligation. They are not tragic heroes but merely heroes of irony. They retreat before the ultimate tragic ordeal: the fullness of tragic awareness itself. This is a fact the form of the novel supports.

Time, we know, leaves the characters suspended in the void which their failures create; the hints of regeneration are barely audible. Morris Bober dies in bankruptcy; Helen continues at her dreary job, dreaming of a better life; Frank slaves at the store, trying to provide for the Bobers, send Helen to college, and win back her love. The fate of each remains less than what it could be in heroic tragedy, less even than what it usually amounts to in realistic fiction. Thus, for instance, does Helen evaluate the life of her father: "People liked him, but who can admire a man passing his life in such a store? He buried himself in it; he didn't have the imagination to know what he was missing. He made himself a victim. He could, with a little more courage, have been more than he was." And thus does Frank reflect upon his incessant labors: " 'Jesus,' he said 'why am I killing myself so?' He gave himself many unhappy answers, the best being that while he was doing this he was doing nothing worse." Whatever awareness time brings to the characters, whatever qualified dignity it confers upon their failures, every act in the novel is whittled by irony, every motive is mixed with its opposite.

Because time cannot unravel the knotted relations of the characters—what could be more gnarled than the relation of Gentile to Jew, of savior, seducer, and thief to those upon whom he preys, those from whom he gains an identity—the point of view of *The Assistant* dissociates itself from the protagonists, veering toward one then the other in friendly detachment. The characters are simply there, and they criticize each other's behavior; the point of view encourages us to perceive how ludicrous pain can be, and how unhappy virtue. The subtle, incredible twists of the plot, the reversals and accidents which affect the fortunes of the Bobers, are finally envisioned in a moral as well as dramatic perspective which acknowledges no certainties except the fact of suffering. (It is appropriate that Morris Bober should be an unorthodox Jew, and that at his funeral the rabbi should say, "Yes, Morris Bober was to me a true Jew because he lived in the Jewish experience, and with the Jewish heart. . . . He suffered, he endured, but with hope.")

The achievement of Malamud's style, which survives his ironic play, lies in the author's capacity to convey both hope and agony in the rhythms of Yiddish speech.

"I think I will shovel the snow," he told Ida at lunch-time.
"Go better to sleep."
"It ain't nice for the customers."
"What customers—who needs them?"
"People can't walk in such high snow," he argued.
"Wait, tomorrow it will be melted."
"It's Sunday, it don't look so nice for the goyim that they go to church."
Her voice had an edge in it. "You want to catch pneumonia, Morris?"
"It's spring," he murmured.

There is a Hemingway cleanness in this dialogue, a kind of humility and courage, but also a softness Hemingway never strove to communicate.

Morris, however, does catch pneumonia and die. Nor can the poetry of the style persuade us to forget that the search of Frank Alpine for an identity ends, in the last, brief paragraph of the novel, with the ritual of circumcision. The act is one of self-purification, of initiation too, in Frank's case, but it is also an act of self-repudiation, if not, as some may be tempted to say, of symbolic castration.

JOHN HOLLANDER

To Find the Westward Path

Easterners have used up many versions of the American Far West. Fact, historians' hypothesis, entrepreneurial dream; repository of Kitsch mythologies; a coast, mostly; a vast ideological blur, ranging from Southern California, an allegory of Inauthenticity, through San Francisco, a Real City, to the vaguer reaches of the healthy North: the whole expanse seemingly christened after the author of *Miss Lonelyhearts*. But now jets have tied it to New York, academic empires have spawned, San Francisco has invented avant-garde literature and Caligula Hollywood died and has been deified as a cherished dream. Sociological, moral and sexual frontiers have long since bleached out the significance of the historical one, and for some time the West has seemed to be unusable for the American imagination, having become so, perhaps, while the South was seizing its title to The Other Place.

But in Mr. Malamud's latest novel [*A New Life*] we are given a new vision. "My God, the West!" exclaims his hero at the beginning of the book; it is a Pacific North-west, a world of geniality and frankness at which Levin has arrived to start teaching at the agricultural and engineering branch of a state university (not, as he had innocently supposed before getting there, at the central campus itself). It is the gradual decay of that world which the book unfolds. A garden of promise where simplicity seems to have been purchased only at the expense of crowding and desperation falls to an American reality where local political battles can seem to be mental fight and where sexual fulfillment passes as the only morally authentic enterprise. In the opening sentence we see "S. Levin, formerly a

From *Partisan Review*, vol. 29 (Winter 1962). Copyright © 1961 by *Partisan Review*.

drunkard, after a long and tiring transcontinental journey" getting off a train to confront a disarming hospitality, nice people with funny names, and an almost emblematically hopeful landscape. By the end of the book, after the fable-like anonymity of "S. Levin" has become the "Sy" that his academic colleagues call him and the "Lev" of his girl, experience ejects him into a real world cleared of any visionary gleam. And the garden of paradise has become a National Park. As he sets off for a real new life at last, with a newly acquired family and no concrete plans for a future, he is able to read correctly the allegory of the landscape:

> Levin drove to the edge of town for a last look at the mountains. The clouds were a clash of horses and volcanoes.
> "Beautiful country."
> "If beauty isn't all that happens."

Life has, of course, happened, and the "new life" of the title can now be known to dawn only in the heart. But at the beginning of the story, the West does indeed appear to be a *Morgenland* of renewal, just as, traditionally, spaciousness of scene seems to mean Possibility. As we first see it, the new life is an innocently modest version of the American Dream. Levin has come west from high-school teaching and personal despair in New York to what he hopes will be the first of the steps to a Parnassus of worth and accomplishment. Levin is not the typical, sophisticated exile from the Eastern graduate school who, to use an analogy from the world of Mr. Malamud's first novel, is being farmed out to a minor-league ball-club after serving as a bat-boy in the majors. He is uniquely capable of accepting the drudgery of four sections of freshman composition, the tears of co-eds and the parochial inanities of English Department politics with something more than passive tolerance. From this viewpoint, Mr. Malamud has been able to write what is among other things the best academic novel so far. Minor bureaucratic types, using the Academy as an alternative to either a Cloth to which no calling has come or a Management which seems to threaten, are reverently portrayed. Levin's sincerity and *engagement* throughout his attempt to keep faith with The Word by championing better textbooks and eventually running, in a mad way, for the chairmanship of his department, enable the author to treat what Dr. Johnson would have called the difference in size between a flea and a gnat without the cruelty of distant observation. Even though he is fired at the end of the year, Levin manages to institute some reforms.

But these can constitute no victory for him. Mr. Malamud never divides his hero's private world of love from a public one of affairs and decisions: Levin is by no means a C. P. Snow-bound man with *troubles* at home but *problems* to be faced around a conference table. His love affair with Pauline Gilley, the wife of a colleague, connects the realms of school and bed just as it helps to pour the pain of the old life into the shining cup of the new. It is only after that cup has been dissolved by its very contents that Levin can set out on what is truly a pioneering journey, his old Hudson sedan laden with impediments and responsibilities sexually incurred. This journey can finally move traditionally westward, at least in the sense that it rides heavily and dreamlessly, on creaking wheels, toward an unreceding future.

Admirers of Mr. Malamud's previous fiction will be interested in some new facets of his work which emerge in *A New Life*. The first of these is his splendid writing about sex. Ours is a time in which the description of lovemaking has become a literary convention, when "hot scenes" are almost mandatory in fiction with any pretensions to seriousness, and when there can occur the paradox of a novelist like Wright Morris, who writes all the more intensely, apparently, about the war between men and women by avoiding specificity in sexual description. It is thus reassuring to the spirit of literary realism to find Mr. Malamud using encounters in and out of bed so effectively and convincingly. Levin's women in the book include a co-ed with whom he has a dream-like, unreal weekend, a wonderfully funny pseudo-picaresque encounter with a waitress, in a barn, and, finally, the reality of his complicated and protracted affair with Pauline.

Another interesting question raised by his third novel is Mr. Malamud's treatment of Levin's Jewishness, which, in the reasonable air of North-western democracy, practically vanishes. He is thought of by everyone else in the book as an Easterner only. Even the glimpse we have of his family background shows us something different from any of the typical modes of Jewish life in America. Only at the end of the book does Pauline reveal to him that the crystallization of her love for him was catalyzed by his resemblance to a Jewish boy she had once known. Here again, it is almost as if the author were reacting against something more than the direction of his own earlier work, against a budding convention which has led to the trotting-out of even the most assimilated of Jewish middle-class backgrounds as a treasure-trove of Experience in college creative-writing courses. The character of Levin poses its author some problems, and while he has not gone so far with an uneasily-willed *persona* as Saul Bellow with Henderson or Norman Mailer with O'Shaughnessy, there seem to be some inconsistencies of identification and fictional distance between Mr. Malamud and his protagonist.

A *New Life* may, however, represent Mr. Malamud's attempt to break out of a limited, almost regional area of performance in which, like such different writers as Flannery O'Connor and J. F. Powers, he has been most successful. One may have to have been an academic to like his latest novel as much as I did; I hope not. But its new version of an old American pastoral encounter redeems it from the provinces of any smaller genre. It is a unique kind of book, and for its author's future work, it promises excellent results.

ALFRED KAZIN

The Magic and the Dread

The stories of Bernard Malamud are a striking example of the opportunities—and hazards—that are faced these days by "minority" writers who have rejected special pleading in favor of modern art. Writers like Ralph Ellison and James Baldwin are no longer tempted to sing the chain-gang blues once favored by Negro writers in this country; originals like Saul Bellow, Daniel Fuchs, and Bernard Malamud are not likely to retrace the kind of sentimental or aggressive pathos that has afflicted so many recorders of Jewish experience in this country, from Fannie Hurst to Michael Gold—a style that has found its last haven in the Hollywood of Irwin Shaw and other nostalgic readers of PM.

The newer writers (who seem "new" not because they are young but because it has taken them so long to climb out of the depression and war and to discover themselves as individuals) have turned their backs on what James Baldwin has jeeringly called "everybody's protest novel"—Uncle Tom, the Negro or the Jewish Christ dead of American capitalism, the saintly victim. But agile and really gifted as these new writers are, they have been just as unwilling or unable as Jewish and Negro writers always have been to let their experience alone, to describe it as something that may be valued for its own sake. It is here that one sees the peculiar nemesis of writers who feel that they can fit themselves to American life only by trying to give universal meaning to each piece of their experience.

The patron saint of these writers is always Dostoevsky—the supreme example of the novelist whose characters must always search for meaning, who cannot for a moment allow life to exist without scrutinizing intervention. But where Dostoevsky had equal ability to embody the emptiness and sloth of nineteenth-century Russia, these new American writers itch with symbolism. They have been exposed so continually to modern literature and modern art that they find it hard to find their way back to what Herbert Gold has called the lesson of Blazac's "stupidity." Although these writers have produced a peculiarly penetrating kind of fiction, haunting as well as haunted, there is a certain overeagerness in them all to stand and deliver, to be freed of certain painful experiences through the ritualistic catharsis of modern symbolism. The Jewish or Negro writer, far from being mired in his personal pathos as of yore, is now so aware that his experience is "universal" that he tends to escape out of his particular experience itself, to end up in the great American sky of abstractions.

Of all these new writers, Bernard Malamud seems to me the most unnecessarily tempted by symbolism. For he is the most compassionate, the most concerned and involved of them all, and whenever I turn back to the best scenes in his fine novel, *The Assistant*, or to the little masterpiece about a rabbinical student in search of a wife who went to a marriage broker (the title story of this collection [*The Magic Barrel*]), I get something of the same deep satisfaction that I do from the great realistic masters of Yiddish literature.

Malamud's world has its own haunting archetypes: the desperate and sickly storekeeper, the refugee who turns up in Rome or New York to accuse his fellow Jews of heartlessness, the lonely student with ovoid eyes in staring search of love, the American intellectual abroad who finds it impossible to escape his Jewish past. The scene is always the down-at-heels grocery, the winter street, the irreversible hardness of the modern city. Malamud has caught as one the guttural toughness of big-city speech and the classic bitterness of Jewish dialogue. The remarkable story "Take Pity" contains the typical situation of all his work—a great love condemned to ineffectuality. A man who has committted suicide so that he can leave all his property to a widow who always refused to accept him during his lifetime sits in the other world telling a "census-taker" (his name is Davidov) how the woman's husband died. "Broke in him something. . . ." "Broke what?" "Broke what breaks. He was talking to me how bitter was his life, and he touched me on my sleeve to say something else, but the next minute his face got small and he fell down dead, the wife screaming, the little girls crying that it made in my heart pain. I am myself a sick man and when I saw him laying on the floor, I said to myself, 'Rosen, say goodbye, this guy is finished.' So I said it."

This is the talk of people who are not merely on edge but who really live on the edge. Their tense expressiveness is one of the cultural symbols of the Jews, in art as in religion; just as the great Rabbi Hillel could be challenged to give the whole meaning of the Law while standing on one foot, so there is a Doomsday terseness to Jewish speech—as if the book of life were about to close shut with a bang. Malamud has caught this quality with an intimacy of understanding that is utterly remarkable. But in their terseness, his characters fundamentally express despair rather than any spiritual refusal of the great world. His world is all too much an inner world—one in which the city streets, the houses, the stores, seem, along with the people who broodingly stand about like skeletons, some with flesh, always just about to fold up, to disappear into the sky. People talk to each other disbelievingly, as if each felt that the other was about to disappear, as if the world under their feet were itself unreal. People flit in and out of each other's lives like bad dreams.

It is a curious, almost uncanny transformation of the old Jewish mysticism, where earth is so close to heaven—or to hell—that the super-natural and the trivial jostle each other. From the historic standpoint of Jewish theology, of the seemingly incredible Jewish experience itself, every-thing is entirely real. Life is always strange and God always moves in unpredictable ways. In Malamud's stories everything real becomes unreal; we are under the sign not of theology but of surrealism. Sometimes this is unbearably effective; but when the symbols become too explicit, as in "The Lady of the Lake" or "Angel Levine," Malamud's own tone is undecided between the mysterious and the silly. In "The Mourners," an old man, suffering for the guilt of having deserted his family years back, is about to be evicted; the landlord is driven half mad trying to get the dirty old man out of the tenement. The old man begins mourning for him, the landlord, as dead—he is spiritually dead—and the landlord, staring in unbelief, is engulfed in the sudden upsurge of his own shame and becomes a mourner too. The symbolism here is not only explicit, it is positively allegorical. And indeed, Malamud explains, in his Hawthornesque touches, why Haw-thorne and symbolist novelists like Kafka so often read alike.

But Malamud is at his best in those stories which depend not on surprise but on the moment of ungovernable human feeling. In "The Loan," an old friend turns up in a baker's shop to ask for a loan—to pay for a headstone for his wife's grave. The baker's wife, his *second* wife, steadfastly refuses to countenance the loan, and at the end of the story the two friends, each bereft in his own way, "pressed mouths together and parted forever." In the title story, Malamud's usual attempt to escape "realism" is brilliantly, triumphantly justified. It is the marriage broker's own daughter whom the rabbinical student falls in love with, from a photograph, and at the end of the story the ambiguities of life and death are so close that one has the sense of being caught in a dream. Life is never very solid for these Jews, these people "who live on air"; they are always on the verge of saying good-by and departing for the other world.

The otherworldly feeling in the great Jewish writers of the past was supported by a conviction that earth and heaven are connected. Malamud captures the strangeness of Jewish experience brilliantly, but he relies on compassion, not on the covenant. He is so concerned with the dread, the flimsiness of the human material in our age, that he has to outwit his own possible sentimentality. This, as I see it, is why he so often turns to symbolic endings, goes through his material so quickly. The result is that while this book seems to me masterful and indescribably haunting, it is surprising to note, when one closes it, how many of the people fade indistinguishably into each other. What remains in the reader's mind is not a world, *the* world, but the spectral Jew in his beggarly clothes—always ready to take flight.

It is an extraordinary fact that although the great Yiddish writers in Czarist Russia could not call the country their own, they gave the earth of Russia, the old village, a solid reality, as if it were all the world they had left to cherish, like the Jewish graveyard that is lovingly kept up even when the houses decay. Malamud, the closest in wit and depth of feeling to the great Yiddish writers, nevertheless falls into the same abstractness that is the bane of so many new writers in America. Unlike those who are abstract because they have only their cleverness to write from, Malamud is abstract out of despair: despair of the world itself, which can no longer be represented.

In this one sees the curious danger of the American writer who has been influenced by Kafka, Joyce, Eliot, *et al.* Life in America changes so quickly, and people are so quick to change into each other, that the everlasting thinness and abstractness of American writing, which comes from our lack of "society," of a solid core of leaders, manners, tradition, is likely to be intensified by our new writers, who have a society but don't believe in it enough to describe it—to deal with it not merely as it is but as something that *is*. One of the things we now long for in contemporary literature is escape from the tyranny of symbolic "meaning." We want to return to life not as a figure in the carpet but as life in its beautiful and inexpressible materiality—life as the gift that it actually is rather than as the "material" that we try to remake.

Malamud provokes these reflections because he is so gifted. There seems to me no writer of his background who comes so close to the bone of human feeling, who makes one feel so keenly the enigmatic quality of life. The only thing I miss in his work is a feeling for the value of life, for the body of this world—for that which cannot be explained because it is too precious to turn into symbols.

JONATHAN BAUMBACH

The Economy of Love

Without heroes, we're all plain people and don't know
how far we can go.

—from *The Natural*

Anglophiles and Jacobites notwith-
standing, the English novel of manners has never been congenial with us.
The main tradition of the American novel, if such a freewheeling form
can be said to have one, is founded on that ambiguity that Richard Chase
calls the "romance." In *The American Novel and Its Tradition*, Chase, referring to Cooper, Melville, and Hawthorne, defines romance as

> an assumed freedom from the ordinary novelistic requirements of verisi-
> militude, development and continuity; a tendency toward melodrama and
> idyl; a more or less formal abstractness, and, on the other hand, a tendency
> to plunge into the underside of consciousness. . . .

I quote Chase's definition here because, with certain modifications, it also
describes the concerns of some of our best recent fiction. One thinks immediately of *The Natural, Henderson the Rain King, Other Voices, Other
Rooms, Barbary Shore, Wise Blood, Set This House on Fire, The Fable,* and
Invisible Man as novels having, more or less, the qualities ascribed to the
romance tradition. Since 1945 the serious American novel has moved away
from naturalism and the social scene to explore the underside of consciousness (the heart of darkness), delineating in its various ways the burden and
ambivalence of personal responsibility in a world which accommodates

From *The Kenyon Review* 3, vol. 25 (Summer 1963). Copyright © 1963 by Kenyon College.

evil—that nightmare landscape we all inhabit. Perhaps more than any of his contemporaries, Bernard Malamud, in his fables of defeated love and failed ambition, has extended the tradition of the American romance-novel, has made the form into something uniquely and significantly his own. A moral fabler and fantasist, Malamud writes of the conflicting demands of the inner and outer worlds of his heroes, of the tremulous private life confronted by a mythic public scene. Unlike many contemporary writers of allegorical fiction, Malamud is aware that, if a novel is to function as novel, it must deal first of all with human experience; otherwise the symbols are merely window dressings in a vacant store. Malamud's fiction delineates the broken dreams and private griefs of the spirit, the needs of the heart, the pain of loss, the economy of love.

A romantic, Malamud writes of heroes; a realist, he writes of their defeats. In our serious arts as in our popular sports, we demand heroes, men who break records, enact our wildest fantasies, write great novels. And when we discover, as we must, that our heroes are, after all, fallible, we are disenchanted and pillory them for having failed us, for not having transcended the defects of our own poor humanity. In crucifying our heroes, we create after the fact our saints. And this in part is the subject of Malamud's three novels: *The Natural* (1952), *The Assistant* (1957), and, last and least, *A New Life* (1961). The rest is love. Love is the redemptive grace in Malamud's fiction, the highest good. Defeat of love is the tragedy. Love rejected, love misplaced, love betrayed, loveless lust: these are the main evils in Malamud's fictional world where (in contrast to Flannery O'Connor's) a good man is not too hard to find. Yet the world, for all its potential goodness, is not good, and the good man, the man capable of love, is inevitably the sufferer, the sacrifice, the saint.

A New Life is to Malamud's career what *The Adventures of Augie March* on a larger scale was to Bellow's, a breaking away from the airlessness and intensity of his two earlier novels, an attempt to extend the range of his concerns beyond the impulse of his talent. Whereas the worlds of *The Natural* and *The Assistant* are vaguely indicated, have a kind of mythic placelessness, the setting of *A New Life*—Cascadia College in the Pacific Northwest—is obviously a real one. *A New Life* is a new form, a demi-picaresque in which the hero, S. Levin, wanders quixotically through a series of comic misadventures, all taking place in the provincial (micro-cosmic) community of Cascadia College. Levin, "reformed drunkard" and New Yorker, unreformed romantic, comes west (to the land of innocence) to remake his life—he has grown a beard—and to teach freshman composition. A typical Malamud hero, Levin (at thirty) has been a failure all his life and the trip west, the job at Cascadia, constitute a romantic attempt to reverse the pattern of his fate, to escape the stigma of his past, to become nothing less than a new man. In the terms of the novel's melodrama, the instructorship at Cascadia is a first and last chance for Levin to succeed at "the career of his choice." Inevitably, he fails; in Malamud's universe, fate is irreversible. Yet, in the context of the novel, defeat becomes a triumph: Levin rediscovers in his failure the best of himself, the lesson of his old life.

He discovers himself by discovering what he is not. The men on the faculty at Cascadia, who represent the kind of life Levin wants ultimately for himself, disillusion him in one way or another, with one curious exception: Duffy, the failure he has replaced, a man he never meets. The first Levin hears of his predecessor, "the disagreeable radical" who left Cascadia "publicly disgraced," is when Gilley, the Director of Composition, assigns him Duffy's former office. Later, informing Levin of his duties, the Department Chairman (Fairchild) is instinctively reminded of Duffy and warns the new instructor to avoid the pathetic fate of his predecessor—"a broken man, the shadow of himself, quickly abandoned by all." If Levin is to succeed in his new life, Duffy is absolutely not the man for him to emulate, yet Levin is attracted despite himself to the mysterious circumstances of Duffy's career, and goes out of his way to uncover the mystery. Uncompromising with principle and the needs of the heart, Levin gradually discovers that he has been following Duffy's life, error by error, as though it were the predestined pattern of his own. Levin uncovers the secret of Duffy's past by reliving it.

It soon becomes apparent that A New Life has two separate and distinct concerns which, for all of Malamud's matchmaking, never quite come together. As social realism, the novel is a satire on a kind of monolithic land grant college which offers everything its students *need* except the Humanities—the needs of mind and spirit. The satire is occasionally pointed, but even at its best it is second-rate Malamud; and only as plot device is it relevant to the world of Levin's inner life—the real subject of the novel. As psychological fantasy ("romance"), A New Life deals mainly with Levin's double search for self and love and his guilt-ridden affair with Pauline Gilley, the wife of the man who has given him his job. A refugee from the tenements of New York, Levin is romantically enamored of the country, touched by its beauty and mystery. When, in a magical scene, Pauline offers herself to Levin in the woods, Malamud's hero achieves momentarily the fulfillment of his romantic quest—the pastoral idyl—which is the ultimate promise in our literature of the trip west. "He was throughout conscious of the marvel of it—in the open forest, nothing less, what triumph!" Prompted by Pauline's questions about his life, Levin tells her the secret of his past, of how, sick with despair, an alcoholic on the verge of suicide, he had a revelation which convinced him to go on living:

> But one morning in somebody's filthy cellar, I awoke under burlap bags and saw my rotted shoes on a broken chair. They were lit in dim sunlight from a shaft or window. I stared at the chair, it looked like a painting, a thing with a value of its own. . . . Then I thought, Levin, if you were dead there would be no light on your shoes in this cellar. I came to believe what I had often wanted to, that life is holy. I then became a man of principle.

Levin's revelation of the sacredness of life is a discovery of God and by implication the discovery (or illusion) of this own sacred destiny as "a man of principle." When he finishes telling about himself, Pauline says cryptically, "I sensed it. I knew who you were." What she means, of course, is not only that Levin corresponds to her dream image of him but that their destinies are interrelated, that he has come to Cascadia to be, in some way, her savior. At this point, Levin is content being merely her lover.

When the affair with Pauline continues, Levin, the "man of principle," becomes aware of the ambivalence of his idyl; in achieving love (a good), he is betraying Gilley, a man who befriended him when he needed a friend. Levin's melodramatic dilemma is clearly defined: what takes priority in a world of isolation, loss, and pain—love or principle? Malamud resolves this conflict by diminishing Gilley out of existence, by making him so totally despicable that Levin's betrayal of him seems no more than just retribution. That Levin wants desperately to succeed in his new career presents a further complication. He knows that if his relationship with Pauline is discovered he will be summarily fired. To make matters even more difficult for himself, as a "man of principle" he has quixotically committed himself to fighting for certain needed reforms in the college. Malamud's universe is perversely whimsical; it grants boons but tarnishes them in the process; no gain is without loss.

Love is sacred in this universe; if life is holy, love is a holy of holies. At the end of the novel, Levin achieves a kind of unsought heroism in sacrificing his career for the *principle* of love, a love in itself dead, a memory beyond feeling. Accepting responsibility for having once been in love with Pauline, Levin agrees to marry her, to take on the burden of her two sickly children, which also means—Gilley's blackmail demand—that he must give up hope of teaching in a college again. The knowledge of Duffy's death (Duffy also loved Pauline) further influences Levin's decision. In leaving

Cascadia with Pauline and her two adopted children, he is fulfilling an implicit commitment to Duffy, who has been the example of his behavior. In completing the broken pattern of Duffy's life, Levin redeems his spiritual father's failure. Thus, Levin's act of heroism becomes, in another context, an act of love.

The quality of this heroism is defined in his last confrontation with Gilley. When, as a favor to Pauline, Levin asks her rejected husband for custody of the children, Gilley responds by pointing out to his successor the prohibitive drawbacks of marrying a chronically discontented woman and of assuming responsibility for a ready-made family. When Levin, against all logic, seems bent on going through with his decision, Gilley is amazed:

> "An older woman than yourself and not dependable, plus two adopted kids, no choice of yours, no job or promise of one, and other assorted headaches. Why take that load on yourself?"
> "Because I can, you son of a bitch."

A New Life is principally about Levin's heroic destiny: his discovery of what it is and his acceptance of what it entails. The other characters, with the possible exception of Pauline (and Gilley at the end), are caricatures and stereotypes, part of the allegorical landscape of Levin's quest. Malamud is at his best in this curiously flawed novel in illuminating Levin himself—the underside of his consciousness, the arena of his dark, hallucinated dreams, his war with the past and his uneasy peace with the future.

II

Each of the heroes of Malamud's novels undergoes a mythic journey to test the stuff of his heroism. Levin is partly successful; Pauline, barren all her life, is pregnant with his child at the end, a boon of the hero's triumph—the gift of life. However, in the attrition of his guilt-ridden affair with Pauline, Levin loses the ability to feel love, his victory diminished by his loss. The least promising of Malamud's heroes, Frank Alpine (*The Assistant*), is the most successful, renewing in his own spiritual rebirth the saintly life of his exemplary father. Conversely, the most gifted of Malamud's heroes, Roy Hobbs of *The Natural,* fails to fulfill his extraordinary potentialities, compromises with his principles, and is defeated by the retribution of fate. While Levin and Frank are redeemed through the commitment of love which makes possible their heroism (the momentary transcendence of their mortality), Roy Hobbs is destroyed by false love, compulsively sacrificing his destiny to the desire of the moment—"the expense of spirit in a waste of shame."

The least known of Malamud's work, *The Natural* is a curious combination: a serio-comic baseball fantasy in the tradition of "Alibi Ike," and an allegory about the Grail quest and the plight of the mythic Hero (with a thousand faces) in the modern world. The Grail hero, Roy Hobbs (linguistically, king rustic, an analogue of Percival), is a knight of knights, a noble clown, victimized by fate, defeated by circumstances beyond his power to anticipate or control, and yet, in some way, ultimately responsible for the facts of his existence. Hobbs (like Gatsby) is part Grail knight and part absurd, existential hero, whose goal—to be "the greatest in the game"— is only meaningful in terms of a perfect (romantic) commitment to an impossible dream.

An overreacher, Hobbs is struck down by fate for his presumption. En route from somewhere in the far west (the opposite of Levin's journey) to a tryout in the big city, Roy meets Harriet Bird, a beautiful, mad girl in black ("certainly a snappy goddess"), who seems to have a special interest in great athletes. The girl is cool to Roy until he demonstrates his supernatural ability—his identity as hero. In a two-man game (pitcher against batter) played on the side of the tracks during a mysterious train stop, Roy shows his stuff by striking out on three pitches the then American League's leading hitter, Walter (the Whammer) Wambold. As a tribute to Roy's deed and his boast ("I bet someday I'll break every record for throwing and hitting"), Harriet gives him the hero's reward, a silver bullet in the stomach, death to his presumptions:

> She pulled the trigger (thrum of bull fiddle). The bullet cut a silver line across the water. He sought with his bare hands to catch it, but it eluded him and, to his horror, bounced into his gut. . . . Fallen on one knee he groped for the bullet, sickened as it moved, and fell over as the forest flew upward, and she, making muted noises of triumph and despair, danced on her toes around the stricken hero.

When, in the second part of the novel, Roy Hobbs mysteriously reappears, (resurrected) fifteen years after his fatal wound, to play for the New York Knights (managed by Pop Fisher), who in a rainless season have lost a record number of games in a row, the scheme of Malamud's allegory becomes clear. Pop Fisher, an analogue of the legendary Fisher King, rules impotently over a cursed and barren team. It is the task of Roy, the potential Grail hero, to redeem Pop and his Knights (to break the "whammy" which has "jinxed the team") by bringing them the pennant. In *The Natural*, baseball superstition is escalated ironically into myth. Roy's first hit, in which he literally "knocks the cover off the ball," brings as its boon three days of continuous rain, magically ending the drought. Thereafter, the Knights' fortunes miraculously reverse themselves until they become the best team in the league, all but unbeatable. With the grail of the pennant in sight, Roy, deceived again by the temptation of false love, fails in his elected task. The past repeats itself and he relives his own destruction.

Malamud's baseball world is fluid and magical—the landscape of a dream. Characters from the first part of the novel, dead and half-forgotten, reappear in slightly different shapes, giving Roy, as hero manqué, the occasion to re-enact the failures of the past. Whammer, Sam, and Harriet in the first part of the novel correspond to Bump, Pop, and Memo Paris in the second. Like the Whammer fifteen years before, Bump is the league's leading hitter when Roy appears. Hearing Bump's voice for the first time ("a strong, rawboned voice, familiar from his boyhood"), Roy is reminded of the Whammer, only to recall that the Whammer has long since retired. It is also, Malamud suggests, the voice of Roy's father, further suggesting that the Whammer and Bump are intended as father-surrogates in the myth of the novel. And Roy, like Oedipus, like all of us, has a predilection for inadvertently slaying his fathers. In striking out the Whammer, Roy destroys the former slugger's confidence, brings an abrupt end to his career ("Dropping the bat, he trotted off to the train, an old man"). Similarly, Roy is indirectly responsible for Bump's death. His job threatened by Roy's presence on the team—they are both left fielders—Bump, attempting a heroic catch, crashes into the stadium wall, never to regain consciousness. After his death, Roy the bumpkin (the pun is Malamud's) replaces Bump as left fielder, and for awhile seems to the fans indistinguishable from his predecessor. Roy asserts his identity, finally, by being better than Bump, by being "the best in the game." The destruction of the father, however, that ultimate identification, is a prophecy of one's own destruction.

Though no one else blames him, Memo Paris, who was Bump's girl, holds Roy responsible for her lover's death. Vulnerable to the temptation of "snappy goddesses," Roy falls in love with the neurotically vindictive Memo—the conventional dark lady of myth and fiction. (In case the symbolism is unclear, Malamud lets us know that both Harriet and Memo remind Roy of his actual mother, a fallen woman who ruined his father's life.) Pop Fisher warns Roy of Memo: "She is unlucky and always has been and I think there is some kind of whammy in her that carries her luck to other people." A chronic victim of misplaced love, Roy, however, is fatally attracted to the personification of his unlucky fate. Inevitably, she brings about his downfall.

As Bump and Memo are counterparts of Whammer and Harriet, Pop Fisher is an avatar of Sam Simpson, the scout who, fifteen years before, had "discovered" Roy. At that time, Sam was bringing the hero to Chicago for a tryout in the hope that Roy's success ("he is more devoted to me than a son") would redeem his own failed career. Instead of saving Sam, Roy is the occasion of his death. Catching for the hero in his duel with the Whammer, Sam is knocked down by the third strike; he dies a few hours later, victim of his "son's" lethal fast ball. As spiritual father to Roy, Pop is also dependent on the hero for the renewal of his career. In a weak moment, the manager admits the extent of his fondness for his star player:

> "My boy, if you knew what you meant to me—"
> "Don't say it." Roy's throat was thick with excitement. "Wait till I get you the pennant."

The pennant, the grail of Malamud's allegory, is the ultimate gift of hero to Fisher-king (son to father), the renewal of life. When Roy comes to bat for the last time, with two out in the ninth inning, the tying run on third base, Pop pleads with the hero to "keep us alive." In the context of the novel, the myth grown large, winning the game (and pennant) is a matter of life and death. Though we never actually find out what happens to Pop after the pennant's loss, Roy, in failing, for all intents and purposes kills the old man.

Like Bellow's Henderson, Roy (a rain king in his own right) *wants* insatiably, which is at once the impulse of his heroism and the final cause of his defeat. A Malamudian hero, Roy is impelled by dreams of a noble future, of love and children, of the pastoral idyl of his childhood, and, at the same time, haunted by the nightmare awareness of their impossibility, of their irrevocable loss. A *naïf*, he corrupts his ideals by mistaking the occasion of their fulfillment. He rejects Iris Lemon, who loves him, for Memo Paris, and gets the American hero's reward—emasculation and defeat. Starved for Memo's love, Roy becomes a voracious eater in compensation. Playing on his weakness for her, the temptress plies the frustrated hero with huge quantities of food—a counterfeit of love (the analogue of Harriet Bird's bullet)—until Roy collapses with a "colosssal bellyache," a re-enactment of the past. With Roy disabled, his potency lost to the team, the Knights lose their remaining three games, and the pennant race, all but won, ends in a tie.

His ideal of himself compromised beyond repair, Roy accepts a bribe "to throw" the play-off game in order to win Memo by paying, in a double sense, her price. When he decides late in the game that he wants desperately to win ("the most important thing in his life"), it has become too late; he is magically unable to reverse his commitment to Memo. At a crucial point in the game, Wonderboy, Roy's marvelous bat (the symbolic sword of his potency), breaks in two. A further quirk of fate: Roy finds himself confronted in his last at bat by Herman Youngberry, the personification of his lost youth. The rookie relief pitcher, a twenty-year-old farm boy, strikes the hero out (as Roy had Whammer) on three straight pitches. Replaced by Youngberry, Roy is transformed momentarily from hero to scapegoat—a homiletic illustration of the tenuousness of fame. The hero's career completes its cycle. The baseball commissioner announces that, if the rumor of Roy's selling out is true (can Roy even deny it?), "he will be excluded from the game and all his records forever destroyed." This is the ultimate defeat for the natural, who had hoped (his dream of greatness) to live eternally in the record of his triumphs. Given the absurd context of the pennant race, Roy's failure is quixotic, a tragic joke on his romantic dreams and, since they are our dreams too, on all of us.

Though the mythic superstructure of Malamud's first novel is remarkably unobtrusive, expressed for the most part in felt experience, it seems, by the same token, somewhat gratuitous, a semi-private literary joke between author and academic reader. The Natural, as experience, is a wildly funny (and sad) baseball tale, informed by the fantasy of heroism and the nightmare frustration of defeat. Its pleasure is not in its allegory, though Sir Percival as baseball star is a witty idea, but in the hallucinated and idiomatic particulars of its narrative. Committed to its scheme, The Natural, on occasion, seems over-plotted; too much is governed by fortuitous circumstances in the guise of fate. At his worst, Malamud has a predilection for manipulating his characters in order to accommodate the anti-novelistic demands of his moral allegory. This is his major flaw, the vice of his virtue, and it mars to a lesser extent his brilliant second novel, The Assistant, one of the most concentrated and powerful works of fiction to come out of America since the Second World War.

III

The most Dostoevskian of Malamud's novels, The Assistant is about an ambivalent saint; a man who in seeking expiation for a crime succeeds only in increasing and intensifying the burden of his guilt. The hero, Frank Alpine, is congenitally and circumstantially unable to translate his good intentions into moral acts. However, at the end, racked by anguish and suffering, he finds the occasion to redeem his sins, electing to live the saint's life of the old man he has sinned against. *The Assistant* has two central biographies: the life and death of Morris Bober, unwitting saint, and the guilt and retribution of Frank Alpine, saint-elect, the first life creating the pattern and possibility of the second.

Morris Bober, the luckless owner of an unprofitable grocery store, is the center of the first half of the novel. That he is a Jew in a non-Jewish area, a commercial failure surrounded by success, an honorable man among thieves indicates his inescapable isolation—his exemplary role. At the opening of the novel, in a passage which has a kind of gnarled eloquence, Malamud defines the terms of Bober's existence:

> The early November street was dark though night had ended, but the wind, to the grocer's surprise, already clawed. It flung his apron into his face as he bent for the two milk cases at the curb. Morris Bober dragged the heavy boxes to the door, panting. A large brown bag of hard rolls stood in the doorway along with the sour-faced, gray-haired Polisheh huddled there, who wanted one.
> "What's the matter so late?"
> "Ten after six," said the grocer.
> "Is cold," she complained.
> Turning the key in the lock he let her in. Usually he lugged in the milk and lit the gas radiators, but the Polish woman was impatient. Morris poured the bag of rolls into a wire basket on the counter and found an unseeded one for her. Slicing it in halves, he wrapped it in white store paper. She tucked the roll into her cord market bag and left three pennies on the counter.

It is autumn on the calendar but already winter in Bober's world. The writing is empathic, evoking the burden of Morris' day-to-day reliefless existence. The old Polish woman is seen as Morris sees her, "a sour-faced, gray-haired Polisheh." She has no other identity because she has no other existence in the novel except as one of Morris' private ghosts. The routine of this morning, performed every morning for all the waking-suffering days of his life, is ritualistic—attrition by rote. To sell a three-cent roll, he must wake up and go out into the cold an hour earlier than he would otherwise. Though he is an old man, needing his rest more than the three pennies, he feels constrained to serve the dour old Polisheh out of an uncompromising sense of the responsibilities of his office. That he continues to serve her despite her chronic discontent is a part of his burden, his anonymous decency in an indecent and abusive world. Like the grocer in Malamud's short story "The Bill," Morris, despite his practical resolves, extends credit indiscriminately, even in cases where he knows payment is unimaginable.

If it is in his power to satisfy them, he will not ignore the needs of another human being. It is the least one man can do for another. He is therefore an easy mark, a victim of his own undiscriminating kindness. Like Roy Hobbs, he does not learn from the past; he continues to believe human beings are better than their actions; he continues, in spite of all the evidence of his suffering, to extend the grace of trust. Before the action of the novel begins, he has been thoroughly cheated by a man whom he has trusted as his partner; he has had his livelihood diminished by his "friend" Karp, who rents a store across the way to a rival grocer. His victimization is not limited to man's inhumanity but is compounded by the fates; he is a predestined, inexorable sufferer. His daughter Helen, who is a sufferer in her own right, contrasts her father's low estate to his successful neighbor Karp's:

> The grocer, on the other hand, had never altered his fortune, unless degrees of poverty meant alteration, for luck and he were, if not natural enemies, not good friends. He labored long hours, was the soul of honesty—he could not escape his honesty, it was bedrock; to cheat would cause an explosion in him, yet he trusted cheaters—coveted nobody's nothing and always got poorer. The harder he worked—his toil was a form of time devouring time—the less he seemed to have. He was Morris Bober and could be nobody more fortunate. With that name you had no sure sense of property, as if it were in your blood and history not to possess, or if by some miracle to own something, to do so on the verge of loss. At the end you were sixty and had less than at thirty. It was, she thought, surely a talent.

Karp's luck, as if parasitic, seems to improve only when someone else's (usually Morris') gets worse. When two men come to rob Karp's plush liquor store, they end up (as Morris' "talent" would have it) robbing and beating the impoverished grocer. Morris accepts even this unutterable indignity, as he has the long line of lesser ones preceding and anticipating it, with hopeless resignation and a sense of renewed guilt for his failure: "He fell without a cry. The end fitted the day. It was his luck, others had better." Though Morris survives, he is no longer the center of the novel's focus; he is replaced by Frank Alpine, one of the men who robbed his store. The old grocer's Job-like existence provides an anticipatory parallel and exemplar to Frank's penitential suffering and final conversion to Judaism.

Despite Frank's intense (actually religious) desire to do good, he is unable to resist the least admirable of his instincts. Out of acquiescence, he accompanies the degraded Ward Minogue (the son of a local policeman) when he holds up "the Jew's" grocery store. Guilt-ridden for his complicity in Ward's vicious treatment of the grocer, he haunts the area of the store, looking for an opportunity to redeem himself. He makes the occasion, insinuating himself as Morris' assistant without pay. He runs the store while the injured grocer recuperates, and manages through a combination of salesmanship and circumstance to increase the old man's income. Disturbed by his own apparent selflessness (and loss of identity), Frank begins to steal small amounts—negating one impulse by the other. He is not bad; it is only that he finds it prohibitively difficult to be as good as he would wish— a saint's good. This is the essential paradox of his existence: he means to do good, yet compulsively continues to do harm. Early in the novel, before we really know Frank, Malamud introduces us to his romantic admiration for St. Francis, whose pattern of life Frank unsuccessfully imitates. Over a cup of coffee, he passionately explains the saint's concerns to the indifferent candy store owner Sam Pearl:

> "For instance, he gave everything away that he owned, every cent, all his clothes off his back. He enjoyed to be poor. He said poverty was a queen and he loved her like she was a beautiful woman."
>
> Sam shook his head. "It ain't beautiful, kiddo. To be poor is dirty work."
>
> "Everytime I read about somebody like him I get a feeling inside of me I have to fight to keep from crying. He was born good, which is a talent if you have it."

Morris, too, has a talent for goodness, and in his abiding gentleness of spirit Frank senses an essential likeness to his patron saint. Though Frank's devotion to St. Francis as fable is wholehearted, he is ambivalent toward the same qualities in the here-and-now impoverished and suffering grocer. ("His pity leaks out of his pants, he thought, but he would get used to it.") Though repelled by Morris' indiscriminate compassion, Frank is attracted to the grocer's martyred existence. His motive for staying on to help the old man long after his debt of conscience has been repaid is to discover the mystery of Morris' virtue. He feels that Morris' Jewishness has something to do with the grocer's capacity for self-immolation. Frank asks him:

> "What I like to know is what is a Jew anyway?"
>
> Because he was ashamed of his meager education Morris was never comfortable with such questions, yet he felt he must answer.
>
> "My father used to say to be a Jew all you need is a good heart."

Pressed by Frank, Morris insists that it is the following of the Law, the Torah, which makes a Jew. A poor but bountiful man, Morris offers what little information he has. The Law, he tells the boy, means to do what is right, to be honest, to be good. This means to other people. Our life is hard enough. Why should we hurt somebody else? For everybody should be the best, not only for you or me. We ain't animals. This is why we need the Law. This is what a Jew believes.

Frank's quest is not so easily ended. In the terms in which Morris has defined Jewish law he recognizes the Christian doctrine which was taught him as a child. Yet there is a real difference between Jew and non-Jew which Frank has noticed, and he pursues his spiritual quest into a moment of imperfectly shared discovery:

"But tell me why is it that the Jews suffer so damn much, Morris? It seems to me they like to suffer, don't they?"

"Do you like to suffer? They suffer because they are Jews."

"That's what I mean, they suffer more than they have to."

"If you live, you suffer. Some people suffer more, but not because they want. But I think if a Jew don't suffer for the Law, he will suffer for nothing."

"What do you suffer for, Morris?" Frank said.

"I suffer for you," Morris said calmly.

Frank laid his knife down on the table. His mouth ached. "What do you mean?"

"I mean you suffer for me."

A prophet, Morris instinctively defines the nature and consequence of his relationship with Frank. At the end of the novel (after Morris' death), Frank becomes a Jew, not out of religious conviction but because he elects to be, like Morris, a good man; he elects to suffer for Morris, who has suffered and, in a sense, died for him.

Frank's relationship to Morris is as significant to the development of the novel's theme as his unfulfilled love affair with Helen is to the development of its melodramatic action. Frank's attraction to Helen is an uneasy fusion of the sensual and the spiritual: at one moment he rages with lust for her; at another, he is filled with profound tenderness for her suffering. Yet, even after he comes to know her, she remains unreal to him, a personification of the beauty in the world from which the conditions of existence have shut him off. Since he believes that this beauty is justifiably inaccessible to him, he compulsively destroys the relationship at the very moment its realization becomes possible. While they are still strangers, Frank's unrequited desire for Helen impels him to climb an elevator shaft to spy on her in the bathroom, to make love to her inaccessible nakedness with his desperate eyes. In a stunningly powerful scene, Malamud describes the self-induced torments of Frank's shame. Frank peeps through the bathroom window not so much to gratify his lusts as to torture himself ("his passion poisoned by his shame") with the impossibility of their fulfillment. This scene in which Frank symbolically violates Helen anticipates his actual violation of her later on.

All of the sons in the novel (*The Assistant* is about fathers and sons)—Nat Pearl, Louis Karp, Ward Minogue, and Frank Alpine—court Helen's love in one way or another. Helen, the least convincing of Malamud's characters, is both practical and idealistic, less ordinary than her surroundings though not extraordinary enough to surmount them. Her dream of bettering herself is an admixture of bovarism and genuine sensitivity. What she wants, as she puts it, is "the return of her possibilities," though she is only vaguely aware of what her possibilities include. The unambitious liquor clerk, Louis Karp, is not good enough for her, but she is more than willing to settle for the equally shallow Nat Pearl, an ambitious law student who has apparently risen above his surroundings. It is part of her tragedy that the real Nat is not the dream hero she has romantically envisioned. Insensitive to her, he devalues the gift of her love, taking it as his due, and irreparably wounds the giver. Despite the difference in their situations, Nat is the spiritual heir of his father, a good but materialistic man, whose livelihood comes from selling penny candy. That Helen's dream of a better life might be satisfied by marriage to Nat suggests the inadequacy of her apsirations. Whereas she loses the possibility of marrying him by yielding herself too readily, she loses the possibility of a real relationship with Frank by withholding herself too long. Inhibited by the pain of the first experience, she is unwilling to risk the second until her last nagging self-doubt is assuaged. When Helen is finally sure that she loves Frank, it has become, for a number of reasons, too late.

Melodramatic circumstances (fate as authorial prerogative) conspire against the ill-fated lovers. While Helen is waiting for Frank in the park to tell him that she loves him, Ward Minogue, also looking for Frank, appears in his place and attempts to rape her. When, after saving her from Ward, Frank forcibly makes love to her, she feels disgraced, as if Ward had actually consummated his attempt; in the merging of the acts, the two identities seem as one. Though circumstances contrive against them, Helen and Frank are in themselves responsible (fate as character) for the failure of their relationship. A Malamudian irony: Helen is able to love Frank only until he makes love to her; the fact debauches the illusion.

Having lost Helen through is lust, Frank, waking from a guilt-ridden nightmare, has a revelation about himself:

[He] got up to run but he had run everywhere. There was no place left to escape to. The room shrank. The bed was flying up at him. He felt trapped—sick, wanted to cry but couldn't. He planned to kill himself, at the same minute had a terrifying insight: that all the while he was acting like he wasn't, he was really a man of stern morality.

Like S. Levin, Frank discovers (in a comparable illumination) that he is a man of principle, but unlike Levin he is at the same time a compulsive sinner. His own most merciless judge, Frank continually sets up occasions in which he can test his actual self against his ideal of himself. Guilty of imperfection (the presumption of the romantic hero), he debases himself as penance; he destroys his relationship with Helen and continues to steal gratuitously from the grocery store. Since he wants more than anything else to be a good man, his crimes are a means of self-punishment; each time he pockets money from Morris' register, he torments himself with guilt. Moreover, he increased his debt (psychologically and financially) to the grocer, which means he must punish himself still further to make requital. As penitent, he must fall deeper and deeper into his interior hell before he can allow himself salvation. This is the pattern of his life and a central concern of the novel.

Malamud uses the changing of the seasons and the seasons them-selves as physical symbols, providing his timeless and placeless New York landscape with a kind of metaphysical climate. The novel starts in early November and ends in mid-April, symbolically covering the Fall, the Death, and the Redemption of Man. The seasons mirror the inner condition of the central characters. Winter is the longest season in Malamud's bleak, lonely, suffering world. Throughout that almost endless period, Frank, Morris, and Helen suffer their wounds in isolation, waiting for the spring as if it were some sort of relief-bringing God. The February day on which Helen decides to accept Frank's love is warm, springlike, and carries with it an illusory sense of flowering. She discovers, however, after her night-marish experience in the park, that she has been victimized by her romantic illusions, that it is still winter—the season of death, the destroyer of love.

Morris too is destroyed by the conspiracy of a protracted winter and an illusory spring. Winter reasserts itself late in March with a heavy snow-fall. Morris, refusing to acknowledge the winter cold ("tempting fate"), goes out to shovel snow without a coat. As a direct consequence ("every move he made seemed to turn into an inevitable thing"), he gets pneumonia and dies. Among the ravages of a protracted winner, Morris' death, like his life, goes unnoticed, soundless as the falling of the snow which covers the path he has sacrificed his life to clear. Yet spring ultimately does come, and with its coming Frank, almost triumphantly, renews Morris' existence.

At Morris' burial, when Helen tosses a rose into the grave, Frank falls in after it, landing feet first on the coffin. It is an absurd accident, embarrassing the solemnity of the occasion; yet it is also a kind of spiritual communion between son and father. In entering the grave, Frank achieves final identification with Morris, which is the ultimate act of self-sacrifice. His rising from the grave as Morris is a symbolic resurrection; the season aptly enough is spring, shortly before Passover and Easter.

Ironically, Frank's rebirth leads him only to the assumption of Morris' living death in the tomb of the grocery store. In a hauntingly bitter passage, Ida and Helen console each other.

> "Your father is better off dead," said Ida.
> As they toiled up the stairs they heard the dull cling of the register in the store and knew the grocer was the one who had danced on the grocer's coffin.

Like Morris, Frank becomes wholly committed to the store, sacrificing his energies to support Ida and Helen. Totally committed, he even gets up an hour earlier, as Morris had, to sell a three-cent roll to the Polisheh. In continuing Morris' life, Frank fulfills the possibilities of the grocer's actual son, the son who died while still a child. It is the least Frank can do for the man he has wronged, and the most. In suffering for Morris and, in Morris' role, for all of us, Frank achieves his own redemption, becoming at last a wholly honest and good man. In Frank's purification through pain and suffering, Malamud unites the disparate concerns of mythic ritual and conventional realism. *The Assistant* ends on a transcendent note. As a consequence of Morris' death, Frank finds the occasion to fulfill his no longer self-conscious quest for sainthood.

Frank's redemption is made possible by his uncompromising love for Helen—which provides the impetus for his commitment to the store. A similar commitment is made by the shoemaker's assistant in Malamud's tender short story, "The First Seven Years." In the beautiful ending to that story, we get an illumination of the informing spirit of the novel and, as such, the romantic impulse at the heart of all of Malamud's fiction:

> But the next morning, when the shoemaker arrived, heavy-hearted, to open the store, he saw he needn't have come, for his assistant was already seated at the last, pounding leather for his love.

The amount of love a man is able and willing to commit to life is, in Malamud's universe, the measure of his grace.

HERBERT LEIBOWITZ

Malamud and the Anthropomorphic Business

Malamud is a sort of waggish minstrel of misery. He is a homilist whose stock of canny folk proverbs contains the distilled wisdom of the politics of survival. Since his characters usually live in a kind of psychic jail, they defend their self-respect by crying out in protest against an unhearing, uncaring world; by laughing, wailing, groaning, or shouting threats at the bullying powers that balk them. In a way, they are intrigued by their dramatic predicament, and like strutting actors, they emote, soliloquize, and substitute gesture for action until they are forced to remember their hopeless misery. Reaching out for communication, they are misunderstood, or left with their inner selves unexpressed; when they feel most defeated, they lapse into an "eloquence almost without vocabulary."

Malamud seems to have arrived at an impasse rich in unsettling perceptions of the moral nature of life. Most of his characters suffer in excess of their offense or are encumbered, to paraphrase Kafka, by a state in which they find themselves guilty, quite independent of sin. They raise troubled questions: whether man is free or bound by necessity, whether the world is governed by pitiless, inescapable laws or by love. With the zest, tenacity, and occasional weariness of a scholastic disputation, the quarrel is carried on in story after story: who are the guilty, who is responsible, is atonement possible? Even the titles of these stories strangely reverberate

From *The New Republic* 25, vol. 149 (December 21, 1963). Copyright © 1963 by Harrison-Blaine, Inc.

the terms and perplexities of the debate: *The Cost of Living, Life Is Better Than Death, Still Life, The Death of Me.*

In the quasi-allegorical title story [of *Idiots First*], the old, poor, dying Mendel rushes frantically about trying to collect enough money to send his idiot son to California where he can be properly cared for. Running into dark closed doors, he is stalked and finally stopped by Ginzburg, a spectral avenging Fury (Death) who tells him: "I ain't in the anthropo-morphic business . . . the law is the law . . . what will happen happens." Mendel's embittered question, "Don't you know what it means human?" illustrates Malamud's perpetual struggle to humanize the impersonal and the irrational, to give it a local habitation and a name. At times, these forces are homely and identifiable, but they usually turn out to be agents of some supernatural case; like the landlord in *The Cost of Living* who drives the old grocer Tomashevsky out of business and out of his wits by renting an empty store to a supermarket chain. Even nature mourns, as if in uni-versal assent to the hardship of Being. *The Cost of Living* begins and ends in winter, and the change of seasons ritually parallels the grocer's dislocation and loss of hope. The weather in Malamud's stories is generally cold (*Still Life* and *Naked Nude*) or unbearably stifling (*A German Refugee*), and is a gauge of a person's spiritual discomfort: "Tomashevsky's face was a blizzard"; Mendel put on "the cold embittered clothing."

Malamud's characters are often idiots in the sense of being fools and clowns, or of being incapable of rational conduct or logical reasoning. But the root meaning of the word "idiot" is "private, own," that sanctity of the human personality that Malamud wishes to protect against the assault of a faceless, autocratic will. And paradoxically, this temperamental quirk assures man's freedom, even though he uses it foolishly, destructively, and inhumanely, as, for example, the rich businessman Fishbein, in *Idiots First*, who substitutes Philanthropy (organized charity) for Love of Man.

The locked door and the hidden cross—these are the symbols of Malamud's fictions. As in Kafka, what thwarts is often matter-of-fact, but invisible. In the Jewbird's words: "That's how it goes. It's open, you're in. Closed, you're out and that's your fate." But more often, the Mendels and Oskar Gassners are trapped in the dark, stuffy rooms of the mind, worn down by their nagging obsession with what they have done or failed to do. In *Still Life*, a droll sex comedy with an undertone of melancholy, the failure to permit absolution for one's past deeds results in a denial of the ebullient spirituality of the flesh, to a crucifixion without tenderness or love. An-namaria Oliovino (oil and wine, the ingredients of the sacrament), the ripe, earthy but capricious *pittrice*, paints still lifes and huge abstractions "exploding in all directions, these built on, entwined with, and ultimately concealing a small black religious cross." She cannot, however, still the life within her or her remorse; she desires abasement as penance for her sins. A voluptuary of religious purity, she must confess to a Fidelman dressed as a priest and then be taken sexually in a slightly fraudulent communion. Passion becomes The Passion, a crucifixion necessary for the power to will resurrection, to be reborn by the single redemptive act that will erase the shame and iniquity of the past. (Fidelman is the meek, bumptious artist, dreaming of bold conquest, sexual rapture, and ultimate victory, who suffers his own hilarious crucifixion at the hands of Annamaria: "He considered jumping into the Tiber but it was full of ice that winter.") The story is also a witty spoof of abstract expressionism.

Like the Aeschylus of *The Oresteia*, Malamud explores the dialectic of law and love. His human solidarity inclines him to a Whitmanesque faith in the radical goodness of creation and man, but the evidence of his senses, of his moral experience, and of modern history seems to erode that faith. The German Refugee, in the most moving story of the volume, bitterly disquieted by his forced uprooting, tries to rouse himself from spiritual torpor and quotes with apparent affirmation Whitman's creed that "the kelson of the creation is love," only to lose faith entirely and kill himself. His suicide is due not merely to despair at the gruesome evil of Hitler and at the failure of brotherhood; it comes also from a personal guilt, a failure to love; he had abandoned his Gentile wife, who had later been converted to Judaism and thrown into the common grave by the SS. Sober hope dwindles into dark pessimism. Neither love of God, of others, nor of self seems possible: to the Germans, the love of death has led to the death of love; to Oskar, the death of love has led to the love of death.

Detachment from another's cross, then, is a perilous moral position. If one orders one's life by carefully distancing someone else's woes, either from a gruff reluctance to know the full measure of another's suffering or from fear of being taken advantage of, then the heart is deformed. Yet benevolence and involvement may be futile. The tailor in *The Death of Me* is stunned and saddened by the eerie violence of his workers' enmity. His exhortations, eloquence, and kindness are respected, but locked into their self-pity and irrational hatred, their selfhood somehow threatened, they fight with incoherent rage and break his heart. But unless love balances the bleak negativism of the law, Malamud seems to be saying, there can be no rebirth, no triumph of the spirit against egotism and evil. Perhaps through accepting imperfection yet risking ourselves we can change and live wholly. That, for Malamud, is the responsibility of freedom, the "gaiety transfiguring all that dread."

F. W. DUPEE

The Uses and Abuses of Commitment

Looking up Malamud in Leslie Fiedler's capacious *Love and Death in the American Novel* I find that the treatment of him there is surprisingly brief and unenthusiastic. Given Mr. Fiedler's well-known prepossessions I should have expected him to award Malamud high marks. Fiedler is carrying the torch for "mature genital sexuality"—something that he finds deplorably lacking in the erotic life of the American novel. I have myself just read, not only the recent *Idiots First*, but all of Mr. Malamud's work that I can find in print; and it is my impression that the sexual norm of his world is eminently normal, as in fact it would have to be since his people are mostly too busy establishing themselves and their families in an elementally hostile world to feel desire in excessive or distorted forms.

True, they often suffer mildly from an *insufficiency* of sexual fulfillment, especially when they are young. But this suffering is apt to seek relief in the simpler forms of action, namely in going to bed with the opposite sex, or trying to. At worst, the deprivation manifests itself in a sexual curiosity so candid as scarcely to deserve the fancy term "voyeurism." In no other author, surely, are so many pretty girls so sweetly obliging about getting undressed in front of their boy friends. "Would you mind if I peeled and went in for a dip?" the girl student asks her teacher in "A Choice of Profession," a story in *Idiots First*. "Go ahead," the teacher says happily, and she does. But "A Choice of Profession" is not, as this scene by itself might suggest, one of those steamy romances with a campus setting. The student turns out to have been a call girl in her past life; and the teacher, on her telling him this, recoils from her in fear and disgust even though he is so far from being a lily himself that he has been entertaining furtive designs on her. But he is only a prig, not a creep; and the point as finally voiced by him is that "It's hard to be moral."

In Malamud's novel, *The Assistant,* to be sure, we have in the Italian youth, Frank Alpine, a bad case of distorted sexuality. He is a thief, a peeping Tom and, just once, a rapist. But Frank is by definition an outsider, especially in the Jewish family that shelters him. Even so, he finally atones for everything. He settles down, marries the girl he raped, has himself circumcised and becomes a Jew. The lesson is as clear as the lesson is in *The Golden Bowl,* where James's Anglo-Saxon girl succeeds in reforming *her* beloved Italian, the adulterous Prince Amerigo. Essentially the lesson is the same in both authors. Mature sexuality culminating in marriage is the norm. And so potent a force is the norm that it accomplishes not only the regeneration of the erring ones but their actual or virtual assimilation to another culture. Indeed "assimilation," but with the Jew seeking the moral assimilation of the non-Jew, is a basic principle of Malamud's work. And as concerns sex, the power of the Jew is reinforced by his relative normality.

If Mr. Fiedler fails to credit Malamud with his own sexual values it is because he has other tests that Malamud's work fails to pass. Fiedler is carrying a second torch: for the "Gothic" strain in American fiction. Gothic fantasy, he believes, "provides a way into not only the magic world of the baseball fan . . . but also into certain areas of our social life where nightmare violence and guilt actually exist." The reference here is to Malamud's first novel, *The Natural,* which is about the heroics and horrors of professional baseball. Influenced, apparently, by Nathanael West's mordant dealings with American folklore, *The Natural,* true to its Westian prototypes, explodes at one point into bloody fantasy. This is what Mr. Fiedler means by "Gothic" and it is what he likes about *The Natural.* And so, while praising that book for its "lovely, absurd madness" he reproaches its author for the "denial of the marvellous" implicit in much of his later work, where, says Fiedler, "he turns back to the muted, drab world of the Depression as remembered two decades later." For Fiedler, "the denial of the marvellous" seems to be the gravest of apostasies, a dereliction of one's duty to be Gothic. But as I see it, the "marvellous" requires of its user the rarest of talents. The mode of it established by one writer seldom survives imitation by another (consider the fate of Kafka's imitators). And the presence in a novel of standardized Gothic machinery—for example the secret staircases and come-alive portraits in Hawthorne—often substitutes for true literary invention. In any case, so irrelevant are Gothic fancies to Malamud's sturdy characters, so little can they afford the luxury of a "lovely, absurd madness," that they are easily imagined as retorting: "So what's lovely about madness that we should play Ophelia?"

All this by way not so much of quizzing Mr. Fiedler, who has his better moments, but of trying to define Malamud, especially his differences from the "Gothic" or "wacky" strain in contemporary novels from *Catch 22* to *Naked Lunch* to *V*. The differences are notable and tend to align Malamud with such a writer as J. F. Powers rather than with most of the Jewish-American novelists of today to whom he is generally compared. Like Powers, Malamud is a mildly conservative force in writing at present, a fact that he, like Powers, perhaps owes in part to his interest in the short story with its necessary economy and—in old-fashioned parlance—its highly "conscious art." Not for Powers or Malamud, in any case, those specialities of the modern Gothic or wacky novel: the "sick" hero, the "stateless" setting, the general effect of improvised narrative, the marathon sentence which, in its attempt to deliver instantaneously a total physical experience, leaves the reader feeling as if he had been frisked all over by a peculiarly assiduous cop. For the people of Malamud and Powers, Bellevue is out of bounds; they are not *that* sick. Moreover, a distinct localism rules their choice of settings; even when foreign, they are never "stateless" in the sense given to that word by Mary McCarthy in her account of *Naked Lunch*. In addition, neat patterns are traced on the reader's mind by the movement of the "story lines" of a Malamud or a Powers narrative; there is no effect of improvisation. And their prose avails itself of the special authority, so thoroughly exploited by the early Joyce, that is inherent in the short declarative sentence. Norman Podhoretz has noted Malamud's genius for getting the maximum authenticity from the maximum economy of such a statement as, "And there were days when he was sick to death of everything." Here are familiar words and a familiar rhythm for one who is "sick," presumably, in the sadly familiar way of hard-pressed people.

Malamud's ability to persuade us of the reality of his characters—their emotions, deeds, words, surroundings—remains astonishing. In most of the twelve stories that make up *Idiots First*, that ability is quite as evident as it was in *The Magic Barrel*, his earlier short story collection, and in those long stories (*The Assistant*, *A New Life*) we call his novels. There is no accounting for this elusive gift except by terms so trite as to seem like abstractions. His identification with his people tends to be perfect, and it is perfect because, on the one hand, they are mostly Jews of a certain class, as he is, and on the other (to quote Mr. Podhoretz further), they are "copied not from any models on earth but from an idea in the mind of Bernard Malamud." The idea brings about a grand simplification, or specialization, of historical fact. For one thing, Malamud's Jewish community is chiefly composed of people of East European origin. For another, they tend to retain, morally speaking, their immigrant status. Life is centered in the home and the workshop and remains tough and full of threats. The atmosphere is not that of the 1930's Depression alone, as Fiedler says, but that of the hard times ever immanent in the nature of things. His people may prosper for a while and within limits. But memories and connections continue to bind them to the Old World, in some cases to the world of the Old Testament where Jacob labors for Laban and Job suffers for everyone. Some of them, it is true, progress to the point of acquiring ineffably Anglo-Saxon first names ("Arthur Fidelman," for example). Some are found claiming that all-American privilege of the post-war period, "a year in Italy." But in Italy they become, or fear to become, immigrants all over again, and the old American theme of innocents abroad is updated. Golden Italy so confounds the professor of "The Maid's Shoes" that he dares open his heart to it not at all. The art student Arthur Fidelman is made of different stuff but not of stuff dependable enough to prevail against the glorious menace of golden Italy. In the story about him in *The Magic Barrel*, his first days in Rome were shown to be haunted by a crafty alter ego (a "refugee from Israel") and Fidelman lost his notes on Giotto, the "Christian artist." In the two stories about him in *Idiots First* he is still being badly hustled in Italy and his few victories are painfully Pyrrhic.

The Fidelman stories are beautifully done and very funny. Something about them, however, suggests the rigors of a punitive expedition on the part of the author and possibly at his own expense. I remember his earlier tales of would-be artists and intellectuals—those dreary youths who lie all day on their rooming house beds trying to concentrate on the reading of *Madame Bovary* or on writing novels themselves. And I suspect that in these cases Malamud's identification with his world is carried beyond the point of perfection to a certain guilt and fear. His people seem to be watching him, rather than he them, to make sure that he doesn't get out of line. And then there is the story ("Black Is My Favorite Color") in which Mr. Malamud tries to motivate the love of a Jewish liquor dealer for a Negro woman by giving the liquor dealer a good deal of wry sensibility. "That was the night she wore a purple dress and I thought to myself, My

God, what colors. Who paints that picture paints a masterpiece." This strikes me as a mere stereotype of Second Avenue folksiness. Nor are the author's powers of invention quite equal to the demands of the metaphysical fantasy which serves this volume as title story. Here an old man is pursued by Death until at last he acquires the courage to look Death squarely in the eye, thus winning the desired extension of his borrowed time. Meanwhile each has clarified his position to the other in the artificially racy speech of what sounds like a bull session. Challenged to explain his lack of "responsibility," Death says, "I ain't in the anthropomorphic business." And the old man yells, "You bastard, don't you know what it means human?" Nor does it help that Malamud, humorizing, calls Death "Ginzburg." He sets out, perhaps, to disinfect Kafka's universe of its total tragedy and ends up approximating the whimsical affirmations of Paddy Chayefsky. Such are the occasional failures of a first-rate talent bent upon maintaining his "commitment" (in the sloganeering phrase) to his own people and trying to be as positive as possible. In these cases, commitment, that very necessary stage in anyone's development towards freedom of self and imagination, seems to have become an end in itself, a commitment to commitment.

Among the many fine stories in *Idiots First*, two are very fine. One, "The German Refugee," simulates reportage rather than fable—perhaps it *is* reportage—and is the most profound rendering of the refugee theme I know. The other, "The Death of Me," is the epitome of the author's whole matter and manner—his fabling, as distinguished from his reporting, manner. Marcus, a former tailor, has risen to the level of clothier only to be harassed to death by the furious quarrels of his present tailor, a thin bitter hysterical Sicilian, and his presser, a beefy beery sobbing Pole. Their fury flows from their consciousness of old unhappy far-off things in their lives. And the prose in which Malamud renders their deliberate squalor and pain-wrung cries makes their troubles sound like all the troubles that ever were in the world.

To Malamud, Mr. Podhoretz says, "the Jew is humanity seen under the twin aspects of suffering and moral aspiration. Therefore any man who suffers greatly and also longs to be better than he is can be called a Jew." True, and the special appeal of "The Death of Me" comes from its giving the thumbscrew of this theme a decisive turn. Here are two men whose sufferings exceed those of Marcus the Jew until, realizing that they are beyond assimilation by his own ethos, he experiences the supreme suffering of total despair and gives up the ghost. There is true "madness" in this story—the madness not of Fiedler's prescription but of art.

EARL R. WASSERMAN

"The Natural":
Malamud's World Ceres

The doges of Venice dropped a ring into the Adriatic to renew annually its marriage to their city and to assure that the sea be propitious. The British monarch ceremonially opens the annual session of Parliament that it may undertake its care of the kingdom. In the United States the President annually sanctifies baseball by throwing the first ball of the season into the field; and, having received its presidential commission, baseball proceeds to its yearly task of working the welfare of the national spirit. The wonder is that we do not have a whole library of significant baseball fiction since so much of the American spirit has been seriously poured into the game and its codes until it has a life of its own that affects the national temperament. Just as a personal indiscretion can topple an English government, the White Sox scandal stained the collective American conscience, and Babe Ruth's bellyache was a crisis that depressed the national spirit nearly as much as the bombing of Pearl Harbor infuriated it. Like any national engagement, baseball, especially in that form that Ring Lardner called the "World Serious," has had not only its heroic victories and tragedies but also its eccentricities that express aspects of the American character and have become part of our folklore: Vance, Fewster, and Herman, all piled up on third base; Hilda (the Bell) Chester, the Dodger fan; Rabbit Maranville's penchant for crawling on window ledges, especially in the rain; Wilbert Robinson's attempt to catch a grapefruit dropped from a plane; Chuck Hostetler's historic fall between third and home when he could have won the sixth game of the '45 Series.

From *Centennial Review* 4, vol. 9 (Fall 1965). Copyright © 1965 by *Centennial Review*.

These are not merely like the materials of Malamud's *The Natural;*
the items mentioned are among its actual stuff. For what Malamud has
written is a novel that coherently organizes the rites of baseball and many
of its memorable historic episodes into the epic inherent in baseball as a
measure of man, as it once was inherent in Homeric battles or chivalric
tournaments or the Arthurian quest for the Grail. Coming, like Babe Ruth,
from an orphanage, Roy Hobbs, unknown pitcher of nineteen on his way
to a try-out with the Cubs, strikes out the aging winner of the Most Valuable
Player award and then, like Eddie Waitkus in 1949, is shot without apparent
motive by a mad girl in her Chicago hotel room. The try-out never takes
place, and the years that follow are degrading failures at everything. But
at thirty-four, having switched—as Ruth did—from pitcher to fielder and
prodigious batter, Roy joins a New York team and, with his miraculous
bat, lifts it from the cellar into contention for the league championship.
Like Ruth, too, his home run cheers a sick boy into recovery, and a
monumental bellyache sends him to a hospital, as it did Ruth in 1925, and
endangers the battle for the pennant. Like the White Sox of 1919, Roy
and another player sell out to Gus, an Arnold Rothstein gambler, to throw
the crucial game for the pennant, and the novel ends with a heartbroken
boy pleading, as legend claims one did to Shoeless Joe Jackson of the
traitorous White Sox, "Say it ain't true, Roy." In fact, nearly all the baseball
story derives from real events, and to this extent the novel is a distillation
of baseball history as itself the distillation of American life: its opportunities
for heroism, the elevating or dispiriting influence of the hero on his community, the moral obligations thrust on him by this fact, and the corruption
available to him. By drawing on memorable real events, Malamud has
avoided the risk of contrived allegory that lurks in inventing a fiction in
order to carry a meaning. Instead, he has rendered the lived events of the
American game so as to compel it to reveal what it essentially is, the ritual
whereby we express the psychological nature of American life and its moral
predicament. Pageant history is alchemized into revelatory myth.

I

But the clean surface of this baseball story, as a number of critics have
noticed, repeatedly shows beneath its translucency another myth of another
culture's heroic ritual by which man once measured the moral power of his
humanness—another and yet the same, so that Roy's baseball career may
slip the bonds of time and place and unfold as the everlastingly crucial
story of man. Harriet, mad maimer of champions, conceives of Roy's strike-

out of the Whammer as a "tourney"; Roy's obscure, remote origin and clumsy ignorance have their archetypal form in the youth of Sir Perceval; the New York team he ultimately joins is the "Knights"; and one opponent, sick at the thought of pitching to him, sees him "in full armor, mounted on a black charger . . . coming at him with a long lance." Of the mountain of gifts Roy receives on his Day at the ballpark one is a white Mercedes-Benz, which he drives triumphantly around the field and stops before the box of Memo, coldly disdainful lady of courtly love, to ask for a date. By subsuming the chivalric tourney and the Arthurian quest, baseball expands beyond time, and Roy's baseball career becomes, not merely representative, but symbolic of man's psychological and moral situation. Because of the *trompe l'oeil*, Roy at bat is every quester who has had to shape his own character to fulfill his goal, whether it be the Grail or the league pennant. By drawing his material from actual baseball and yet fusing it with the Arthurian legend, Malamud sets and sustains his novel in a region that is both real and mythic, particular and universal, ludicrous melodrama and spiritual probing—Ring Lardner and Jung.

Sir James Frazer, Jessie Weston, and T. S. Eliot have transformed the significance of the Arthurian myth for the modern mind, and their anthropological and psychological interpretation now almost necessarily invests the legend. To the twentieth century the Grail story is the archetypal fertility myth embodying, in Miss Weston's words, "an ancient Ritual, having for its ultimate object the initiation into the secret of the sources of Life, physical and spiritual." Malamud's syncretism of baseball and the Arthurian legend therefore invites a further consideration of the novel in these terms: the psychological, moral, and communal needs of the baseball champion—the American hero—to gain access to the "sources of Life." Roy long since had made his own bat out of a tree, a sort of Ygdresel, and named it "Wonderboy," and a miraculous bat it is, with an energy of its own. Derived from nature's life and shaped by Roy for the game in which he is determined to be the hero, it flashes in the sun, blinds his opponents with its golden splendor, and crashes the ball with thunder and lightning. It is, in other words, the modern Excalibur and Arthurian lance, which Weston and others have identified as talismans of male potency and re-productive energy. The phallic instrument is the raw vitality and fertility he has drawn from the universal "sources of Life." After Roy's fruit-full night with Memo, Bump says to him, "I hear you had a swell time, won-derboy," and during Roy's slump Wonderboy sags like a baloney.

With Wonderboy, Roy joins the dispirited last-place Knights in a remarkably dry season, and the manager, Pop Fisher, who laments, "I shoulda been a farmer" and whose heart "feels as dry as dirt," suffers, as his form of the Fisher King's affliction, athlete's foot on his hands. Even the water fountain is broken, yielding only rusty water. But when Wonderboy crashes the ball, its thunder cracks the sky, the rains leave the players ankle-deep, the brown field turns green, and Pop Fisher's affliction vanishes. When Roy first appeared and merely entered the batting cage, the flagging Knights suddenly "came to life." The Quester has brought his virility to the Waste Land, and, like Jung's mana-personality, he restores the dying father-king. Roy, the questing Knight, by access to the sources of life, has restored virility to his community and the vegetative process to nature. In the radical sense of the word, he is the "natural."

The Grail vegetation myth has been precisely translated into its modern American mode and is carefully sustained in this baseball story. The "Pre-Game" section, in which young Roy is shot, takes place in early spring, prior to the baseball season. When the story is resumed years later, Roy joins the Knights in summer, a third of the baseball season having passed; and with Roy's failure in the last crucial game the novel ends in a wintry autumn to complete the fertility cycle inherernt in both the Grail Quest and the schedule of the baseball season. The traditional Arthurian dwarf who taunts the hero and beats him with a scourge takes his place in the bleachers as the dwarf Otto Zipp, who reviles Roy, honks a Harpo Marx horn at him, contributes razor blades on Roy's Day with the advice, "Here, cut your throat." This stunted growth, who also embodies a good deal of Homer's Thersites, is that portion of the community envious of and antagonistic to the hero's regenerative potency that spreads to the entire team, although Zipp had worshipped Roy's predecessor Bump, whose sterile triumphs were wholly his own while the team slumped; and Zipp exults over Roy's downfall with the empty gesture of hitting a phantom ball for a visionary home run. Merlin the Magician and Morgan le Fay have evolved into the league of Gus the "Supreme Bookie," who plays the percentages, and Memo, Morganatic in every sense, the temptress for whom Roy sells out. Because of the complementary parts played in King Arthur's life by Morgan, who works for evil and slays knights, and the Lady of the Lake, who works for good and beneficently aids them, Arthurian scholars have claimed they were originally one. Correspondingly, of Roy's two women, red-haired Memo is customarily clad in black, and black-haired Iris, complementarily, in red; and it is Iris who knows Lake Michigan intimately and whose presence restores the power of Wonderboy, his Excalibur. Like the Grail fertility hero, Roy displaces the current hero whose power has waned. In the "Pre-Game" section, like Perceval slaying the Red Knight, he succeeds to the hero's office by striking out the thirty-three-year-old

Whammer, thrice chosen the Most Valuable Player, who now knows he is, "in the truest sense of it, out" and trots off, an "old man." In the main narrative Roy gains his life-giving position with the Knights by inducing the death of Bump, who, although the leading league hitter, has transmitted no potency to his team. (Le Roi est mort, vive le Roy.) And at the novel's end thirty-four-year-old Roy's spiritual death is his being struck out by the young pitcher whose yearning, like Pop Fisher's, is to be a farmer, just as years before Roy had struck out the aging Whammer. Yet at one point Roy confuses the Whammer with Bump, at another sees Bump when he looks in his own mirror, and later dresses exactly like the Whammer; and when Roy succeeds the dead Bump the newspapers marvel at the identity of the two in body and manner. For in fact they are all the same fertility hero, displacing each other with each new seasonal resurgence and decline of potency. In nature, quite independently of moral failures, life and strength are forever renewed.

Besides the hero's charismatic power to restore the maimed Fisher King and bring the fertile waters to the Waste Land, Arthurians have added that the characteristics of the seasonal Grail hero are possession of a talisman, like Excalibur or Wonderboy, representing "the lightning and fecundity of the earth," and "marriage to the vegetation goddess." In every respect, then, Roy seems to fulfill his role as fecundity hero, except for the marriage, despite his yearning for Memo and his passing affair with Iris. His tragic failure therefore is linked with this omission; and the search for the reason takes us to the core of the novel, where we must seek the psychic and moral flaw within the fertility theme—which is embodied in the Arthurian Grail myth—which has been assimilated to the baseball story—which is purified out of actual events.

II

Superficially, Roy's moral failure is his lust for Memo, who induces him to throw the final game for a bribe, supposedly that he may marry her. He is further tempted by knowledge that his athlete's heart will allow no more baseball seasons; the season god is fading, and he would harvest for himself alone. But this hardly touches on the grounds of his inner corruption. The very opening of the novel establishes a condition that will repeatedly symbolize the central psychic theme: nineteen-year-old Roy, awakening from sleep, kneels in a Pullman berth and strikes a match to see his reflection in the window as the train passes through a tunnel. Crouched in this fetal position, in his berth, during passage through the uterine tunnel he then feels "a splurge of freedom" on seeing the world of pre-dawn early spring while lulled by the mothering train. Throughout this prelude the subtly muted intimations of Roy's infantilism persist in what appears mere naiveté like that of the young Perceval. The porter treats Roy as a child who must be led by the hand to the men's room and humored with mock misunderstanding and exaggeration.

"I'm going to Chicago, where the Cubs are."

"Lions and tigers in the zoo?"

"No, the ballplayers."

"Oh, the ball—" Eddie clapped a hand to his mouth. "Are you one of them?"

"I hope to be."

The porter bowed low. "My hero. Let me kiss your hand."

Without solicitous, fatherly Sam, the scout who had discovered him and is taking him for a try-out with (appropriately) the Cubs, Roy is completely infantile: clumsy, embarrassed, spilling water on the tablecloth as though he were wetting his diapers. The region in which his spirit is anchored becomes clear when, instead of writing down his order in the dining car, he absently prints his name and date of birth. The train taking him from his origin on the Pacific Coast to Chicago is obviously something more than motion through space: travelling "over long years," it is the time of Roy's life translated into space, and, having carried him to his youthful wound and failure in the Midwest, it will later take him to his heroic tragedy with the Knights in New York. The completion of transcontinental space will be identical with the fulfillment of the season cycle of fecundity and with the transformation of Roy the pitcher who strikes out the aging Whammer into Roy the aging batter struck out by youthful Youngberry. When, therefore, in "Pre-Game" the train is halted by a doctor who has a mysterious telegram about a sick passenger and does not know it is that failing fertility hero the Whammer, it is appropriate that the train stop beside a carnival with its "kiddie rides" and "try-your-skill booths" and that in this childish setting with the Ferris wheel looking "like a stopped clock," Roy strike out the Whammer, slay the aging hero, "bury" him, as Roy thinks of it.

We shall come closer to the meaning of this infantilism when we recognize that in striking out the Whammer, Roy also slays Sam, his fatherly scout who, serving as catcher in this trackside "tournament," is mortally shaken by the pitch that puts the Whammer out. During alcoholic Sam's three years in baseball long ago, he had slumped badly at bat but, as catcher, had never made an error. No hero, he is the flawless receiver and support for that conqueror, the pitcher. On him Roy leans like an infant, and Sam has accepted his role as substitute father. The young hero's symbolic slaying of the waning baseball god and thus his accession to his own potency role is simultaneously the slaying of the father image to which he had been a servile appendage. The severance from the father image is not traumatic. Despite Roy's "No, oh no, Sam, not without you," self-effacing Sam accepts his own disappearance into death, orders Roy on alone to Chicago, gives him his wallet and thereby his name. The mother image is another matter.

Aboard the train had come Harriet Bird guarding a hat box as jealously as Roy guards Wonderboy's case. The two objects—bat and hat—correspond to the Arthurian symbols, sword and chalice, which Jessie Weston and others have identified as talismans of male and female potency. Each has selfishly made the talisman for himself and will not relinquish it to others. Yet, through Harriet Roy feels "a great longing in his life" and a tenderness towards her "as if she might be his mother (That bird)." Repressing his incestuous attachment to his real mother as hate (later he will call her a whore), Roy has unconsciously substituted Harriet for her. But the quality of Harriet as mother image must be determined by Roy's psychic state. Having struck out the old hero and mortally wounded the father substitute, Roy seems to have free possession of his life-energy, or, in psychoanalytic terms, his libido: "I'll break every record in the book for throwing and hitting," he tells Harriet; "I'll be the best there ever was in the game." But Harriet submits him to the hero's "test": "Is that all?" And Roy flunks, unable to understand the question or the implication that such self-centered triumph leaves one alone and is purposeless, just as the Grail Knight fails by neglecting to ask whom his talisman is meant to serve. For Roy admits that Wonderboy is something he made "for myself." With Roy's blindness to the communal and reproductive purpose of his vitality, Harriet becomes what Jung has called the "terrible mother," *mater saeva cupidinum*, and not ("snappy goddess" though she seems to Roy) the Mother Goddess of fertility, not the World Ceres. Consequently, when the train again enters a tunnel Roy slips his hand on Harriet's breast and, compelled by the infantile regression to the tunnel, tweaks the nipple. With a scream she contorts head and arms, "Look," she says, "I'm a twisted tree"—a distortion of the tree of life from which Roy had drawn his talismanic bat.

It is the infantilism of the American hero that Malamud is concerned with, the psychic and therefore moral regression of the gifted "natural" who could vitalize society and reveal to it the capacities of human strength; the selfish attachment to the "terrible mother" that introverts and blocks the psychic energy that could flow outwardly from the mature hero and restore the Waste Land. "When will you grow up, Roy?" Iris, that Lady of the Lake, will later ask. Alone in Chicago and regressively "sick for home," Roy is summoned to Harriet's hotel room. Wonderboy in hand, he reaffirms his determination to be "the best there ever was in the game," and the nude terrible mother reaches into her hat box, fits the talismanic hat on her head and pumps a spirit-shattering silver bullet into his guts, into his vital force. Harriet is the psychic mother from whose dual nature Roy has evoked the destructive, for when she dances about the stricken hero she makes noises of both triumph and despair. Eddie Waitkus would have been startled to learn what really hit him at the Edgewater Beach Hotel in 1949.

III

The main narrative now evolves out of the brief prologue of infantilism in the same manner that from the childish stuff of its opening pages Joyce evolves his *Portrait of the Artist,* that other novel about growing up and releasing creative power by cutting free from inherited bonds.

The moral world Malamud postulates—the one Roy, like all of us, enters—is Satan's by more than half. The land no longer belongs to the Fisher King, for the manager, Pop Fisher, whose only concern is the human team and the game they play, has been forced by need to sell sixty percent of the Knights' stock to the Judge, a scripture-quoting Mammon whose favorite element is darkness, whose profits increase in proportion as he weakens the team and debases the game, and who is trying to squeeze out the Fisher-father entirely. The Judge is the futility of all codes artificially imposed from without—religion, the law, codified morality, golden maxims; and he is an illustration of how they can be hypocritically applied for selfish material ends. But if the satanic Judge—who, like Wagner's Klingsor, lives in a dark, crooked tower above the field and who has something of both Charlie Comiskey and Branch Rickey in him—has gained major control over the material world, Fisher, frustrated father-god of human strength, has sold only with the understanding that he control all player deals "as long as he lives." Human values are in his hands so long as psychic vitality is a possibility. "Keep us alive," he begs Roy at the moment of last hope in the final game. But the contest is hardly an equal one, for the something over Setebos, the power behind the Judge, is Gus, the Supreme Bookie, who knows that the long-range odds of chance are on his side and that the threat of a vitality-hero like Roy can probably be removed by a bribe. Into this world Roy enters to make his psychic choice: his accession to heroic life-force, an *élan vital* that will give itself to his team and win Pop Fisher the pennant, or infantile, self-centered security that will betray his fellows and human values. For although Roy is the "natural" athlete, possessing the same energy that lives in nature, he must make a decision. Miraculous though Wonderboy is, Roy also hits at bad pitches, at "lemons": "I mistrust a bad ball hitter," says Pop. "They sometimes make some harmful mistakes." But moral discrimination is not presented as a conscious act of the reason; it is a psychic condition and has something to do with the will to be mature.

The libido, in Jung's formulation, naturally yearns to retreat from harsh reality into the fantasy indolence of maternal protection; but because this incest tendency is checked by society's prohibition, the consequent repression drives the psychic energy backwards into infancy and locks it inertly in the mother image. The mother so defined is the "terrible" mother of death, the destroyer who drowns man in his own source. This retrogressive mother must be renounced; yet, creative strength must derive from the mother, and hence, paradoxically, renunciation of Mater Saeva is access to Mater Magna, the life-giving mother. Through this other mother one is mature, and the libido is freed to flow unselfishly into the world of reality, rather than backwards into the subjective fantasy world. In Jung's words, "as long as the libido is satisfied merely with fantasies, it moves . . . in its own depths, in the mother. When the longing . . . rises . . . to escape the magic circle of the incestuous and, therefore, pernicious, object, and it does not succeed in finding reality, then the object is and remains irrevocably the mother. Only the overcoming of the obstacles of reality brings the deliverance from the mother, who is the continuous and inexhaustible source of life for the creator, but death for the cowardly, timid and sluggish."

The relation of Jung's two mother images is that of Lilith to Eve, Morgan le Fay to the Lady of the Lake, red-haired, black-clad Memo to black-haired, red-clad Iris; and Roy's maturity and hero-role will hang on his choice. Occasionally Roy reflected of Memo: ". . . what if the red were black and ditto the other way? Here, for example, was this black-haired dame in red and what about it? He could take her or leave her . . . but with Memo, flaming above and dark below, there was no choice." And in a delirium he thinks of Iris and Memo exchanging heads and bodies. Memo is mistress to Bump, leading hitter of the league, self-centered practical joker in this life-game, who, though "full of life," transmits none of his energy to his team and wants to be released from it. Identical in body and batting style with Roy, he contrives that Roy occupy his bed so that un-suspecting Memo sleep with unexpecting Roy. Their sexual possession therefore is a kind of unwilled incest, and the episode symbolically repeats his encounter years before with Harriet. Before Memo's entrance into the bedroom, he had been dreaming of the horrifying, aimless train of time roaring out of his origin into the world, "a place where he did not want to go," then of Harriet, who had cut him down in his youth, and then of a fantasy love affair in an indolent rural scene. The psychic scene having been set, Memo now enters his bed and slashes his hot body with her icy hands and feet, just as that terrible mother had once slashed it with a silver ghost-killing bullet. The oedipal pattern is then completed by Roy's driving Bump into competition with his flawless fielding so that Bump kills himself in a Pete Reiser crash against the wall. Roy now replaces his mirror-image on the team, wonders whether he had willed his death, and hungers for his predecessor's mistress, who detests him for their night together and violently mourns for Bump as women once violently mourned the broken season gods Tammuz, Adonis, and Osiris. Roy half recognizes that his yearning is regressive: "It was a confusing proposition to want a girl you'd already had and couldn't get becauses you had; a situation common in his life, of having first and then wanting what he had had, as if he hadn't had it." The significance of Memo's name should now be clear, but we can call on Jung to annotate it more richly: "the libido sinks into its 'own depths'. . . . and finds there below, in the shadows of the unconscious, the substitute for the upper world, which it had abandoned: the world of memories . . . , the strongest and most influential of which are the early infantile memory pictures. It is the world of the child, this paradise-like state of earliest childhood, from which we are separated by a hard law." Being the destructive and infantile, not the nourishing life-mother, Memo pretends to Roy that her breast is "sick," and Pop warns, she "will weaken your strength."

On Roy's day of tribute at the ballpark, Memo relents for the first time and agrees to a drive, longing to see the ocean. In view of the presence of the Waste Land theme, we do not need Jung to connect water with the maternally derived life-energy in the unconscious; but Jung does make much of the "maternal significance" of water, of the fact that the libido wishes "the black water of death might be the water of life," and that the black water of death "represents the devouring mother." In Harriet's presence infantile Roy could not manage the water, spilling it on the table; and the description, "the pitcher thumped the pitcher down" can be read either way. Sam, the fading father figure, sneaks a shower in the train crew's compartment because the life-water is not the privilege of coach-travellers;

and Sam deliriously foresees his death in terms of being thrown off the train of time and being carried off by a foaming river. Harriet had seen Roy defeating the Whammer as Sir Perceval slaying Sir Maldemer—the water-sick, failing hero. Before his infantile assault on Harriet, Roy had seen through the train window the "black water" and "tormented trees"; and beyond her fatal hotel room he saw "the endless dark lake." The Judge confesses his childhood nightmare was drowning and, unaware he is admitting repression and consequent fixation in the terrible mother, boasts that through discipline—that externally imposed restraint—"water is my favorite beverage." On the drive with Memo, then, Roy, who naturally "liked the water," does not care if they never reach it; Memo intends only to wade in some pond; and when they reach a stream, the sign reads, "Danger. Polluted Water. No Swimming." Memo of the poisoned water is not the Great Mother because she herself is regressive. Father-abandoned (just as Roy had been mother-abandoned), introverted, and yearning for protection from reality, she is allied, like the Judge, with Gus the Bookie, whom she considers a "daddy" and over whose battered body she at length makes "mothering noises."

IV

Before continuing with Roy's drive with Memo it is necessary to consider a few other symbols. Roy has a recurrent subconscious image of himself as a boy sheltered within a silent, moonlit forest filled with bird cries. Moon and bird, not unexpectedly, are among Jung's major symbols of the mother, as the forest is of psychic energy. Murderous Harriet's name is Bird, and Roy had seen in her a resemblance to his own mother, adding, "That bird." Memo, corrupting Roy by playing on his sympathy, looked "like a little lost bird." To the fading Whammer the ball Roy pitched to him recalled a boyhood image of a "bird-form"; when Roy is at the height of his power the ball he hits plummets "like a dead bird," the terrible mother having been defeated for the moment; and, in his perfect fielding, he instinctively catches a flying object that turns out to be a bird he has crushed into a bloody mess. The vision of the boy, moreover, is associated in his mind with going back home and withdrawing from the hardships of reality; and, in its inwardness, it is juxtaposed to the train, symbolic of the inexorable movement of time in the world and of Roy's worldly ambitions. The boy in the woods is symbolic of his entirely private, mother-protected self that, because of the womb-like security, he refuses to mature. When, then, beside the polluted water he makes advances, Memo, cross-eyed with fear, takes the wheel of the car, and, like a bacchante, this demon mother drives insanely in the total dark. Understandably, the vision of going home returns to Roy, and with it the boy in the moonlit woods. In the horror of his hallucinatory experience Roy convinces himself the boy is real and that, the maternal moon suddenly vanishing, Memo has struck the boy down with the car as he emerges from the guardian maternal woods. "I heard somebody groan." "That was yourself," Memo says. It was indeed, for Roy's incestuous yearning for the mother of the "world of memories" has released the wild terrible mother to shatter his treasured infantile image of his private self. In the dark, Memo crashes the car into a tree, that psychic living strength from which Roy had fashioned Wonderboy. Back in his hotel, the vision of moon, woods, and smashed boy returns to him as a reality, and when his own shadow falls over this vision of "his lost youth" and replaces him, Roy feels "a burning pain in his guts." Like Harriet earlier, Memo has shattered the spirit, drained his psychic energy. A day later his slump begins, as years before Harriet's silver bullet, cutting across a vision of water, had caused his years of failure.

For her own security from reality, Memo has allied herself with Gus the Bookie, and for his benefit she sets out to corrupt Roy. Meanwhile, Roy's regression has moved his sexual libido back to the related but even more infantile "hunger libido," and Babe Ruth's big bellyache has begun. In Jung's terms, the libido has regressed to the "presexual stage." Unlike his incestuous desire for Memo, which was a regressive wanting of what he had had, hunger is the ultimate regression, food, like breast-feeding, giving him "a feeling of both having something and wanting it the same minute he was having it." Through this monumental hunger, Memo, carrying in her name the memory of the infant's nursing, plans to corrupt Roy and wreck the Knights' quest for the pennant. "Food," she says like a Jungian, "is a woman's work" and, with Gus's money, prepares a Circean feast for Roy and the team the night before the crucial game. Even after the gluttonous feast, Roy goes out for hamburgers that look and taste like "dead birds," the symbol of the destructive mother. To complete this destruction, Memo has at last agreed to sleep with him that night, combining Circe's unmanning seductions of bed and board; but when he enters, the great bellyache, like a shaft of lightning, hits "the shattered gut," to repeat the recurrent pattern of the psychic wound. Here the story reaches through the baseball narrative, beyond the Arthurian legend, to an earlier culture-hero myth, for Memo has played Circe to Roy's corrupt anti-Ulysses, Roy refusing to leave the feast or tell the Knights to leave, although they would have listened to their leader. As he sinks in delirious pain, he has a vision of Memo as a "singing green-eyed siren" and then of being sucked down in a whirlpool of dirty water—the polluted water of maternal death—in a nearby toilet. Roy has succumbed to the temptresses—Circe, Siren, and Charybdis—whom Ulysses overcame in order to return to his responsibilities as king and father. In Roy the baseball champion, Arthurian knight, and Homeric hero have betrayed their fellows because of selfish infantilism of spirit. It is the wonderful irony of fate (and Malamud) that rushes stricken Roy to a maternity hospital and allows him to escape under the disguise of a visiting father.

V

Iris Lemon is obviously Memo's reverse, the extrovert's mother image, the other half of what Jung has called "the dual mother role"; and Roy does not want her even though she willingly gives herself. As her name tells, she is a kind of Flora or Ceres, but her mythic origins are manifold. Seduced at sixteen by something between a rape and a yielding to a man's hunger, she has devoted herself to her fatherless daughter. Self-sacrificing acceptance of this burden of the present has freed her of fear of looking at her past and earned her the mature self-possession that opens up the future; and yet she now repeats with Roy her girlhood act. Not only a mother, she is now a grandmother at thirty-three; and the fact sticks in Roy's throat, terrifying him and spoiling "the appetizing part of her." For the grandmother, mother of the mother, is the Great Mother, mother but not wife, both young and old, and, as Roy observes of Iris, a girl above the hips and a woman below. Unlike Memo and Roy's own mother—the terrible seductive mothers whom Roy identifies as whores—the Great Mother is the matrix of psychic powers; and through her, to use Jung's terms, the libido is redirected from its inward, ennervating prison to flow outwardly to the real world, exactly as Iris has gained possession of her self by giving it up to her daughter. Roy's failure is his self-centered inability to turn to her and sacrifice the Memo too vividly recorded on his spirit. What horrifies him is that marraige to Iris would make him a grandfather, which is to say the responsible hero-father who completely possesses his miraculous psychic strength and unselfishly directs it to his human community. "Man leaves the mother, the source of libido," Jung wrote," and is driven by the eternal thirst to find her again, and to drink renewal from her; thus he completes his cycle and returns to the mother's womb. Every obstacle which obstructs his life's path, and threatens his ascent, wears the shadowy feature of the 'terrible mother,' who paralyzes his energy with the consuming poison of the stealthy, retrospective longing. In each conquest he wins again the smiling love and life-giving mother." For acceptance of Iris would not be selfish Circean delight; fruity though her name is, she is a "Lemon."

Iris makes her first appearance at the depths of Roy's slump, his strength robbed by Memo. The episode is founded on a famous event in Babe Ruth's career and transforms it into a mythic version of the true hero-father's role, the "grandfather" role Roy might have filled. A grievously injured boy, his psychic energy having flagged, is not exerting his will to live, and because he is a fan of Roy's his father lies to him, claiming Roy has promised to hit a home run for him. Now the father pleads with the weakened Roy to fulfill the promise. Afraid of the "responsibility," Roy promises only that he will do the best he can. "A father's blessing on you," the truckdriver calls after him. Pop Fisher, convinced Roy's slump is due to Wonderboy, has benched him for refusing another bat. At this point, wearing the white rose that throughout symbolizes the glory granted by the Great Mother to the hero who accepts the burden of reality, Iris assumes her Great Mother role as Aphrodite and unaccountably rises from a "sea" of faces in the stands, with electric results. A subrational murmur spreads among the fans; a stranger next to her, as though her atmosphere were aphrodisiac, feels "a strong sexual urge"; and the air is filled with "unbelievable fragrance." Her purpose in remaining standing is to show Roy her confidence in him, to transmit it to him; and, she later admits, the price she paid was giving up her own privacy, the same infantile and self-abortive privacy to which Roy repeatedly flees and refuses to abandon or (psychoanalytically the same thing) make public. Yet for a moment he does. Motivated consciously by the sight of the suffering father and unconsciously by the risen Aphrodite-Iris, he offers to give up Wonderboy, and Pop does an immediate about-face and lets him bat with it: it is his to use because he is willing to give it up. When he then hits the home run, he is for the moment the Great Father and hero through the agency of the Great Mother. Just as Iris' self-sacrifice becomes Roy's strength, so his life-energy flows into another; and "everybody knew it was Roy alone who had saved the boy's life."

The night before her first meeting with Roy, Iris had enacted the ritual of her role. The summer rain that the fertility hero evokes with his talismanic bat has been falling. But life-energy is not purely benign, for ambivalent Wonderboy, made of a lightning-struck tree, also flashes with lightning, and of the lightning Iris has special dread, afraid prophetically "she would be hurt by it." After the rain, Aphrodite-like she had walked barefoot through the flowers in the park. But on meeting Roy next day she assumes another but related form of the Great Mother. Having once driven with Memo to the polluted water, Roy now drives Iris to Lake Michigan, and this Arthurian Lady of the Lake, no dabbler in pools, knows well and is expert in this maternal water of life in the unconscious. Her own life is summed up in her advising Roy that the lake water is cold, "but you get used to it soon." Like Harriet, Iris also subjects the hero to a "test," and Roy still knows only that he wants to be "the best," to break every record. Still selfishly infantile and fearing death, he wants to set records because in that way "you sorta never die," not learning from Iris' life that one gains his self by giving it to others and that one is immortal in the life-energy he gives. Baffled by the "test," Roy again thinks he hears the train of time, going nowhere in particular; and he freezes in dread. "There are no trains here," Iris says; not, that is, at the water of life. "It must have been a bird cry," she adds.

In the water Roy makes as infantile a gesture as he once had with Harriet and asks for a kiss. When Iris is repelled, he dives down into the lake. This plunge into the waters of the unconscious is not a new experience to Roy. When he first joined the ailing-Knights, they were under the care of a hyponotist, whose progenitor is the medicine man of the Arthurian fertility myth and who was as unsuccessful as his Arthurian predecessor, for his efforts through autosuggestion to rouse a winning spirit merely pacified the team. This outside help produced merely euphoria by reconciling the men to their unconscious, instead of releasing from it their life-energy, for that must result from an internal striving. Hypnosis opened to Roy the golden waters of the unconscious that became black as he dived deeper, vainly seeking a mermaid, the water-mother. But, lost in the black depths, he could not find his way back and violently broke off the vision: "no medicine man is going to hypnotize me." Tied to the terrible mother, he could not find his way back from the regression to reality. Roy at least knows the psychic truth: "I want to go through on my own steam." He is both right and wrong, for in fact he wants entirely to avoid facing his unconscious because of all the ugly past he has repressed into it like a dirty closet. Not only does Roy conceal his private self from the sportswriter who considers a private life a personal insult and wants to display it simply for the display; he also hides it from himself. Talk about "his inner self was always like ploying up a graveyard."

In Iris' lake, however, Roy dives down to the liquid mud bottom to find his mind crammed with old repressed memories that disgust him, and after he fights his way up through the iron bars of the current, surprised by how far down the maternal moonlight filters, he sees the golden mermaid Iris seeking him. For Roy has taken what Jung called the "night sea journey": the plunge represents withdrawal from the outer world and adaptation to the inner, and the emergence symbolizes recommencement of progression. "What the regression brings to the surface," Jung adds, "certainly seems . . . to be slime from the depths; but . . . it will be found that this 'slime' contains not merely incompatible and rejected remnants of everyday life . . . but also germs of new life and vital possibilities of the future." Or, as Iris redefines it, we have two lives: one of suffering, to learn with, another to live with in happiness after that. The first existentially constitutes the personal unconscious with all its slime; the second enters that unconscious to release a new life—to use the title of Malamud's latest novel. Or so it should be. But Roy protests, "I am sick of all I have suffered." "All it taught me is to stay away from it." His plunge was a childish withdrawal and a self-concerned determination to make another record, not a wresting of psychic energy from the selfishness in which it inheres.

VI

All the symbolism of the novel now comes powerfully to bear upon the crucial game, which Roy has agreed to throw for the Judge's bribe. As though three strikes were the three times one sinks before drowning, between his second and third drowning strikes two recollections flash into Roy's mind. His sudden childhood memory of his mother's drowning a tomcat is affiliated, of course, with Memo and the polluted water, for Roy is bound to the terrible mother and the deathwater in which she drowns the life-energy. His other vision is of his rejection of the Great Mother, who is available to the maturely unselfish, for Roy recalls that after he had had Iris beside the lake, she "wanted him to comfort her but he wouldn't. 'When will you grow up, Roy?' she said." And Roy, in the grip of the mother-bird, then intentionally misses Vogelman's next pitch. Once again at bat, still intending to throw the game, Roy is taunted by Zipp, the dwarf, and, still regressive, lashes out at that hostile, stunted public world by trying to chop the ball at the dwarf. When he succeeds in this rejection of the world, the ball is deflected from Zipp's skull and strikes Iris, wounds the Great Mother who directs the hero's energy out of himself to altruistic good. Injured Iris, pregnant with Roy's child, persuades him to win "for us" and to "protect me," and Roy returns to Wonderboy lying, appropriately, in the mud near the water fountain, determined now to "save the game, the most important thing he ever had to do in his life." But clearly Roy has learned too late, and with the next ball talismanic Wonderboy splits in half. The psycho-moral decision has come only with the death of the psychic energy. Without Wonderboy, Roy fails to lift the bat, and he is out again.

One last chance remains, and Roy now goes to bat fully determined to save the game of existence, to help Fisher and his team, not to betray them. It is now that Vogelman, that bird-man whose nemesis Roy had been at the height of his strength, sees Roy as the Arthurian hero charging him with a lance. "Take me outa here," Vogelman moans, and after pitching three balls keels over in a faint. But it is too late for Roy to be the father-hero. Twenty-year-old Youngberry, wishing to be a farmer and seeing visions of fields of golden wheat, takes the mound, and with the score at three and two, Roy strikes out. At a "bad" ball. Nature's season cycle has fulfilled itself: the new hero slays his fading predecessor, and Roy joins the ranks of Whammer and Bump.

In the night of defeat Roy performs the ritual of psychic mourning. In the now parched earth he digs a grave for his split bat, his shattered vital power, and, wishing it could take root and become a living tree again, he hesitates over the thought of wetting the earth with water from the fountain. But he knows the futility—it would only leak through his fingers. Because Roy's failure to be the hero is his failure to accept the mature father role, it is properly a boy who ends the novel, begging hopefully in disillusionment, "Say it ain't true, Roy." More was lost by Shoeless Joe Jackson than merely the honor of the White Sox or even the honor of the national game. For in the boy is each new American generation hopefully pleading that those on whom it depends will grow mature through the difficult love that renders the life of the human community the self-sacrificing and yet self-gaining purpose of their vital resources; that they not, selfishly seeking the womb-like security of disengagement, evade the slime that human existence must deposit within, but willingly and heroically plunge into it, with all its horror, to release for others its life-giving power.

With the insight sometimes granted the tourist, Virginia Woolf once wrote that baseball solved for Ring Lardner "one of the most difficult problems of the American writer; it has given him a clue, a centre, a meeting place for the divers activities of people whom a vast continent isolates, whom no tradition controls. Games give him what society gives his English brother." Baseball has given Malamud a ritualistic system that cuts across all our regional and social differences. The assimilation of the

Arthurian myth defines the historical perspective, translating baseball into the ritual man has always been compelled to perform in one shape or another; and the Jungian psychology with which Malamud interprets the ritual locates the central human problem precisely where it must always be, in one's human use of one's human spirit. *The Natural* is the broad formulation of Malamud's world of meaning, for in it he evolved the structure of symbols and the design of thematic patterns and relationships on which he has drawn in *The Assistant* and *A New Life*. In addition to its own artistic integrity, *The Natural* is the necessary reference test for a reading of his subsequent fiction.

V. S. PRITCHETT

A Pariah

This [*The Fixer*] is a Jewish fable: the hero as sufferer and martyr is a characteristic Jewish theme, comic and tragic, and a continuing one in Malamud's novels. They also draw on the traditions of the Russian novel, in which, because Russian society was anarchic, the human being, in his naive, unprotected, passive mind and flesh, could appear as if he were Nature itself. In *The Fixer*, a Jew in abysmal circumstances, orphaned by pogrom, childless, deserted by his wife, tries to free himself, takes one false step, commits a small illegal act, and destiny, i.e., history, is on to him at once. From that moment he goes from disaster to disaster; if there are respites in which the hope of normal felicity throws a gleam, this is only a deceit. Soon the screw will be turned tighter. The moral of *Candide* is that we must cultivate our gardens: The moral of Malamud's story is that you will be left with no garden to cultivate. From him that hath not shall be taken even that which he hath. That, of course, could be what you want: the ultimate sense of your own drama. Better be meek—yet meekness is a corrupting culture; suffering, into which Judaism and Christianity have put so much moral capital, is a miasma. Going to his final trial and probable death, Malamud's hero learns the lesson that the philosophy he has tried to work out with the aid of Spinoza—picked up from a secondhand shelf—was really self-regarding: the virtuous man grows to his proper human dimension and becomes large or noble not by what is done to him but what he does. If you make a break with resignation and go in for active virtue you must continue:

From *The New York Review of Books* 4, vol. 7 (September 22, 1966). Copyright © 1966 by *The New York Review*.

One thing I've learned, he thought, there's no such thing as an unpolitical man, expecially a Jew. You can't be one without the other, that's clear enough. You can't sit still and see yourself destroyed.

Afterwards he thought, Where there's no fight for it there's no freedom.

And so, if he survives his trial, this passive though stoical victim of the anti-Semitic witch hunt that followed the Russian revolution of 1905 will be a revolutionary. The relevance of the fable to the Negro or other minority situations is obvious. But Malamud is getting something native off his chest.

Yakov Bok is a half-starving odd job man whose wife has left him because they have failed to produce children. He has rejected the orthodox Jewish teaching and sets out for Kiev to earn more money, and to continue his self-education. If he can he will struggle somehow across Europe to Amsterdam and ship to America, the promised land. In Kiev he ventures out of the ghetto and one night, against his better judgment, he plays the good Samaritan: He saves a drunken Russian from death by pulling him out of the snow. The grateful Russian offers the good Samaritan a job and Fortune smiles; but only on one side of its face: Jews are forbidden to work in the Russian quarter. Worse, his grateful employer is a leading member of the anti-Semitic movement. Bok is desperate: employer and employee like each other, shall he confess? He decides to conceal his race and breaks the regulation. All goes well; but Bok's job as a foreman of his master's brick works is to prevent the wholesale stealing that is going on. For this he is hated and watched by the workers. One day some wild schoolboys pelt the brickyard offices with stones. Bok drives them off. A week or so later one of the boys is found savagely stabbed to death. The boy, left a long time, is bloodless. The hysteria in the town is useful to the anti-Semitic party: They need a sensational case to distract the people from the campaign for liberal reforms. Bok's Jewishness is discovered and he is accused of ritual murder.

For the rest of the novel, Bok is in prison for prolonged investigation and eventual trial. The examining magistrate is a liberal man and is soon convinced of Bok's innocence. But the anti-Semites organize their prosecution and eventually drive the magistrate to suicide and get the case to themselves. It is an embarrassment, however, to these fanatics. They are driven to wholesale faking of evidence; when this is questioned by liberal lawyers and the press, they go out for confession. Bok may or may not be innocent, but (they say) there is no such thing as an innocent Jew and he had better confess because if he doesn't there will be terrible pogroms. An acquittal will lead to a holocaust. Years of brutal treatment in prison in which he is reduced to a physical wreck do not break Bok. He sticks to his innocence. In the end someone throws a bomb at the wagon on which he is to be taken through the streets to his trial. He is not hurt. But it is after the explosion that he, for the first time in his life, thinks of punishment and violence, and makes the remark that I have quoted.

The material out of which this novel is made is nauseously familiar. We have been instructed to the full about anti-Semitism and we have been made to understand that its horrors are paralleled in the attitude to other racial groups. We know all about witch hunts. Mr. Malamud's danger, as a novelist, was that he would write one more scathing tract, and tracts get merely stock responses of good will. He is also open to the charge of being rather ardent in ill-health. If I were a Jew I would think it necesary to turn my hysteria into a passion for moral consciousness. The fable, as a form, is made for this and here Malamud tremendously succeeds. Yakov Bok has to suffer all the obscenities of Russian anti-Semitism, which was medieval in 1905. The modern anti-Semite might be shocked to see what images of medieval bestiality he has in his unconscious: it is a stye. So, first of all, Malamud is not generalizing. He has a precise, historical scene in mind; and a precise theme: the ancient accusation of ritual murder. Left on this level, Bok's story would have been no more than lacerating and Bok himself one of those casualties whom our despairing minds cannot help. Like the victims of massacre, they lose identity. But Malamud's Bok is not that. The novel is original because it is focussed on another drama: the drama of the crisis of moral consciousness in a pariah who has been forced to think for himself. He is forced out of animal cunning, out of the whimper of the kennel to become, little by little, a man. He is blind to everything except his one drive—to get away. This blindness makes him even clownish. His intensity invites absurd calamity, and one of Malamud's triumphs is that he does not forget that Bok has a saving core of the Jewish comic in him, if we understand he is playing black comedy. For example, he is manacled in his cell by day. The prosecutor visits him at night. The sadistic prosecutor tells him worse is to follow:

"I warn you, you will be publicly unmasked and seen for what you are."

Bok replies:

"What do you want from me here, Mr. Grubeshov? Its late at night. I need a little rest for the chains in the morning."

In another scene with his friendly lawyer:

"The thing about life is how fast it goes," said Ostrovsky.
"Faster than that."

Suffering has made Bok a wit. He can also get in a temper; or drop into sly naivety:

> I'm sick of prison.

He is prudish and shockable; it takes years of prison to make him forgive his wife. He is continuously human, something of a folk-tale character; his mind wonders as it wanders. It is even comic—in the sense that Don Quixote is comic—that his growing moral consciousness is like a load on his back: being ignorant did he take on too much when he tried reading Spinoza? Was he a mug to make a break? What is he?—simply a peasant, a Jew, a man in a temper, a little man in a muddle who can be certain of only one thing which appears to have no relevance: that he is innocent.

> Once you leave [the shtetl] you're out in the open; it rains and snows. It snows history, which means what happens to somebody starts in a web of events outside the personal. It starts of course before he gets there. We're all in history, that's sure, but some are more than others, Jews more than some. If it snows not everyone is out in it getting wet. He had to his painful surprise stepped into history more deeply than others—it had worked out so. Why he would never know. Because he had taken to reading Spinoza. An idea makes you adventurous. Maybe, who knows?

As for "the open":

> It was anywhere. In or out, it was history that counts—the world's bad memory. It remembered the wrong things.

Malamud gets in Bok's mind by a kind of passive cunning—very much a feature of this novelist's writing. He is also a master of means: all the sound views and good feelings count for nothing in a novelist who is not skillful in suspense, the tightening of the drama chapter by chapter, surprise moving from sentence to sentence. The shock of the suicide of the magistrate is marvelously timed. The lesser characters are seen with an original eye. They fill out the design, but never distort it. And all the time, slyly, step by step, the fantasies and lies which the anti-Semites have built up are revealed. The murdered child's mother is a whore, living among criminals. The whole story slips out vividly. Bok's wife is forced to see him in prison—they hope to get her to persuade him to confess—and she, the sly peasant, agrees; but what she is after is to get Bok to sign a paper saying he is the father of her bastard. Everywhere Bok is betrayed. And what is to happen in the end—guilty or not guilty, dead or alive? It is brilliant not to let us know, for although we long for Bok to win, we also hope he will not, for his strength lies in his tragedy and in the doubt about his future.

After all, doubt about general views about life have made him push on and on. Success at this stage would be an insult. It is possible to complain that the prison scenes are repetitive; and that—as usual with Malamud—there is something *malsain* about the women; and that Bok's dreams are too convenient. The last one about the Tsar almost frivolously so; but the whole fable is unexpected, inventive, and compelling.

SIDNEY RICHMAN

The Stories

There are unseen victories all around us. It's a matter
of plucking them down.

—BERNARD MALAMUD

"THE MAGIC BARREL"

One of Bernard Malamud's early short stories, "The First Seven Years," has an opening sentence so arrestingly simple and clumsy that it demands repeating: "Feld, the shoemaker, was annoyed that his helper, Sobel, was so insensitive to his reverie that he wouldn't for a minute cease his fanatic pounding at the other bench." A good many of Malamud's other stories, both later and earlier than "The First Seven Years," begin in a similarly rough-and-ready fashion. Here, for instance, is the opening of "The Mourners": "Kessler, formerly an egg candler, lived alone on social security"—and here the start of "Take Pity": "Davidov, the census-taker, opened the door without knocking, limped into the room and sat wearily down." The beginning of another story, "The Loan," varies the formula only by the position of the name but enlarges the clumsiness with the intrusion of a rhyme: "The sweet, the heady smell of Lieb's white bread drew customers in droves long before the loaves were baked."

Whatever is apparent in these beginnings, drawn from the first collection of Malamud's short stories, *The Magic Barrel*, it is assuredly not their grace. If anything, they seem, for their matter-of-factness as well as

From *Bernard Malamud*. Copyright © 1966 by Twayne Publishers, Inc.

for their suggestion of a rough and untutored speaking voice, to belong to a tradition so old that its reappearance is slightly unnerving. The last thing to expect from the modern author is the author himself. But Malamud never seems to fear his own voice, even if it means sounding like an immigrant out of night school translating the prophets, as in the opening of "Angel Levine," the story of an East Side Job:

> Manischevitz, a tailor, in his fifty-first year suffered many reverses and indignities. Previously a man of comfortable means, he overnight lost all he had, when his establishment caught fire and, after a metal container of cleaning fluid exploded, burned to the ground. Although Manischevitz was insured against fire, damage suits by two customers who had been hurt in the flames deprived him of every penny he had collected. At almost the same time, his son, of much promise, was killed in the war, and his daughter, without so much as a word of warning, married a lout and disappeared with him as off the face of the earth. Thereafter Manischevitz was victimized by excrutiating backaches and found himself unable to work even as a presser—the only kind of work available to him— for more than an hour or two daily, because beyond that the pain from standing became maddening. His Fanny, a good wife and mother, who had taken in washing and sewing, began before his eyes to waste away.

Needless to say, it has been a long time since an author could pass off a line like "His Fanny, a good wife and mother," and make it work. It has been an even longer time since an author's own compassion could convince one of the reality of pains so directly evoked. If one of the tests of a successful author is his ability to make convincing what should *not* be convincing, then Malamud has surely passed the test. In reading his better stories, one has the strange sensation of entering a world in which the most complex of realities masquerades with ease in a motley of folk-wisdom and genuine naïveté. Although the subjects are, as in the novels, the thorny ones of spiritual growth and decay, the terrors of alienation and salvation, there is about many of them an echo of a long dead voice intoning directly, "I will tell you now of dragons."

It goes without saying, of course, that the only thing that can sustain such artlessness is art of a very difficult kind; and so it is that, as a writer of short fiction, Malamud seems to have emerged full-grown and mature with his first collection. Published in 1958, the year after his second novel, *The Magic Barrel* not only received the National Book Award, but more importantly it represents, along with *The Assistant*, his major achievement. If assuredly uneven, the thirteen stories in the work contribute to a triumph rarely granted a writer so early in his career. With them he achieved what many writers, and even better ones, must struggle for years to attain: a voice which is distinctively his own.

Literary Traditions

For this very reason, however, it is also difficult to assess the stories. Norman Podhoretz wrote that the tales possess a quality which "very nearly beggars description." And the general critical response to *The Magic Barrel* bears him out. Blending in some indeterminate way both the resources of naturalism and symbolism, a vernacular steeped at one and the same time in the rhythms of European Yiddish storytelling, and a laconic irony reminiscent of Hemingway, the stores have inspired oddly divergent searches after influences. As a short-story writer Malamud has been called a disciple of I. L. Peretz, a Sherwood Anderson and Chekhov of the East Side, and frequently an amalgamation of all these things. Nor is the obverse side of the coin slow to rise: one often learns that the Jewish elements in the stories are neither essential nor even particularly significant—even from those critics who readily agree that the "Jewish" stories are precisely the best.

But there is no reason to deny the efficacy of the comparative approach. That Malamud has mastered his craft with the aid of "models" is as true of the stories as of the novels. A good many of the pieces, especially the shorter ones, are approximately if not precisely in the tradition of Yiddish folk-realism; and there is about them, in their pained but rarely bitter evocation of suffering and inhumanity, a narrative echo, as Earl Rovit beautifully put it, "of the eternal chant."

But if the intonations are reminiscent of the literature of the Pale, Malamud's handling of form reveals a sensibility "keenly aware," as Rovit adds, of the "formal demands of the short story." Not only do many of the tales, and even the most "Jewish" of them, rely heavily on the technique of epiphany, but they reveal a formal concentration as spare and as devoted to symbolic design as the stories of Chekhov or Joyce. Moreover, there are times when the stories, both in their fusion of poetry and outright horror, as well as the reiterated images of alienation and psychic crippling, sound curiously like Sherwood Anderson's tales of the grotesque.

The Stories and the Novels

But comparison with other authors, by virtue of the extensiveness of the possibilities, is misleading. For Malamud, borrowed technique seems only the means of shoring up and extending a vision that is essentially his own. That is why, perhaps, the novels themselves offer the readiest and the most illuminating approach to the stories. For not only do the shorter pieces recapitulate the central themes of the novels, but they also reflect in their variety and in their unequal value all the pressures that went into the creation of the three longer works. Variously, and sometimes at once, the stories move from the extremes of symbolism to realism; from a deft and conscious use of myth and ritual to a seeming artlessness; from fantasy to naturalism. In each case, the reader finds also the same interrelationship of fictional modes and successes-and-failures which undercut *The Natural*, *The Assistant*, and *A New Life*.

It might be expected that the finest achievement in the collection would belong to those stories which share most closely the techniques and the vision of *The Assistant*. Such, in fact, is the case. The half-dozen best stories, and preeminently the title story, though reminiscent of the ethical folk tales of Aleichem and Peretz, unfold in a remarkably tough-minded and spare crucible. In each case the major ingredients are the same. The Jewish heroes, most of them elderly, sit behind closed doors (the essential setting) in a twilight tenement world. With their hungers stripped to fundamentals and their bodies shaken by memories of ancient lore, they manage to translate misery into a bemused humanity. In each case, the dramatic conflict, to which all else is subordinate, is between man and assistant, man and enemy, the pursued and the pursuer. The conflict is so intense at times that it breeds angels and *luftmensch*, *doppelgangers* and ghosts; but finally it breeds a miracle, a moment of painful unmasking which resolves the conflict and often transforms the hero into something more than he was originally.

The Tales of New York Jews

The initial tale in the collection, "The First Seven Years," might illustrate them all; for the opposition and final integration of Feld, the shoemaker, and Sobel, his assistant, is pure Malamud. The aged Feld is the real center of the story by virtue of the special moral demands imposed upon him. Like most of the protagonists in the stories, Feld must choose between alternate values; and the choice, made in terror and suffering, distinguishes finally the shoemaker from the *mensch*.

Like Morris Bober, Feld is in part the victim of his own goodness. Spinning daydreams out of the February snow, and agonizing over memories of his youth in a Polish *shtetl*, the shoemaker has sworn to create for his daughter Miriam a better life than he has known. But the dream, with true Malamud irony, redounds not to Feld's glory but feeds the guilt which tortures his relationship to Sobel, a spectral young-old refugee who five years before had saved Feld from ruin by becoming his assistant. Aware without full consciousness that Sobel labored only for love of Miriam, Feld arranges a date for his daughter with a young accounting student who is the harbinger of a better life. For this action, Feld immediately loses his infuriated assistant and, for his guilt, his own sense of well-being.

A single date convinces Miriam, who had already been won by Sobel, that the budding accountant is an inveterate materialist; and when a new assistant proves a thief, Feld in despair takes to his bed with a damaged heart. Later, driven by a complex of needs, the old man pushes himself to Sobel's cluttered rooming house and the kind of confrontation which is Malamud's special province: a meeting in which the denied self begins, in pity, to leak past one's guard and for a decisive moment pours forth in a sanctified stream. Listening to Sobel's tearful declaration of his love, Feld shuttles from exasperation to a compassion that proves his undoing:

> Watching him, the shoemaker's anger diminished. His teeth were on edge with pity for the man, and his eyes grew moist. How strange and sad that a refugee, a grown man, bald and old with his miseries, who had by the skin of his teeth escaped Hitler's incinerators, should fall in love, when he had got to America, with a girl less than half his age. Day after day, for five years he had sat at his bench, cutting and hammering away, waiting for the girl to become a woman, unable to ease his heart with speech, knowing no protest but desperation.

Though Feld feels a gripping sorrow for his daughter's future, he submits to the relationshp and the return of the assistant. But Feld exacts from the now young-looking Sobel the promise that he wait two years before the marriage (and so invokes the mythic cycle of fertility). That is all of the story; but for Feld there is an instant of real though muted triumph, a gesture which, despite the winter night and the continuous poverty for himself and his daughter, stamps the story with a spectral promise of salvation through love. His success is no more perhaps than the ability to walk the whitened street "with a stronger stride," or to hear, without anxiety, the consecrated labor of his assistant, who, himself now the father and provider, sits at his work desk "pounding leather for his love."

Despite the brevity of the form, Malamud's ability to evoke a sense of full experience with an odd verbal twist, as in the last line, or to intimate the Biblical parallels of the story, seems to raise behind the actual story a canvas far larger than the described one. But what sustains "The First Seven

Years" most effectively is what sustains *The Assistant,* an alteration of techniques which continually shifts the character into a strange borderland
world which becomes the emblem of the author's belief in the possibility
of a leap beyond determinism. The intensity of Feld's emotion, the fragments of myth, the grotesque beauty of Sobel, and most particularly Malamud's own beautifully clumsy and compassionate voice charge the story
not only with the suggestion of human mysteries but human miracles. Here,
for example, is the description of Max, the poor accounting student: "He
was tall and grotesquely thin, with sharply cut features, particularly a beak-
like nose. He was wearing a loose, long slushy overcoat that hung down
to his ankles, looking like a rug draped over his bony shoulders, and a
soggy, old brown hat, as battered as the shoes he had brought in."

That Max might pluck a magic flute from the folds of his monstrous
coat seems only the result of the faith of the teller himself: that weirdly
ironic, poetic voice which reminds the reader—by an occasional clumsiness,
a halting rhythm, or the folk tale form itself—that what he is relating is
more than just art. What finally makes the miracle most believable, however, is that it does not occur. Malamud's tongue is "forked"; for, though
it rings at times with the visionary simplicity of a child, it is nonetheless
thick with the sour disaffection of a cynic which enforces upon the whole,
despite the clear drift toward sentimentality, a drama of pained possibility.

Techniques so delicately balanced, however, can easily become un-
coupled and spill over either into outright fantasy or the grotesque. While
it is true that Malamud rarely loses control of his Jewish tales, he does
occasionally slip. Stories like "The Mourners" or "Angel Levine" illustrate
this tendency.

"The Mourners," the second of the tales, recounts an incident in
the life of a sixty-five-year-old retired egg candler who seeks to end his days
closeted in a wretched little flat at the top of an East Side tenement. But
unlike Morris Bober or Feld, the protagonist, Kessler, is frankly a Jewish
grotesque: an aged isolato who had long before forsaken wife and children
and now, in filthy old age, devours himself in loneliness, speaking to no
man and, for his contempt, being shunned by all. For this reason "The
Mourners" is assuredly one of the most dismal stores in the collection,
overburdened with a sense of futility that is enlarged by Kessler's fanatic
resistance to the landlord's efforts to evict him. The weight of despair is
so intense, in fact, that the resolution, despite numerous anticipatory clues,
offers less relief than a weird shock.

Climbing to Kessler's flat, Gruber, the landlord, agonizes over his
guilty conscience even while intent on reaping the financial rewards that

Kessler's eviction promises. Once in the room he finds the old man in a state of mourning, "rocking back and forth, his beard dwindled to a shade of itself." Although Kessler is mourning for himself, for his past misdeeds and for his abandoned wife and children, Gruber, "sweating brutally," decides that Kessler is mourning for *him*. In a gesture that plunges him out of the role of landlord and back into Jewish history, Gruber wraps himself in a sheet and drops to the floor as a fellow mourner. While spectacular and even haunting, the epiphany of "The Mourners" is simply too abrupt and too meaningful to be supported by the two-dimensional characters and the unrelieved weight of horror. It is, finally, *only* the conclusion which remains in the mind, a sudden frozen tableau.

However, it is quite otherwise with "Angel Levine," the fourth fable in the collection and one which, while drenched in fantasy, exercises a bold, unmistakable magic. By virtue of its very extremes, the story also serves as a map for the implicit fantasy of the other tales. Manischevitz, whose tribulations remind one of a latter-day Job, is offered salvation if only he will recognize in the form of a mysterious visitor—a large bonily built Negro named Alexander Levine—a heaven-sent Jewish messenger. But in outrage against what he believes to be the pretensions of the Negro, and, wonderfully, his own naive inclination to believe, Manischevitz denies Levine. Moreover, he persists in his denial despite the evidence that Levine's mere presence relieves both the former tailor and his wife Fanny of some of their pains. For his disbelief, however, the pains return in greater fury; and Fanny sinks quickly toward death.

And so Manischevitz, with unwilling willingness, sets out in search of the black angel through the streets of Harlem. His feet carry him to such unlikely spots as a Negro synagogue where a Talmudic disquisition is occurring, then to a satanic honky-tonk where Levine, denied the salvation of Manischevitz's trust, is succumbing to Bella, the Circe of the establishment. In the end, Manischevitz does credit Levine as a Jewish divinity; and for this act he experiences a moment of vision in which he sees the Negro mount heavenward on a pair of magnificent wings. Rushing home to the magically recovered Fanny, the tailor whispers the tag-line to a millennium of Jewish encounters with the unexpected forces of humanity: "A wonderful thing, Fanny," he breathes. "Believe me, there are Jews everywhere."

Because of the supporting fantasy, "Angel Levine" is the only one of Malamud's stories to deal explicitly with the religious implications that offer subtle support to many of the other stories, as well as to *The Assistant*. But the difference is only a question of degree, and the story relies on the same kind of formal tension and resolution that directs the drama in most of the author's fiction. Like Feld, Manischevitz is required to acknowledge the divine essence in another, an act which redeems both the truster and the trustee. Because Manischevitz must extend his trust beyond the confines of differing skins, he has only a more difficult burden than most. What Manischevitz must learn, in fact, is the author's theme that Jews are indeed "everywhere"—in Protestants, in Catholics, in Negroes who can intone Chassidic wisdom in synagogues. As Norman Podhoretz has suggested of Malamud's characters, "The Jew is humanity seen under the twin aspects of suffering and moral aspiration. Therefore any man who suffers greatly and who longs to be better than he is can be called a Jew."

But if Jewishness generalized into metaphor and construct is Malamud's subject, the Jew particularized is his triumph. This particularization is certainly true of Manischevitz, whose every gesture or intonation reveals not only superficial Jewish aspects—superbly rendered—but the deeper attitudes and postures which have developed through ages of accommodating ethical vision to historical necessity. The Jobian parallel, in other words, is funny; but it is no joke. In Manischevitz's relationship to God, which runs from mild despair to the sense of abandonment, there is only loving reproof, never disbelief. His prayers, in fact, reveal an elemental closeness to God: " 'My dear God, sweetheart, did I deserve that this should happen to me? . . . Give Fanny back her health, and to me for myself I shouldn't feel pain in every step. Help now or tomorrow is too late. This I don't have to tell you'."

That Malamud loves his old Jews, and particularly those in whom misery has only induced more kindliness and gentleness, is unquestionable. Moreover, through them he has managed, as Dan Jacobson has suggested, to achieve "what has baffled and defeated greater writers: the capacity to make goodness of the most humble and long suffering kind real, immediate, and attractive."

"Angel Levine" is, however, only one of the better stories of its kind in the collection. It is certainly not the best, and the trouble seems to be that the fantasy is so enlarged in the service of victory that the story lacks the second property which cinches conviction in Malamud's best work. It lacks failure, the sense of continuing despair. However, in two others of the fables, "The Bill" and "The Loan," the blend of the real and the fantastic, of horror and triumph, borders on the miraculous.

"The Bill," structurally the more complex of the two stories, sounds again the problems of trust, of Jewish-Gentile relations, and of imprisonment in a grocery store which marked *The Assistant;* but it does so with an economy and directness that is remarkable. The opening paragraph is a weird blend of cameo realism and symbology that is sharply angular and impressionistic at the same time:

> Though the street was somewhere near a river, it was landlocked and narrow, a crooked row of aged brick tenement buildings. A child throwing a ball straight up saw a bit of pale sky. On the corner, opposite the blackened tenement where Willy Schlegel worked as janitor, stood another like it except that this included the only store on the street—going down five stone steps into the basement, a small, dark delicatessen owned by Mr. and Mrs. F. Panessa, really a hole in the wall.

Though the relationship of the Schlegels and Panessas supplies the tale with its dramatic center, the story proper belongs to Willy, for he observes the progress of the store and broods upon the disconsolate weariness of his life in an East Side wasteland that promises neither escape nor relief. Wandering into the Panessa store one day, Willy finds himself relating to the attentive Panessas the horrors of his barren life; and, as he speaks, he buys item after item. When he cannot pay, Mr. Panessa offers credit, ennobling the act with the thought ". . . because after all what was credit but the fact that people were human beings, and if you were really a human being you gave credit to somebody else and he gave credit to you."

But the tale is not about goodness alone, nor in this case even about particular forms of Jewish goodness. Instead, the subject is the depressing one of how, in a world ruled by the ineluctable demands of economics and accidents, even good can turn rank. Or better, it is a story which depicts the manner in which the soul descends into an embittering nightmare when the need to extend goodness is denied. And Willy Schlegel encounters such a nightmare when, after weeks of frantic buying on credit, the Panessas are forced to ask him for payment. Unable to pay, he retreats from the store, nursing an obscure grievance. As the season turns toward winter, Willy spends the nights dreaming of repaying and the days lamenting his inability to do so. In time, the pain of his guilt transforms his sympathy for the aged couple to hatred. In the spring, there is a momentary turning, a flash of redemption that hovers for a moment over the stony streets. Rising from a dream-filled sleep, Willy dashes to a pawnshop, receives ten dollars for his overcoat, and rushes to the Panessas' store.

When he arrives, a hearse is standing before the grocery and two men are carrying a coffin from the house. Told it is the grocer who lies within, Willy plunges into inarticulate despair in which only the author's words can find a grotesque glory: "He tried to say something but his tongue hung in his mouth like a dead fruit on a tree, and his heart was a black-painted window." The following paragraph, the last, belongs only to the narrator, who is now in full retreat; and it closes out the story with granitic objectivity: "Mrs. Panessa moved away to live first with one stone-faced daughter, then with the other. And the bill was never paid."

Though only eight pages long, the impact of "The Bill" is unaccountably powerful. One senses in it the impersonal weight of a naturalistic universe that balances precariously on the moral give-and-take of a few struggling nonentities—and then quickly crushes them. And in the second of the two stories, "The Loan," the method and the intent are similar—a swift fragment of action that freezes despair into permanent ice and yet leaves within, like Willy's "black-painted window" of a heart, a forlorn and foolish flicker of hope.

Fantasy supports "The Loan," but only as an undercurrent; for the aptly named baker, Lieb, blinded by cataracts and grey with sorrows, is also the dispenser of a strange communion. Though his pastries do not sell, his bread, after thirty years of failure, now "brought customers in from everywhere." The yeast was tears, the misery he wept into the dough. Successful but ill, Lieb tends the ovens while his second wife Bessie serves customers and worries over finances. It is Bessie who first notices the arrival of Lieb's skeletal friend Kobotsky entering the store with a face that "glittered with misery" to greet Lieb after a separation of fifteen years.

Overjoyed by the reunion, Lieb seats the grim Kobotsky on a tall stool in the back room, and forgetting the misunderstanding over a debt that had long ago ended their friendship, they recall their early days in America. But Kobotsky, it is soon revealed, has not come for memories but for money; and this fact fills Lieb with apprehension and Bessie with horror. In fury, as she swirls about the room, she recalls to the anguished Lieb the deceptiveness of their prosperity, the bills, the impending operation on his eyes. Kobotsky, rising like a ghost, prepares to leave, but he stops long enough to pour out a tale of woe. The money would have been used, he tells them, to purchase a stone for the grave of his wife, dead more than five years.

As Kobotsky catalogues his misery, it is not only Lieb who cries but Bessie as well. For a moment, the baker is reassured: "She would now say yes, give the money, and they would all sit down at the table and eat together." But the last word is not Lieb's nor Kobotsky's. The finale belongs to Bessie, and it is her tale which transforms the incipient sentimentality into a dreadful glance at demonic frustrations:

> But Bessie, though weeping, shook her head, and before they could guess what, had blurted out the story of her afflictions: how the Bolsheviki came when she was a little girl and dragged her beloved father into the snowy fields without his shoes; the shots scattered the blackbirds in the

trees and the snow oozed blood; how, when she was married a year, her husband, a sweet and gentle man, an educated accountant—rare in those days and that place—died of typhus in Warsaw; and how she, abandoned in her grief, years later found sanctuary in the home of an older brother in Germany, who sacrificed his own chances to send her, before the war, to America, and himself ended, with wife and daughter, in one of Hitler's incinerators.

Against Bessie's past and her wretched dream of the future, Kobotsky's woe expends itself. Woe and woe, fused together in opposition, deny them the expression of anything but compassion. As the loaves in Lieb's ovens turn into "charred corpses," Kobotsky and the baker embraced ". . . and pressed mouths together and parted forever."

"The Bill" and "The Loan" thus share alike the terrible consequences of morality and poverty in collision; and both gain their power from the nature of the theme itself: the horror attendant on the frustration of man's need to give. Another fable in the collection also sounds the same message, but it does so with such unmitigated directness that, like "The Mourners," it is more dismal than affecting. Entitled "Take Pity," the story is narrated in a sustained and brilliant Yiddish idiom, and tells how Rosen sought to give all to the widow Eva and her children; and, because of her repeated rejections, he finally assigns his possessions to her and commits suicide. But now in limbo, and narrating the story to Davidov, the census taker, Rosen and the widow suffer a weird turnabout. Having nothing left to give, Rosen inveighs against Eva who pleads for him with upraised arms: "Whore, bastard, bitch," he shouts at her. "Go 'way from here."

That "Take Pity" falls short of the other two stories stems in part from the discrepancy between the abrupt conclusion and the supporting structure. Most of all, however, it fails because the author's own voice is missing. In the better fables, it is primarily his voice which lends the ambience of religious sensibility—enough at any rate to convince us that, as in "The Loan" and in "The Bill," the world may pervert the overt act but not the resources of communion. But in "Take Pity" Malamud employs, for the first time in his career, extended first person narration. With his own voice gone, the story slips quickly into an almost Gothic evocation.

The New York Tales Without Jews

What is most revealing about Malamud's difficulties in manipulating the fable form, however, stems from his attempts to apply it to an investigation of similar themes without Jewish characters, as in "The Prison" and in "A Summer's Reading." The first, the better of the two, is again concerned with the accidents which despoil communion. Trapped in a candy store (the prison of the piece) by his criminal past and by an arranged marriage, Tommy Castelli seems in many ways a prototype of Frankie Alpine—a young man yearning for release from the blight of possibilities. Unable himself to escape, Tommy in part discovers the means of salvation through a surrogate, a ten-year-old girl who steals candy from the shop, and whom Tommy dreams of rescuing from the mistakes which had forced him into his time-rotting corner of the world. Though he prepares for the moment of confrontation with calculation, his wife discovers the girl's thievery. When Tommy interferes in the child's behalf, he finds himself refuted not only by his wife but by the girl herself.

In the same fashion as Tommy, George Stoyonovich, the young man of "A Summer's Reading," seeks unavailingly to escape the prison of self and a jobless East Side existence by telling his friends that he is spending the summer reading a hundred books. For the lie, George reaps the respect of his neighbors and a bemusing sense of personal worth. But the lie quickly turns rank when George realizes that Mr. Cattanzara, an early father image, suspects his dishonesty. George flees the recognition, but Mr. Cattanzara proves to be a giver of trust, one of those elderly saints whose goodness forces its way into the heart of its "victims." In the final paragraph George appears closeted in the public library, ticking off a hundred titles and settling down to a season of protracted reading.

While deft and compelling, both these stories are curiously unlike "The Loan" or "The Bill"; and the difference, of course, is the absence of a central Jewish character. Far from being a small difference, however, it accounts precisely for what the stories lack: the sense of the pertinacity of spirit, an indefinable aura of "goodness" which, through the agency of the Bobers and the Felds, transforms the most extreme of failures into a sad redemption. "The Prison" and "A Summer's Reading" are in fact naturalistic tales which reveal more of Malamud's virtuosity than his fundamental skills.

The same losses and gains are also apparent in the five remaining stores in *The Magic Barrel*—all of which either depart from the folk tale or seek to extend it into more elaborate and significant forms. Among them are Malamud's best and his worst stories, but even the worst possess power. The first, "The Girl of My Dreams," swings irresolutely between realism and symbolism; but it resolves itself ultimately into a farcical, ebullient account of the breakthrough into communalism of a shattered young Jewish novelist, Mitka by name, whose literary failure, curiously enough, has to do with an inability to record experience directly. Locked in his tiny room,

Mitka tortures himself with the sense of failure and agonizes over his land-lady, Mrs. Lutz, who unavailingly bears love and chicken soup to his door. To all her entreaties, however, Mitka presents closed ears with a tenacity humorously reminiscent of Raskolnikov's masochistic misanthropy. But Mitka, for all his self-incarceration, is one of Malamud's fractured young men who find their need for love and communion welling up in a strangling ooze; and, while resisting it, they are ripe for success. Success comes, moreover, through the appearance of a mysterious female writer whose newspaper stories had deeply affected Mitka and with whom, half in love, he had arranged a meeting. But "the girl of my dreams" turns out to be no girl at all; instead, she is a "lone middle-aged female . . . Hefty . . . Eye-glassed, and marvelously plain."

Mitka, however, is a man of character; and Olga, the "girl" of the story is also a cosmic mother. Steeling himself to her ordinary face, Mitka indulges in a lengthy colloquium, is fed, admired, and advised; and, under the influence of her faith, he opens like a spring flower. Returning home from the encounter with this new version of Iris Lemon, a woman who had suffered her way into humanity, Mitka vows to go on with his writing; and, more importantly, he decides to fling wide his door to Mrs. Lutz with whom he imagines a new relationship: "They would jounce together up the stairs, then (strictly a one-marriage man) he would swing her across the threshold, holding her where the fat overflowed her corset as they waltzed around his writing chamber."

Despite the humor, and the fact that "The Girl of My Dreams" is the first and only story in the collection to deal with sexual communion (one of Malamud's favorite novel subjects), the story remains, at best, only interesting. It lacks not only the concentrated effect of "The Loan" or "The Bill," but also the tangible persuasiveness that Malamud seems always to derive from his ancient Jews. The primary difference is of course Mitka himself, who, like S. Levin, is a young ostensible intellectual and so resists the kind of reduction to bedrock properties upon which Malamud's stories depend. To render Mitka viable to his theme, the author must rely too exclusively on satire and farcical symbolism—as, in fact, he does with almost all of his stories which deal with second-generation American Jews.

The Italian Stories

This same problem, moreover, comes to the fore in two of the three stories in the collection which deal with young Americans in Italy, a setting which Malamud seems to delight in almost as much as in New York's East Side—and for similar reasons. At once real and fabled, Italy (and particularly

Rome) surrounds the *angst*-ridden Malamud protagonist with the smell and detritus of ancient lore at the same time that it benumbs moral hunger with fanciful romance. In some ways, in fact, Italy serves Malamud in much the same way it served Henry James in his depiction of the naïve American in an international world: a fairyland supported by the thinnest of ice that, upon breaking, precipitates a plunge into depths of feeling hitherto overlooked, denied, or transmuted.

The first of these stories, "Behold the Key," is the most enigmatical. The protagonist, Carl Schneider, a student and a lover of things Italian, comes to Rome with his wife and children and spends his time, not with books, but in apartment hunting. Guided by an inexplicable Virgil, one of those shabby ministers of grace who frequently appear in Malamud's stories, Schneider encounters all manner of deceptions and intrigues, criminal landlords and outright knaveries until, at the end of his patience, a "perfect" apartment is found which can be his if he will tender a bribe. Carl refuses and not only loses the apartment but bears on his forehead the mark of the key thrown by the outraged former tenant, the individual who had insisted on the bribe.

If deceptive, there is at the heart of the story a grim, telling theme. What is being tested is not only Carl Schneider's patience but his humanity: his ability to understand the behavior of a people who, because of war and poverty, bear little resemblance to the literary curiosities that had nourished his dream of an ideal Italy. Because he fails to comprehend, he bears the mark of his failure—a failure of brotherhood—upon his brow.

The second of the Italian stories, which also deals with the failure of a young American in Europe, is perhaps closer to the center of the author's real interests in that it imports into the ancient setting a New York Jew: a thirty-year-old former book clerk who, "tired of the past—tired of the limitations imposed upon him," has come to Europe in search of adventure, romance, and, though he hardly dare name it, love. Entitled "The Lady of the Lake," the story is, like all the Italian pieces, longer, less concentrated, and more indebted to symbolist techniques than are the New York tales. Indeed, these stories which deal exclusively with young men in Europe clearly evoke in the author a technique closer to that of *The Natural* than to *The Assistant*.

However, the themes are the writer's in any setting. In "The Lady of the Lake" Henry Levin, who calls himself Henry R. Freeman, is precisely the kind of out-of-touch, past-denying, and self-denying specimen of incompletion that Malamud can stick wriggling to the wall with telling effect. Rushing through Europe, his heart bubbling with need, Levin finally finds romance and love (in a perfumed garden on the Isolo del Dongo) in the

stories, the means he employs to liberate them often strike new and vital ground.

Perhaps the most obvious symptom of this change lies in the absence of those remarkable fables like "The Loan" and "The Bill" which represent some of the most impressive achievements in *The Magic Barrel*. Only two stories in the new collection, "The Cost of Living" (first published in 1949) and "The Death of Me" (first published in 1950), employ the folk-tale form which Malamud had perfected in his first volume. "The Cost of Living" seems, in fact, to be a preliminary sketch for *The Assistant*—a tale which recounts how Sam Tomashevsky, an old and gentle grocer, was ruined by a neighboring supermarket and a guilt-wracked landlord. In the second, and the better story, the reader is also on familiar ground. One of those tragi-comic little tales (recalling, as many of Malamud's critics have indicated, Marc Chagall's affecting blend of bitter comedy and wistful nostalgia), "The Death of Me" is concerned with a saintly old clothier's efforts to reconcile his two warring assistants. Both stores, needless to say, are powerful; and even if not so powerful as the better tales in *The Magic Barrel*, they serve as clear reminders of the earlier collection.

The Transformation of the Early Fables

But what is so instructive about the new volume is that, beyond these two pieces, the fable form either disappears entirely or survives by virtue of a rather remarkable transformation that appears in two more recent stories—the title piece and "The Jewbird," both of which were written within the last few years. In both cases, it is quite clear that Malamud's interest in the semi-folk tale persists only by virtue of his ability to undo or perhaps exaggerate the weird mixture of fictional modes which made the earlier stories so memorable.

"Idiots First," which begins the collection, is a case in point. Though structurally it *seems* like the early fables, the resemblance is more deceptive than real. Indeed, the story seems somehow less a case of Malamud the neo-folk realist than a case of Malamud the writer of moralities. And that, precisely, is what "Idiots First" is: a morality *à la Everyman* in which the sense of a real world (if only the sense of it) is utterly absorbed by a dream-landscape, a never-never-land New York City through which an elderly Jew named Mendel wanders in search of comfort and aid. Where the settings in the earlier stories threatened to disappear, in "Idiots First" the threat is realized.

A summary of the plot clarifies the differences. Mendel is not only a dying man but one who has made a compact with death (personified by a bearded Jew, Ginzburg) and has been given part of an evening in which to gather the thirty-five dollars needed to send his idiot son to an uncle in California. The story, which follows the father from the moment he draws on "his cold embittered clothing" to the moment he confronts Ginzburg at the train depot, is a striking mixture of gothicism and sudden touches of realism. After an encounter with a "red bearded" pawnbroker who stinks of fish and inhumanity, Mendel conveys his son Isaac to the home of the wealthy Fishbein, a philanthropist who gives money *only* to institutions, and who orates in a masterly mixture of dialect and phony phrases: "Show this party where is the door—unless he wishes to partake food before leaving the premises."

Failing with Fishbein, Mendel hurries through a strange park in which leafless trees reverse their branches, runs screaming from a stranger (Ginzburg) who shouts "Gut yuntif," and ends up at a synagogue where a dying rabbi, resisting his young wife, allows Mendel to steal his fur-lined kaftan and then is striken with a heart attack. From there Mendel flees to the pawnbroker and at last to the station where the California-bound train is about to leave. However, Mendel is past the appointed hour. Ginzburg stands before the gate, barring the way to the train, and resists the old man's pleas in a voice edged with doom and guilt: "I ain't in the anthropomorphic business. . . . The law is the law." But Mendel, wasted and past his time, is also the carrier of human possibilities. Like a gnarled Prometheus he seizes Ginsburg by the throat, shouting, "You bastard, don't you understand what it means human?" Ginzburg, about to destroy the old man, sees in Mendel's eyes his own iron wrath and relents long enough for Mendel to place Isaac on the train and return.

Though there are echoes in its form of such pieces as "The Loan" or "The First Seven Years," the story creates a totally different experience. If in the earlier stories the author seemed an East Side Anderson, in "Idiots First" he seems an East Side Bunyan. What is most curious, however, is that where "Idiots First" undoes the close unity of the fables by placing comparatively real characters in wildly imaginary gardens, the second of the transformed fables, "The Jewbird," reverses the process. The setting of "The Jewbird" is real enough—Harry Cohen's apartment near the lower East River; but the protagonist is a bedraggled crow-like Jewbird named Schwartz who one evening flies into the kitchen and to Harry Cohen's preliminary swat cries: "Gevalt, a pogrom!" Beyond the initial shock, however, the story unfolds in a manner strikingly realistic; and it is soon clear that if Schwartz is a bird, he is also an exemplary image of the Malamudian victim. Half Bober and half Susskind, Schwartz is constantly pursued by anti-Semites and by fate. Moreover, and most importantly, Schwartz is also the compound image of opportunist and saint who tests to the extreme the humanity and the compassion of others.

In particular it is Harry Cohen, head of his family (a wife Edie, and a not-so-bright son, Maurie) who is tested. Stubbornly resisting Schwartz's presence, the effluvia of herring, the woebegone look of misery—as well as the bird's usurpation of his role as father—Cohen loathes Schwartz from his first appearance. As Cohen's guilt feeds an ever-growing hatred, his schemes to torture Schwartz become more diabolical. The climax occurs one winter evening when Cohen throws the bird from the window and in the process flings redemption, wisdom, and fatherhood with it. Later, in the spring, the weeping Maurie recovers the battered body, and when he begs his mother to name the murderers he receives the eloquent reply: "Anti-Semeets."

Like "Idiots First," "The Jewbird" retains the frame of Malamud's earlier short stories but largely alters the sense of reality. Because of his difference, it is difficult to measure the power of either tale. Of the effectiveness of the first, its deft application of allegory to Jewish themes, as well as its refined sense of terror, there can be little question. Nor can there be any question of the comic gifts in "The Jewbird." The style is delightful, and the reader succumbs willingly to its sustained realism-within-madness. But however that may be, neither story is so successful as the better pieces in *The Magic Barrel;* and the reasons seem peculiarly a matter of the self-conscious exaggeration of technique which, ultimately, does not support the conclusions. In "The Jewbird," the naturalistic end is simply too flat: the inevitable fall is too traditional to overcome the weight of the fantasy. The conclusion of "Idiots First" is similarly marred. One suspects finally that the allegorical presentation has teased Malamud into a victory he could hardly have employed in his earlier stories—or perhaps only in a fantasy such as "Angel Levine." Though more powerful than "The Jewbird," "Idiots First" ends at the moment Mendel leaps at Ginzburg's throat and not, as Malamud has it, when Ginzburg relents. The conclusion is not Malamud at his rigorous best—at those moments when he must rescue affirmation out of the inevitabilities of natural law. In succumbing to the temptations of allegory, Malamud has not only invested his vision of human misery with a new horror but, paradoxically, with a new optimism.

However, it is unnecessary to press the point because Malamud himself seems to have grown disenchanted with the form. Of the remaining seven stories, four are Italian pieces, one is a tale of a college professor which is strongly reminiscent of *A New Life,* and, most importantly, two are very recent stories which resist close comparison with any of Malamud's earlier works.

New Techniques

. . . . "Black is My Favorite Color" and "The German Refugee" return to a favorite setting, New York City; both are concerned with Jews under the stress of guilt; and both are about the terror of masks and of love corrupted. The ingredients, in other words, are the same as those which made up the better stories in the earlier collection. However, in both cases the resemblance to past stories is only slight, and in reading them one senses a whole new direction as well as an entirely different sense of reality.

Perhaps the element most notably absent from these stories is fantasy. In both, Malamud seems to be pitting his vision against a firmer reality, to be working with objective experience in a way he had never before done. The most important sign of this approach is that his own presence in the stories is absent. The two pieces represent the first time in his writing career that he has entirely forsaken the omniscient point of view. Both stories are told through a first-person narrator—one, in fact, is a monologue—and by virtue of this technique the author has automatically divested the stories of the most persuasive though most elusive element in his Jewish tales—the sense of his own mitigating compassion.

This latter fact is especially true of the longest of the two stories, "The German Refugee" (1963), which is told by a twenty-year-old college student who has been hired to teach English to a middle-aged refugee from Hitler's Germany. Moreover, the refugee. Oskar Gassner, is totally unlike the refugees in The Magic Barrel. An intellectual writer and critic, Gassner is one of the great men of the world who have fled the incinerators of the old country to take their chances in America. Indeed, in framing his story about this new kind of refugee, Malamud has also broadened it—for the first time in any of his shorter works—to a full and overt sense of the world at large. The problems of world-wide insecurity and inhumanity parallel, and in time dove-tail neatly, with the personal wound that lies at the heart of Oskar Gassner's character. Apparently like the Fascists, Gassner is riding the crest of an awful death wish. Having willfully left his Gentile wife of twenty-seven years in Europe—along with his anti-Semitic mother-in-law—Gassner must tend the twin sorrows of alienation and a sense of personal unworthiness. Unable, because unwilling, to learn English, he has succumbed to a paralysis of the will. But, since his survival in America depends upon his ability to deliver in the fall a lecture for the Institute for

Public Studies, Gassner has called in the narrator, Martin Goldberg, who through a blistering summer attempts, first optimistically and then by an act of despairing sympathy, to teach the despondent refugee the intricacies of the unfamiliar tongue.

In time, with the language at least, Goldberg succeeds. The lecture, however, is something else. Though he begins it a dozen times, Gassner can never get beyond the first page, and he vows, "If I do not this legture prepare, I will take my life." The pronouncement rides ceaselessly over the dark encroachment of two separate but interrelated leitmotives: the Nazi-Soviet Pact and Grassner's perpetual torment because of the wife he has left behind.

That Malamud is trying to connect the two strands seems clear. The general failure of humanity—the shadow of genocide and hate as a generalized death wish—is bound up and particularized in Oskar Gassner's guilt for his actions toward his wife. Yearning for death, the refugee finds himself in dreams identifying with the Nazis and the forces of anti-life generally. The problem is rooted in some failure or corruption of love; and its corrective lies in a sudden affirmation of love through an act of love.

The agent who brings about Oskar Gassner's temporary salvation is the narrator himself, whose faith in the old refugee carries him to the library where he reads about Gassner's subject: the influence of Whitman on German literature. When Martin takes his notes to Gassner, the ensuing scene suddenly rights an elemental wrong. Listening with sadness to Martin's ideas, Gassner suddenly rouses himself: ". . . no, it wasn't the love of death they got from Whitman—that ran through German poetry—but it was most of all his feeling for Brudermensch, his humanity. . . . But this does not grow long on German earth . . . ."

Gassner's pronouncement, in effect an affirmation of life through love, prompts him to complete the lecture. In the fall, with the coming of cooler weather, he delivers it without flaw, reading the words as if they were a screen against the world's impending catastrophe. Warsaw has just fallen, but the words of the poem rise bravely:

> And I know that the spirit of God is the brother of my own,
> And that all the men ever born are also my brothers, and the women my
>   sisters and lovers,
> And that the kelson of creation is love, . . .

This quotation is the limit of the story's affirmation. The theme of realization too late, a theme that haunts so many of the earlier stories, again is given the last word. Here perhaps there is more reason than ever before, for the worst barbarity of history is simply too monstrous to be mitigated. Two days after the lecture, Martin returns to Gassner's apartment to find the old man a suicide. Later, he discovers the cause in a letter sent to the refugee "by his anti-semitic mother-in-law":

> She writes in a tight script it takes me hours to decipher, that her daughter, after Oskar abandons her, against her own mother's fervent pleas and anguish, is converted to Judaism by a vengeful rabbi. One night the Brown Shirts appear, and though the mother wildly waves her bronze crucifix in their faces, they drag Frau Gassner, together with the other Jews, out of the apartment house, and transport them in lorries to a small border town in conquered Poland. There, it is rumored, she is shot in the head and topples into an open tank ditch, with the naked Jewish men, their wives and children, some Polish soldiers, and a handful of Gypsies.

"The German Refugee" is assuredly Malamud's most ambitious as well as his saddest story. Not only does it provide a new "method" but it also replaces the insulated settings of the earlier tales with a concrete social canvas. Moreover, the transition involved a larger, more intricate structure than any of the previous stories. For this reason one is tempted to overrate the attempt at the expense of the actual response. But even if it is not one of Malamud's most realized stories, "The German Refugee" is still impressive, especially in its effort to balance large social issues on the slender strand of individual torment. If Martin Goldberg's vision does not really support the use of the first-person narrator, the alteration of method has supplied the author with dramatic possibilities he has never before employed and which, on the whole, he has used to good effect. Perhaps most importantly, this story has opened up new fictional possibilities.

That Malamud can take full advantage of these possibilities is amply demonstrated by "Black is My Favorite Color" (1963), which is not only one of the best stories in the entire collection but one which deserves to stand with some of the finer pieces in *The Magic Barrel*. At once comic and terrifying, the story again involves the author in the problem of racial antagonisms and, for the first time since "Angel Levine," in the specific problems of Jewish-Negro relations. The story, however, is not a fantasy; and the narrator, Nat Lime, a naïve liquor store owner of "forty-four, a bachelor with a daily growing bald spot," is no angel-encountering Jobian tailor. Instead, Nat is a victim amid victims, whose special fate, as a boy and as a man, is to bang his balding head against the facts of blackness. Black "is still my favorite color," Nat says in the opening; but he can add, "you wouldn't know it from my luck."

What animates and reveals the story is Nat Lime's magical voice, picking its way between knowledge and ignorance, vulgarity and saintliness, with almost acrobatic skill. At times, in his despair over the failure of communion, he can sound like Frankie Alpine bewailing the impossibility to communicate through the baffling screen of misunderstanding: "If they knew what was in my heart towards them, but how can you tell that to anybody nowadays? I've tried more than once but the language of the heart either is a dead language or else nobody understands it the way you speak it." At other times he can sound like an aggressive Frankie nursing his failure in a self-pity that hides hostility: "That's how it is. I give my heart and they kick me in the teeth."

Ostensibly, the "kicks in the teeth" dominate the story, both in the recounting of Nat's early and later life. There was, first, Buster Wilson, the Negro boy who had accepted from young Nat such tokens of friendship as money and candy only to turn on him unexpectedly and scream: "Take your Jew movies and your Jew candy and shove them up your Jew ass." Later, there had been the Negress, Ornita, whom he had loved and then lost on a cold February night when a group of Negroes had accosted them in the street and assailed Nat as a "Jewish landlord" and Ornita as a traitor. Presently there is Charity Sweetness, the cleaning lady from Father Divine's who refuses to eat her lunch at Nat's table but, with a distant smile on her face, retreats to the bathroom and locks the door.

In this regard—as a story of love and friendship defeated by the world—"Black is My Favorite Color" could hardly be better, nor its sense of reality more persuasive. However, this is only one aspect of the story, and in some ways the least important. The full measure of Nat's frustration lies less in the collision of self and the world than in the collision within Nat himself. Like Frankie Alpine, Nat in effect speaks two tongues, and his motivations persistently double back in a dialogue in which good and bad, the *mensch* and the non-*mensch*, collide. To Ornita's apprehensive "What about children? Were you looking forward to half-Jewish polka dots?" he can reply, in an echo of Frankie's admonishment to Helen's talk of Jewishness, "I was looking forward to children." But at another point, describing Ornita, he can say: "Her face was pretty, with big eyes and high cheek bones, but lips a little thick and nose a little broad." Such disparate reactions, as well as Nat's consummately fractured gestures and intonations, dramatize the narrator's dilemma. As with all of Malamud's heroes, Nat's problem with self-integration is the crucial one. But the drama is compounded by the nature of the subject, and particularly by Nat's lack of insight, into a story more ambiguous and perhaps more agonized than most. Moreover, Malamud's irony is unrelenting, for Nat's human assaults on the barriers which separate him from self as well as from Negroes persistently turn rank in the noses of those who receive them. In effect, Malamud is saying that even the gestures of good carry their own peril in the real world. Altogether, the story could not be more baffling, nor, for this very reason, more convincing. In the conclusion there remains only the awful scene: the divided victim, a poor benighted Everyman, alone in his kitchen unavailingly screaming for a way through the barriers that deprive him of communion: "Charity Sweetness—You hear me?—Come out of that goddamn toilet!"

JAMES M. MELLARD

Four Versions of Pastoral

Bernard Malamud has achieved a no-
table variety in his four novels to date, for having begun with a baseball
novel in *The Natural* and a city novel in *The Assistant*, he has since produced
an academic novel in *A New Life* and a historical novel in *The Fixer*. But
Malamud has also achieved a steady development in the handling of his
own special fictional mode in the novels, and the latest work, *The Fixer*,
represents the most powerful demonstration of its range and effectiveness.
Nothing more than a modernization of the pastoral, a putting of the complex
into the simple so that "something fundamentally true about everybody"
may be expressed, this method has been contemned by critics like Marcus
Klein and novelists like Philip Roth because it lacks realistic specificity.
But the truth is that the failure of the realism is the success of the pastoral.
For Malamud, the pastoral mode is his greatest strength as a writer of fiction,
because it has given him an archetypal narrative structure of great flexibility,
a durable convention of characterization, a consistent pattern of imagery
and symbols, and a style and rhetorical strategy of lucidity and power.
Although Malamud employs different versions of pastoral in each novel,
The Fixer not only does all that the others do in developing his major
themes but also pushes the mode into areas never quite reached in *The
Natural*, *The Assistant*, or *A New Life*.

The very flexible structural archetype the pastoral offers Malamud
is the pattern of vegetation rituals and myths. Based upon the seasonal
cycle of change, this pattern gives Malamud a central controlling form in
the pastoral fertility myths of dying and reviving gods, of youthful heroes

From *Critique* 2, vol. 9 (1967). Copyright © 1967 by the Bolingbroke Society.

replacing the aged, of the son replacing the father, the primary expression of which is found in vegetation life rituals, myths of the Fisher King, and its historical successor, the Grail quest. The form that this archetype takes in each of Malamud's novels is that of the son finding and replacing the father or of the young hero or leader replacing the old. In *The Natural*, though there are other mythic associations, the central myth is the pastoral, bringing together vegetation rites, the Fisher King motif, suggestions of Grail quest, and, perhaps most importantly, the relationship of youthful son and aged father. The Fisher King reigning over a desolate wasteland is, of course, Pop Fisher, the veteran manager of the New York Knights baseball team, and the heroic "youth" who revives the team (and the outfield grass) is Roy Hobbs, the thirty-four-year-old rookie who leads the Knights to the verge of a pennant and then sells out to the forces of corruption. In *The Assistant*, the "wasteland" is the Lower East Side of New York City, the weakened and dessicated "king" is the old Jewish storekeeper, Morris Bober, while the youth who replaces him and brings new life to the female Bobers is Frank Alpine, the indigent westerner who does penance to Bober and eventually takes over the store after Bober's death. The Fisher King of *A New Life* is Gerald Gilley, the chairman of freshman composition at Cascadia College, which serves as spiritual and intellectual wasteland, and the new king who takes Gilley's place as husband of the previously barren Pauline is the English instructor from New York, S. Levin, who both finds and creates a new life. Although discovered only very late in the novel, the ineffectual king who reigns over desolation, "a valley of bones," in *The Fixer* is Tsar Nicholas II, who is symbolically confronted by the new hero, the Jewish repairman Yakov Bok, in the hero's vision at the end of the novel.

Adapting this archetype in each of his novels, Malamud devises two important strategies that both conceal the pattern's simplicity and expand its significance: one, the use of multiple levels dependent upon the basic archetypal relationship, and, two, the assimilation of the significant nodes of the narrative to a *seasonal* rhythm. Used partially to "display" the features of the archetype, the multiplying of father-son relationships in each novel serves primarily to reinforce and to extend its meanings. In *The Natural*, for example, Malamud sets up the central *tragic* plot by having a fuzzy-cheeked nineteen-year-old Roy Hobbs strike out thirty-three-year-old "Whammer" Wambold, the American League's leading hitter, in the novel's opening section, "Pre-Game." The novel's central relationship, between Pop Fisher and Roy, is foreshadowed, moreover, in the same section, where the scout who discovers Roy, Sam Simpson, becomes like a father to the youth, but dies after the contest between Roy and Whammer when one of Roy's fast balls hits the old man in the chest. The situation that gives the novel a tragic form, if not a tragic tone, is also created by a variation of the central pattern, for actually Roy Hobbs, older than "Whammer" in the novel's central narrative, should not have replaced Bump, the carefree young slugger, but, barring the near-fatal wound inflicted by Harriet Bird, he should now be giving way to the younger hero. What happens, of course, is that Roy's pursuit of greatness forces him to try things for which he is not now actually suited, his flaw being symbolized by the midseason slump and the climactic splitting of the mighty bat, "Wonderboy," a symbolic sword, lance, and phallus. This multiplication in *The Natural* is only structural, preparing for and explaining Roy's "fall," but in *The Assistant* it operates structurally and quite effectively to increase the novel's thematic implications as well. The "father-son" relationships between Morris and Frank, Karp and Louis Karp, Pearl and Nat Pearl, and Minogue and Ward Minogue involve many areas of man's life—family and society, the letter and the spirit of the law, morality and justice, idealism and materialism, love and duty. Here is probably the cause of *The Assistant's* superiority over *A New Life*, for, although it also uses the device of multiplication, *A New Life* increases the numbers but not necessarily the significances. For example, Leo Duffy foreshadows Levin's role, but he does not add to it; similarly, as Levin replaces Gilley with Pauline, so Gilley replaces the old department chairman, Fairchild, but the changes seem only an academic musical chairs and there are no important themes clearly visible.

In this respect, therefore, *The Fixer* is comparable to *The Assistant*, for its variations of the central pattern add many levels to the novel's theme. Early in the novel, the important "father-son" pair is Yakov Bok and Shmuel, Yakov's father-in-law. Soon, however, this is replaced by the obviously untenable relationship of the anti-Semitic Lebedev to Yakov, who has allowed himself to be romanced by Lebedev's daughter, Zinaida. After this episode, at the end of which Yakov is imprisoned for alleged child-murder, Yakov finds a parental surrogate in the kindly Assistant Prosecutor Bibikov, who seeks to defend Yakov as well as to instruct him. And, finally, after his two-and-a-half-years' imprisonment, Yakov recognizes his last paternal figure in the Tsar, Nicholas II, "Little Father." In addition to these variations, Malamud also increases the novel's thematic range by offering variations in other ways. For example, he implicitly contrasts Shmuel's relationship to Yakov with Marfa Golov's murder of her son, Zhenia. Along with this, there are extensions of the pastoral scapegoat ritual in many ways: Yakov is sacrificed for the Golov child, who supposedly was ritually murdered by the Jews; Bibikov is sacrificed for Yakov, who also becomes a "martyr" to the Russian Jews; and the prison guard Kogin dies for Yakov's freedom. Finally, juxtaposed to all these, is the figure of Christ, who serves throughout as a powerful archetype for the scapegoat figure. All these variations, as they should, serve to embroider the central theme by thrusting it into almost every aspect of man's life: Schmuel and Raisl, Yakov's wife, introduce themes of justice and law on the family and religious levels (Raisl, an anagram for Israel, is clearly identifed with Judaism itself); Lebedev and Zinaida and Kogin and his son Trofim shift the interests to personal and economic relationships; Bibikov raises the central ideas to a philosophic and theoretical plan; and, finally, Nicholas the Second shifts the center of interests to practical politics, the concern that seems most vital to Yakov, and to Malamud, by the novel's conclusion.

Whereas the multiplying of the basic patterns is a device for variety and extension, the device by which Malamud gives his simple narratives a sense of unity and movement is the seasonal rhythm and variations of it. The baseball season of *The Natural,* for example, offers Malamud a handy seasonal rhythm and he uses it pretty carefully, the first section, "Pre-Game," taking place in spring and coinciding with spring training, and the major portion, "Batter Up," taking place mostly in summer (late spring is the period of the Knights' terrific slump) and early autumn. It is almost as if Roy Hobbs were only a sun god whose fate is decreed by the seasonal movement, for he bursts into stardom on June 21 (the last day of spring) and suffers his tragic fall *after* the official beginning of autumn on September 23, the day on which the Knights clinch a tie for the pennant, have their victory celebration, and Roy gorges himself until he becomes dreadfully ill, leaving himself vulnerable to Judge Banner's bribery. Consequently, it appears that Malamud has used the seasonal cycle for structuring a tragic narrative, but, unfortunately, the tone of the novel is rather comic and one feels a lessening, rather than a heightening, of man's dignity because of Roy Hobb's fall. Here, again, *The Assistant* seems to use the pastoral conventions more effectively, for, though the seasonal rhythm also controls the narrative, it does not obtrude or seem contrived as in *The Natural. The Assistant* opens on a windy day in early November and closes after April and Passover, showing along the way the moral and religious rebirth of Frank Alpine, the physical deterioration and death of Morris Bober (as the result of shoveling an unexpected April snow), and the spiritual death and revival of Helen Bober, Bober's daughter and, ultimately, Frank's lover. But here, instead of forcing all the changes into one short half-year, Malamud shows Frank replacing Bober in the first cyle from November to April and then allows Frank another year, from Morris' death to another April, to win back the affections of the daughter. Like *The Natural*, *A New Life* uses a single unit but the time allotted is slightly longer, for it follows the pattern of the academic year. It is divided into four major parts to coincide with the seasonal cycle as well as to the important aspects of the death and rebirth pastoral motif. The first section, summer, shows Levin arriving at Cascadia College (located in a truly pastoral setting), getting settled, and finally being told by Laverne, the moonlighting waitress, that he "ain't a man." The second section, fall, begins with the first day of the fall quarter and ends with Levin's recognition that Gerald Gilley (the "Fisher King") is his enemy; subsequently, in the third section, corresponding to winter, Levin begins, consummates, and ends (he thinks) his affair with Pauline Gilley; in the fourth section, opening with "May sunbursts" and corresponding to spring, Levin takes up his departmental causes, replaces Leo Duffy as the "political" liberal, gives Gilley a losing fight for the position of department head, but wins Pauline away, and leaves Cascadia with her, her two adopted children, and a child soon to be born, having found both a new life and a new identity.

Although Malamud pays careful attention to the rhythm of the seasons in *The Fixer*, he also uses it more freely and successfully assimilates it to a broader, though still pastoral, cycle. Because the central event of *The Fixer* lands Yakov Bok in prison, there is inevitably less *action* than in the other novels, the narrative interest focusing on Yakov's ability to withstand pain and torment and to maintain his innocence. But for this reason the sense of narrative *movement* depends even more on the fixer's noting the seasonal changes. Consequently, Malamud gives us frequent details to suggest seasonal change and he notes months and seasons carefully, Yakov's tale beginning in November when he leaves the Pale for Kiev, and going through the arrest and imprisonment in April, followed by a detailed account of the first year and foreshortened accounts of the second and third years, ending in autumn about the same time of year it had begun. More important than the seasonal rhythms, however, is the pattern of Biblical myth that the novel incorporates: the story coincides rather carefully with the period of Christ's ministry, since Yakov leaves his family and community at the age of thirty, "ministers" to his people for three years, and goes to his trial and possible death at the age of thirty-three. Obviously, there is a great deal of irony in such a use of a "Christ-figure" by a Jewish novelist, but Malamud's point in using it is to insist upon the universality of the pattern, an implication admirably accounted for by the *pastoral*, rather than the simply Christian, aspects. Broadly pastoral or narrowly Christian, *The Fixer* insists as strongly as *The Assistant* upon the cyclicality of life, the necessity for endurance and hope, and the value of suffering as well as its needlessness. Yakov Bok's ministry, the heart of his teaching, is in fact the two and a half years in prison he maintained his innocence and became a hero and a "potential savior" of his people, a people including not only the Jews but all men who suffer without cause. Thus one feels strongly that Yakov will die, like Zhenia Golov, Bibikov, Kogin, and Christ, but one feels as well that his death will presage a better life for man.

Because of the pastoral conventions in Malamud's novels, the vegetation cycles to which the human lives are attached, the most important source of imagery and symbolism for Malamud is the world of nature, its benevolent elements of fields and streams, groves and parks, birds and fish and flowers contrasted to its demonic wastes, sinister forests, torturous mountains, and tomblike caves. Inescapably related to the cycles of the narratives, the kinds of imagery normally revolve from one pole to another in the novels, the final form being determined by the structure of the work. At least a parody of tragedy, *The Natural,* for example, opens in spring, in the American West, among virgin forests, then shifts to the probably too obvious "wasteland" of the Knights' ballpark. After Roy Hobbs's emergence as "hero," rain comes, the diamond regains its greenery, and the climate becomes more temperate. By the novel's end, however, there are many hints not only of autumn, which actually arrives, but also "thoughts of the barren winds of winter." Illustrating the same principle, but reversing the movement, *The Assistant* and *A New Life* have a comedic structure and thus their patterns of imagery conclude with details of spring and summer. In *The Assistant,* for example, Malamud finds an objective correlative for the attitudes of his characters in the mutations of weather, Morris Bober feeling buffeted by life as November's winds blow upon him, Helen feeling "tormented" by winter, but thinking of Frank Alpine when the rains come, and both Helen and Frank feeling life within them awakening when flowers begin to bloom and trees to bud in the spring. Similarly, in *A New Life* Levin's personal preoccupation with the world of nature in the West takes on an appropriate academic cast in his careful study of *Western Birds, Trees and Flowers,* a book perused in summer, laid away "all winter", and taken up again at a hint of spring. Pursuing the tragic implications of *The Natural,* as well as its interests in the "hero," *The Fixer* both opens and closes in a wasteland, wintry setting. And during Yakov's imprisonment, in order to show its importance to human life, nature imagery is brought in through Yakov's memory of and desire for it. We are told, for example, that Yakov "felt the change of weather in his head" and, later, that he imagined the "scent of spring."

Related to these patterns of natural imagery are the ways Malamud depicts characters and character relationships. The most satisfying sexual relationships are almost invariably at least begun in natural settings; Roy Hobbs, for example, makes love to Iris Lemon, who becomes pregnant, beside a grove on the beach of Lake Michigan, Frank Alpine first has Helen Bober in a city park, Levin makes love to Pauline the first time in the woods, and Yakov Bok, who goes often to the woods with Raisl, tells her, "You got me in the woods." As one might guess, principles of life and fertility in Malamud's novels are associated with women and, more specifically, with their mammalian traits; consequently, in them the female breast has unusual significance. Women associated with infertility and death, therefore, have "sick breasts," like Memo Paris (*The Natural*) and Avis Fliss (*A New Life*), or very small ones, like Helen, Pauline, and Raisl before they are revitalized by their lovers. Full-breasted women like Iris Lemon and Zinaida Lebedev seem always to offer the promises of life.

For Malamud, the arcadian, as opposed to the naturalistic, aspects of nature represent a kind of ideal of beauty and peace and fulfillment. Consequently, all of his protagonists long for them when they are not present in their lives, often remembering pleasant natural scenes in their pasts or dreaming of them in their futures. In the midst of a hot pennant fight, Roy Hobbs yearns for a family life and "going fishing in a way that made it satisfying to fish" and "with this in mind he fished the stream in peace . . ." Frank Alpine and Helen Bober both dream of spring time in the midst of winter, and when they are together they often feel that the edge has been taken off the cold winds. Levin finds his real love in the idyll with Pauline in the woods, looks back to it, and forward to a similar state in the future. For Yakov Bok, bound in solitary confinement, a beam of sunlight showing momentarily on his cell wall is enough to recall to him thoughts of a better life; a brief trip from the cell to an interview with Grubeshov, the Prosecuting Attorney, and the sight of imitation flowers on a woman's hat reaffirm for him the existence of a less malevolent nature. He too dreams of his mating with his woman in the woods, and he prays to a sky that he seldom sees for deliverance.

Because of his idealization of benevolent nature, Malamud finds his dominant symbols in natural objects, the major symbols in the novels being unusually consistent with the symbolism of vegetation myths and Grail quests. For example, three symbols consistently used are birds, fish, and flowers. As in vegetation rituals, fish in the novels are associated with principles of fertility and life, so when Roy Hobbs dreams of fishing and eating the fish he reveals a concern that he has not devoted his life to the right pursuits, a failure to achieve all life has to offer that is symbolized later in his mad orgy of gluttony. In *The Assistant*, incorporating the symbolism of the emblematic names of *The Natural*, a devotion to life is represented by birds, rather than fish, Frank Alpine being associated with St. Francis and the innocent mating of pigeons with the love of Frank and Helen. More complex as symbols than in *The Natural*, birds are also linked, in *The Assistant*, to the flower symbolism: at the end of the novel, St. Francis, "with scrawny birds flying around over his head," plucked out of a garbage can a wooden rose that Frank had carved, "tossed it into the air and it turned into a real flower" that he caught and gave to Helen, suggesting, of course, that Frank's sterile lust has now become life-giving love. With more nature *imagery*, but fewer fully developed symbols, *A New Life* brings in the fish symbolism through Gilley, the avid fisherman, a dream Levin has of struggling with a fish and pulling its tail off, and Pauline's dropping tuna fish in Levin's lap. Bird symbolism, although rather negatively, also comes through name associations, the plagiarist, Albert O. Bird*less*, being an unusually uninspired, unidealistic student (apparently the bird as symbol also represents the ideal, for that seems to be what Harriet Bird, of *The Natural*, represents). More suggestions of such symbolism are Levin's being a bird watcher and his carefully noting their return in spring. The bird symbolism of *The Fixer*, in keeping with the novel's dominant interests, is associated with the double-headed eagle of the anti-Semitic Black Hundreds and thus brings together in ironic juxtaposition a symbol of fertility and socio-political revolution: "A black bird flew out of the sky. Crow? Hawk? Or the black egg of a black eagle falling towards the carriage?" Having seen and wondered thus on his way through Black Hundreds mobs, Yakov shudders in terror a few moments later when he sees a bomb like a "black bird" seem to fly out of a "white hand clawing in the air." But it is also unironically associated with life and freedom: for example, when finally freed to begin his trial, "through a window [he] saw a bird in the sky and watched with emotion until he could not longer see it." Although one must recognize that Malamud's symbols in the novels are essentially pastoral, one must also recognize that the novels' power comes not so much from the sometimes obvious symbolism but from the total complex of pastoral conventions.

In some ways more important than the myth, the imagery, or the symbolism is the convention of characterization that the pastoral affords Malamud. Empson has said, "the essential trick of the old pastoral . . .

was to make simple people express strong feelings . . . in learned and fashionable language. . . ." Rather pedantically denigrated at times for being unrealistic, Malamud's simple characters are germane to the pastoral's major strategy. Thus in each novel Malamud has chosen as central characters people who are less wordly, more innocent, inexperienced, or naive than most human beings. Roy Hobbs, for example, is tremendously unfamiliar with the sophistications of modern life, and Malamud creates some cheap comedy at his expense in the novel's opening section. Similarly, Frank Alpine, though he has seen the world, gets into trouble because he is naive about crime and people, getting involved with Ward Minogue because he does not recognize evil when he sees it and with Morris Bober because he has such a simple idea of penance. Even Levin, the New York M.A., is considered naive and by people who in New York City would be only country bumpkins. And Yakov Bok, the simple "fixer," always insists that he is ignorant, uneducated, cowardly, a stranger "from the provinces," a "country boy." But these rustics, whether ballplayer, indigent, academic, or peasant, implement the pastoral's strategic contrast of simple and complex characters, of the *eironic* pastoralite and the *alazonic* cosmopolite. Thus Malamud, through this convention, achieves a great deal of irony, both comic and tragic. It is comic, for example, that the antagonists in *The Natural* take Roy Hobbs at face value, assuming that he is nothing more than "hayseed," only to discover that he is an adept "magician" who can play tricks on the gambler, Gus Sands, and an accomplished actor who can dupe the sportswriter, Max Mercy, with his portrayal of a dish-dropping waiter. And it is quite tragic that Yakov Bok should assume that one like Lebedev who quotes from the Sermon on the Mount should practice its principles or that he should believe he will be freed simply because his accusers can look into his face and see that he is not a child-murderer. But comic or tragic, irony is a major result of the contrast between the apparently naive protagonists and the obviously misguided antagonists, for there is always some kind of disparity between principle and action underlined by the protagonists' innocent assumptions.

In many ways, the most important result of the pastoral's convention of simple characters is the consequent simplification of style in the handling of rather complex materials. An aspect of pastoralism since Theocritus and Virgil, a simple style has immeasurable advantages to a novelist because it frees him to do other things, particularly to develop themes that could be handled only obtrusively in a complex, highly reflexive style, like, say, Faulkner's, at times. In Malamud, style is primarily a function of character, and not only in dialogue, because the author's point of view almost always is assimilated into that of the characters. Because of the simplicity of the characters the style necessarily is relatively elemental in syntax, diction, imagery, and symbol, and yet Malamud's language *is* fashionable and learned—an astonishing feat, perhaps, but still his most distinctive stylistic achievement. He can do this in the novels because the general concerns of pastoral art happen to be the concerns of modern literature and criticism. In *The Natural*, for example, he treats the same materials as Eliot in *The Waste Land*, but he does it in the combined idioms of baseball journalism and the Grail romance. The idea of "the hero" is a major theme here and in *The Fixer*, but Malamud could have found no less complex way of underlining it than to have Iris Lemon tell Roy, "I hate to see a hero fail. There are so few of them. . . . Without heroes we're all plain people and don't know how far we can go." Roy paraphrases even more simply: "You mean the big guys set the records and the little buggers try and bust them?" and Iris answers, "Yes, it's their function to be the best and for the rest of us to understand what they represent and guide ourselves accordingly." Established on a sports pages level—"There are so many young boys you influence"—the theme, as witnessed in John F. Kennedy, has undeniable connection to modern intellectual and emotional concerns. *The Assistant*, like so many modern novels, probes the question of identity, but so much more directly, Frank Alpine saying to Bober, "I don't understand myself." It is also concerned with death and rebirth, and, though at the time she has little direct evidence, Helen Bober can say, "Life renews itself," stating unaffectedly the basic truth of the novel's pastoral vegetation archetype. It is concerned, moreover, with the problem of "the Law," ostensibly only Jewish Law, though it has manifold implications, and Morris Bober distills a people's infinite wisdom to, "I suffer for you. . . . you suffer for me." And the *theme* of suffering, which may be compared to treatments by Faulkner or Hemingway, is summarized in Bober's funeral eulogy by Malamud's simple rabbi: "He suffered, he endu-red, but with hope." In *A New Life*, the most unacademic of academic novels, even Levin, a New York University Master of Arts, comes to express rather graphically the reason for the most important decision of his life, to marry Pauline and father her children. Answering the sterile Gerald Gilley, he says only, "because I can, you son of a bitch."

Employing devices used occasionally in the other novels, *The Fixer* exploits the pastoral's stylistic simplicity in many ways. Seen through Yakov's consciousness, the story, except for the flashback after the opening chapter, is straightforwardly narrated, the dialogue is uncomplex, and the language is concrete, and in *The Fixer*, as in *The Assistant*, the contrast between the manifest content and the symbolic content is enormous. Himself also an *alazon* like his oppressors, though Malamud uses him as an *eiron*, Yakov continually brings our attention to the ironies of man's existence by uttering a few simple words:

> I am in history, . . . yet not in it. In a way of speaking I'm far out, it passes me by. Is this good, or is something lacking in my character? What a question! Of course lacking but what can I do about it? And besides is this really such a great worry? Best to stay where one is, unless he has something to give to history, like for instance Spinoza. . . .

But, of course, we see, as he himself finally does, that Yakov did not stay where he was and thus discovered that what he has to give to history—himself—we all have to give. Through his attempt to understand Spinoza, moreover, Yakov Bok encounters another problem that "fashionable and learned" journals (*Life* and *Time*, et al.) take up, though probably not even *Time* solves it so succinctly: "If there was a God, after reading Spinoza he had closed up his shop and become an idea." Also through Spinoza, Yakov Bok is forced to grapple with what finally becomes the novel's major theme, the relationship of politics to freedom. Implied in Yakov's continual protests that he is "not a political man," this theme is expressed most simply in Bibikov's question, "cannot one be free without being politically free?," the answer to which is given by Yakov himself near the novel's end: "One thing I've learned, he thought, there's no such thing as an unpolitical man, especially a Jew. . . . Afterwards he thought, where there's no fight for it there's no freedom. What is it Spinoza says? If the state acts in ways that are abhorrent to human nature it's the lesser evil to destroy it. Death to the anti-Semites! Long live revolutions! Long live liberty!"

Imbedded in the phrase, "Death to the anti-Semites!" is the real heart of Malamud's versions of pastoral. Departing from Leslie Fiedler, who sees "Zion as Mainstreet" and "The Jew as Mythical American," Malamud envisions the Jew as mythical man, having said "All men are Jews" and using the Jew, at least in the last three novels, as the pastoral "swain," emblem of a realizable humanity. In Malamud, therefore, to be anti-Semitic is to be against the human being. And we are consequently forced to see that the people and the settings of Malamud's novels stand to the "real" world in the same way as those of all pastoral writers from, say, Virgil to Robert Frost. Each novel, in an important way, treats a microcosmic view of the macrocosm, and each theme may then be extrapolated to a universal level. Concretely embodied in the relationship of son to father, the universal theme for Malamud is man's relationship to the "Law," and the treatment of the theme of the Law gains in breadth and depth and sophistication from the first novels to the last one. In *The Natural*, the Law is primitive, is simply chance and fate, symbolized by Gus Sands, the "Supreme Bookie"; in *The Assistant* it is Old Testament Jewish Law, or the "spirit" of it represented by Morris Bober; and in *A New Life* it is liberal and humanistic, and is represented by Levin's "Laws"; "Levin's Law II: One becomes his victim's victim. III. Stand for something and somebody around will feel persecuted." But in *The Fixer*, it is all these and many more, for the Law is Christian, " 'But it is easier for heaven and earth to pass away, than for one dot of the law to become void.' " It is Judaic, "Don't look for God in the wrong place, look in the Torah, the law," Shmuel tells Yakov. It is legalistic, "As for the law it was invented by man," Yakov replies to Shmuel. And it is humanistic, "The law lives in the minds of men," Ostrovsky, Yakov's lawyers says; "If a judge is honest the law is protected." But most of all, as Shmuel tells Yakov, the Law is God, and even if God has been reduced to an idea, in the Idea, God exists and therefore embraces every facet of existence, whether personal, social, religious or historical.

In *The Fixer*, the universality of Yakov's role and the effectiveness of his suffering is shown in the influence he has on other men—and these are willing to die for him: Bibikov, a socialist, Kogin, a Catholic, and Shmuel, a Jew. And it is for these, "and for a lot more that I won't even mention," that Yakov is himself prepared to die by novel's end. More tragic in vision than any of the first three novels, *The Fixer* is also more affirmative and more convincing in its affirmation, for there is a sense at the novel's conclusion that at last someone has come who may revitalize the law and lead a demoralized people out of a political wilderness. Consequently, *The Fixer*, though much more, is Malamud's finest expression of pastoral, and one suspects the fact that Yakov (Jacob) is named both *Bok* (German *Bock*—goat) and *Shep*sovitch (apparently intended to mean "son of sheep") is more than accidentally appropriate to the novel's major strategy.

ALAN WARREN FRIEDMAN

The Hero as Schnook

From the small crossed window of his room above the stable in the brickyard, Yakov Bok saw people in their long overcoats running somewhere early that morning, everybody in the same direction. Vey iz mir, he thought uneasily, something bad has happened.

Tis passage, the opening sentences of Bernard Malamud's latest and finest novel, *The Fixer*, contains the essential Malamudian note: simultaneous passivity and seemingly senseless action, intimations of bitterness and defeat, a vague but certain sense of impending doom.

Malamud's writings are not all of a piece, for only half (two novels and about a dozen short stories) are what I would call uniquely Malamudian, portraying a way of life, an essence, which we recognize as definitively Jewish almost to the point of stereotype. Not fundamentally a realist, Malamud often deploys Gothic elements of fantasy, grotesquerie, surrealism; but in *The Natural* and *A New Life*, his two weaker novels, these elements often seem unearned—too easy or abstract. In *The Natural*, Roy Hobbs, the title character, is almost killed when shot with a silver bullet by a near-naked seductress; he associates his baseball prowess with Wonderboy, his charmed bat; in a dismal slump, he is restored by making love to a thirty-three-year-old unmarried grandmother who comes to him as the fulfillment of a fortune teller's prophecy; and so on. Ultimately, and for all his inherent prowess, the protagonist, a mythical country hick, falls victim to the world's

From *Southern Review* 4, vol. 4 (October 1968). Copyright © 1968 by Louisiana State University. Louisiana State University Press.

essential shoddiness and his own continuing inability to cope with it. Clearly enough, in fact all too clearly, the novel is a reworking of Homeric, Waste Land, and Holy Grail legends, but the baseball formula is too frail to bear the weight of imposed meaning; and the inevitable drive from last place to first, resulting in the play-off loss as Roy's role shifts from superstar to Casey at the Bat, is so predictable it is gratuitous. The novel lacks artistic or "historical inevitability" because Roy Hobbs—swinging wildly from titanic heroism to abject failure and never staying still long enough to become human—exists more as his author's instrument than the world's victim.

A New Life is less surrealistic but more grotesque: Seymour Levin, an ex-drunkard ex-New Yorker, becomes an instructor of English at a small, inbred Western college. He carries on an affair with, among others, the breastless wife of the seedless heir apparent to the departmental chairmanship; Levin himself tries for the chairmanship and fails primarily because his double rival announces the affair on election eve; and he finally goes off with the now pregnant wife and her two small adopted children—having obtained the husband's permission to take them in exchange for, of all things, a promise never again to teach at a college. And as if to underscore the absurdity of it all, Malamud concludes A New Life with the husband, alone and ensconced as chairman, triumphantly snapping a picture of the new-lifers as they drive past the campus, out of his life, and out of the book.

It is obvious that Malamud plays, or rather works, at allegory throughout these two novels—as well as many of his lesser stories—but allegory cannot be earned by sacrificing coherence or perspective. Realism and surrealism must not serve antithetical ends if our sense of incredulity is to be suspended. As one of Malamud's Jewish characters might say, "Allegory is not a novel. A novel is not allegory."

In the writings I take to be predicated on Malamud's essential and unique note, fantasy and grotesquerie are functions of realism. If the Matter of England is Arthur and his nobly chivalric entourage and the Matter of ancient Greece is the Homeric vision of epic confrontation between and among gods and would-be gods, then the Matter of Malamud is the poor schnook who runs a whole-in-the-wall pisher grocery; who has little to begin with and usually loses his little before long; who suffers and endures, suffers and endures, while profits become an ever receding dream and hope an obscenity. Yet he knows that suffering is the Jew's lot and so, having in a sense foresuffered all, he carries on grimly but comically. All Malamud asks of us here is that we accept as given an existentially absurd universe

which manifests itself as the Brooklyn world of permanent Depression or
as virulently anti-semitic Czarist Russia. From these worlds, fundamentally
and irreconcilably at odds with the beauty and dignity of the human spirit,
all the grotesqueness of *The Assistant* and *The Fixer* follow. Here, the assumptions may be impossibly ludicrous, but God knows they are quite real.

The terminology with which we speak of the contemporary novel
is, I think, familiar enough. The protagonist, an anti-hero, is the victim
of a universe beyond his control; he is in anguish to the point of despair
because his life, which he deems of value, evokes only indifference or
hostility; his interminable misery implies, in fact, his insignificance, even
his irrelevance, the sheer gratuitousness of what he is and what he endures.
Here, for instance, is Manischevitz, a true Malamudian sufferer cast in the
form of Job:

> Day by day, hour by hour, minute after minute, he lived in pain, pain
> his only memory, questioning the necessity of it, inveighing against it,
> also, though with affection, against God. Why *so much*, Gottenyu? If He
> wanted to teach His servant a lesson for some reason . . . why then any
> of the tragedies that had happened to him, any *one* would have sufficed
> to chasten him. But *all together*—the loss of both his children, his means
> of livelihood, Fanny's health and his—that was too much to ask one frail-
> boned man to endure. Who, after all, was Manischevitz that he had been
> given so much to suffer? A tailor. Certainly not a man of talent. Upon
> him suffering was largely wasted. It went nowhere, into nothing: into
> more suffering.

The anti-hero is predicated as beaten from the first: he is either will-less
or too feeble to translate his will, his personality, into a viable pattern of
action. Despite the fixer's quest for a better world, such a protagonist does
not meaningfully proclaim himself an adventurer seeking to make the world
yield up its fortunes and its answers to him. Modern man is so very much
smaller than his environment that such a quest is foredoomed to ludicrous
and dismal failure; instead, something like the reverse occurs. The world
thrusts itself against him, eroding his physical and spiritual resources until,
stripped and shivering, he is reduced to a Cartesian minimum: "I suffer,
therefore I am."

But Malamud's characteristic writings not only define themselves
by the force of existential anguish, they derive their special quality from
the ancient Jewish teachings and spirit embodied in the Torah (the first
five books of the Old Testament) and the Talmud (the collection of writing
constituting the civil and religious law). Fundamental to the faith—and to
the people stubbornly maintaining and embodying it long after, by any

ordinary historical reckoning, they have become an anachronism—is the notion that God's ways are righteous and inscrutable, and that man must walk humbly and a little warily to survive from day to day. The vision is dual—simultaneously experiencing the harsh realities of limited mortality and affirming an abiding faith (perhaps a little condescendingly) that God really *is* in control of things and does indeed know what He is doing. Perhaps Shmuel, the father-in-law of *The Fixer's* title character, best expresses the Jew's paradoxical acceptance of the world's inadequacies and God's continuing presence when he warns his son-in-law against anti-Semitism and atheism: " 'Be careful,' Shmuel said, agitated, 'we live in the middle of our enemies. The best way to take care is to stay under God's protection. Remember, if He's not perfect, neither are we.' " Like Job, the Jew is awed by the magnificence and power of his God, yet he knows too much about unjust suffering and his own relative innocence to blot out the experience of the world: "Though he slay me, yet will I trust in him:/but I will maintain mine own ways before him" (*Job*, 13:15).

Unlike both the theater of the absurd and the experimental novel of forty or so years ago, the contemporary novel of the anti-hero is not noticeably marked by distinctive style; its writers are more "realists" than are such technical innovators as Joyce and Virginia Woolf, even Conrad and Faulkner. But Malamud is of special interest for at least two reasons. First, his Jewish victims are not simply realistic, they are naturalistic almost to the point of predetermined misery. *The Fixer* is the *reductio ad absurdum* Naturalistic novel; Yakov Bok, the title character, is a Naturalistic victim-hero with a vengeance, and he not only inhabits but becomes a symbol for the lowest of "lower depths." Macbeth says, "I dare do all that may become a man; who dares do more is none." At the other end of the spectrum, Yakov Bok is stripped seemingly of all that separates man from the beasts below him: in his case, "who dares do less is none."

In addition, Malamud's superb understanding of the endlessly enduring Jewish spirit—simultaneously despairing and comic—best reveals itself in a masterful stylistic and thematic device I call "Talmudic tautology." It is a term easier to illustrate than to define. For example, in one of the short stories, a recent suicide named Rosen, in limbo awaiting judgment, is being questioned by Davidov the census taker about the death of a poor refugee grocer, the husband of the woman Rosen secretly loved:

"How did he die?" Davidov spoke impatiently. "Say in one word."
"From what he died?—he died that's all."
"Answer, please this question."
"Broke in him something. That's how."

"Broke what?"

"Broke what breaks. He was talking to me how bitter was his life
. . . but the next minute his face got small and he fell down dead. . . .
I am myself a sick man and when I saw him laying on the floor, I said to
myself, 'Rosen, say goodbye, this guy is finished.' So I said it."

Talmudic tautology, then, has the wit of a pun, the quiet bitterness of stoic
resignation, the force of sudden truth; it accepts and expresses both the
transcendence of God's ways and the essential crumminess of this world.
" 'What happened then?' [Davidov] asked. 'What happened?' mocked
Rosen. 'Happened what happens.' "

Both *The Assistant* and *The Fixer* are founded on this note, this
attitude; the universe, the given, is impossibly antithetical to human dignity
and worth, and its impoverished creatures struggle gamely to make a go of
things. And usually, as a consequence, out of the dungheap seemingly
conducive only to despair, glimmers of values begin to assert and affirm
themselves. The short story "Idiots First," for example, is a successful
allegory of man's feeble, hopeless existence and the irrelevance of his death.
Mendel, who knows he is to die this night, spends his last few hours
scrounging for money to get his thirty-nine-year-old idiot son, Isaac, a train
ticket to California—where eighty-one-year-old Uncle Leo, drinking tea
with lemon under a warm sky, presumably waits to care for him. Mendel's
steps are dogged by death in the person of Ginzburg, "a bulky, bearded
man with hairy nostrils and a fishy smell," who turns out to be the ticket
collector at the station and who refuses them access to the still-waiting
train because it is after midnight—after, that is, the time when the train
was *supposed* to leave and Mendel was *supposed* to be dead. As he has
throughout the evening, Mendel, in anguish, once again cries out for
compassion, for human relevance—and again receives rules for an answer.
The millionaire he had earlier appealed to had told him, "I never give to
unorganized charity," and now Ginzburg disclaims any responsibility for
Isaac's helplessness.

"What then is your responsibility?" [Mendel asks.]
"To create conditions. To make happen what happens. I ain't in
the anthropomorphic business."

But Mendel persists:

"Whatever business you in, where is your pity?"
"This ain't my commodity. The law is the law."
"Which law is this?"
"The cosmic universal law, goddamit, the one I got to follow
myself."

But Mendel goes Job one better, for after having laid bare the essence of his misery, he refuses to accept inscrutability and power as a valid response. In desperation, he "lunged at Ginzburg's throat and began to choke. 'You bastard, don't you understand what it means human?' " And Ginzburg, though he laughs at Mendel at first, is as astounded as Mendel himself at the dying man's "awful wrath," and he accedes, allowing Mendel to put Isaac on the train and see the train depart. Only afterwards, "when the train was gone, [did] Mendel ascend . . . the stairs to see what had become of Ginzburg."

Scratch a naturalist then and you find a humanist. For Malamud, man has nothing but the misery and intensity of his suffering—but the point is that it *is* intense; he is committed to it because it defines his uniqueness, his humanness. As a consequence, he can—at least at odd moments—impose meaning where God has not. He can make the universe take notice of him and pay some attention to his claims.

The contemporary American Jewish novelist—and writers like Henry Miller who mourn their not being Jewish—no longer feel the need to maintain defensively that "To be Jewish is to be human." Instead their work increasingly demonstrates that "To be human is to be Jewish," for the Jew suffers for us all. Frankie Alpine, the dark-bearded, prematurely old title character of *The Assistant,* is an Italian who comes on like a long-suffering Jew: " 'The week after I was born my mother was dead and buried. I never saw her face, not even a picture. When I was five years old, one day my old man . . . takes off and that was the last I ever saw of him. . . . I was raised in an orphans' home and when I was eight they farmed me out to a tough family. I ran away ten times, also from the next people I lived with. . . . I say to myself, "What do you expect to happen after all of that?" . . . All my life I wanted to accomplish something worthwhile— a thing people will say took a little doing, but I don't. . . . The result is I move into a place with nothing, and I move out with nothing.' "

A goyish embodiment of "Talmudic tautology," Frankie Alpine first does great injury to the long-suffering, hapless Jewish grocer who

> had never altered his fortune, unless degrees of poverty meant alteration, for luck and he were, if not natural enemies, not good friends. He labored long hours, was the soul of honesty . . . coveted nobody's nothing and always got poorer. The harder he worked—his toil was a form of time devouring time—the less he seemed to have. He was Morris Bober and he could be nobody more fortunate. With that name you had no sure sense of property, as if it were in your blood and history not to possess, or if by some miracle to own something, to do so on the verge of loss.

> At the end you were sixty and had less than at thirty. It was, [his wife] thought, surely a talent.

Yet having made an impossible situation still worse, Frankie gives up everything to identify with the Jew and his suffering, and the book ends on this note: "One day in April Frank went to the hospital and had himself circumcised. For a couple of days he dragged himself around with a pain between his legs. The pain enraged and inspired him. After Passover he became a Jew." Thus Frankie, who had complained of moving into a place with nothing and moving out with nothing, leaves a little piece of himself in *this* place—and the little which symbolizes the all of commitment contains, as it were, the seeds of possibility for "the new life" offered in Malamud's next novel.

In *The Fixer*, Malamud has pulled out all the stops and written a searingly brilliant novel. His mastery of dialect achieves new heights of artistry in order to express new depths of misery. Like Morris Bober, Yakov Bok thinks he keeps hitting new bottoms until he learns there are none. He is an archetypal victim with nothing going for him—except the rather dubious advantage of knowing that there is always worse than the worst and that he'd better get ready for it. Yet where Morris Bober, at last two worn out to endure, finally dies, Yakov Bok, though he dies a little on every page, gains kinship with the Mendel of "Idiots First." Out of his nothingness—not despite but *because* he suffers—he asserts and he affirms. He is not a classical tragic hero whose suffering is magnificent because of grandeur of character and the height from which he falls; on the contrary he is a poor schnook distinguished only by misery and his sense of victimization. But because he embraces these, and because, in rejecting a God seemingly obsessed with the perpetuation of injustice, he finds something in himself and in his life to affirm, he becomes a paradigm of a new kind of hero—one who, given the context of his meaningless, arbitrary world and his own feebleness, even irrelevance, when confronting it, triumphs because he endures.

The traditional Jewish attitude expresses itself in an old Yiddish proverb: "God will provide; but if only He would till He does." The characteristic reactions are resignation and complaint. "That's what they live for [thinks Frank Alpine in one of his more cynical yet incisive moments], to suffer. And the one that has got the biggest pain in the gut and can hold onto it the longest without running to the toilet is the best Jew." Malamud's Jews, with the major exception of Yakov Bok, the fixer, are living Talmudic tautologies: they know they are of "the chosen people"; it's just that they wish God would choose someone else occasionally. But it is for Yakov to learn that, like Job, he *too* has been chosen—chosen despite his desires, despite his forlorn plea that he wants only to be left alone. When Shmuel warns him not to forget his God, Bok responds angrily, " 'Who forgets who?' " He maintains that God has rendered Himself irrelevant: " 'He's with us till the Cossacks come galloping, then he's elsewhere. He's in the outhouse, that's where he is.' " But he also begins by rejecting the possibility for reform in *this* world: " 'Where I ought to go is to the Socialist Bund meetings. . . . But the truth of it is I dislike politics. . . . What good is it if you're not an activist? I guess it's my nature. I incline toward the philosophical although I don't know much about anything.' " So Yakov must learn, and by the end he begins to understand both what it means to be a Jew and that there's no such thing as an unpolitical man, especially a Jew.

Yakov starts out then by rejecting both God and his Jewishness. Setting the book in motion, he flees the Jewish town, the shtetl, "an island surrounded by Russia." He leaves because "the shtetl is a prison. . . . It moulders and the Jews moulder in it. Here we're all prisoners . . . so it's time to try elsewhere I've finally decided." A reluctant Jewish Don Quixote, a mock-epic hero once removed, he journeys to Kiev to wrestle with and slay the dragon-windmill—that is, to find what the world has for him to find. His even more reluctant horse, one of the great beasts of literature, is a broken-down, flatulent nag with eroded teeth, whose haphazard motion constantly rouses Yakov's intense but feeble wrath: " 'I'm a bitter man, you bastard horse. Come to your senses or you'll suffer.' " For the fixer, who drinks his bitter tea unsweetened and blames existence, the horse, a semitic Rosinante, becomes a symbol of all the "trials, worries, circumstances" he associates with the shtetl world he is fleeing: "Like an old Jew he looks, thought the fixer," who trades the horse and what he embodies for a surrealistic, equivocal journey across the Dnieper River into Kiev and "a new life."

The virulently anti-Semitic boatman, to whom Yakov gives over his horse and entrusts his own life, embodies and foreshadows the doom which awaits him.

". . . God save us all from the bloody Jews," the boatman said as he rowed, "those long-nosed, pock-marked, cheating, bloodsucking parasites. . . . They foul up earth and air with their body stink and garlic breaths, and Russia will be done to death by the diseases they spread unless we make an end to it. A Jew's a devil—it's a known fact—and if you ever watch one peel off his stinking boot you'll see a split hoof. . . . Day after day they crap up the Motherland, . . . and the only way to save ourselves is to wipe them out. I don't mean kill a Zhid now and then with a blow of the fist or kick in the head, but wipe them all out. . . ."

It is no wonder that, as Yakov later attempts desperately to retain his sanity under insane conditions, the Jewish horse he had given in trade should reappear in a nightmare vision: " 'Murderer!' the horse neighed. 'Horse-killer! Childkiller! You deserve what you get!' "

In Kiev Bok seeks meaning and possibility. "Among the goyim his luck might be better," he thinks, "it couldn't be worse." He thinks: " 'To have luck you need it. I've had little luck.' . . . So the fixer went looking for luck." And what he finds is a drunken "man lying with his face in the trodden snow . . . a fattish, bald-headed Russian . . .," a member of the violently anti-Semitic Black Hundreds. And Yakov saves him. As a consequence, Yakov's position becomes increasingly ambiguous: he rescues a persecutor of his people and he receives money, respect, even the sexual advances of the daughter; he conceals the fact of his Jewishness, and he receives a well-paying job and a place to live.

But this is the high point of Yakov's rise and already inherent is the nightmare obverse world which follows, for he has succeeded in isolating himself as much as Oedipus in the blindness of his self-righteous purpose. He has laid himself doubly bare and vulnerable. Symbolically, he has denied his people, his inherited scheme of values: rejecting his wife, fleeing the shtetl and the God who dwells there, bartering the horse, concealing his Jewishness. On the literal level, not only has he aroused the enmity of the boss's daughter, but his job forces him both to live in an area forbidden to Jews and, as a kind of overseer-policeman, to antagonize all his co-workers. Thus, when the catalytic event occurs—the murder of a Christian boy and the discovery of his mutilated body—all the forces of potential destruction descend on Yakov's wavering, vulnerable head. As a consequence of all he has done and been, he is where he should not be, and he thus becomes a handy scapegoat for those whose ends are served by the cry of ritual blood murder. And while the circumstantial incriminating evidence mounts and his youth dribbles away, he spends almost all the rest of the book (270 pages and two and a half agonizing years) in solitary confinement: brutalized, dehumanized, intimate with pain and misery of every form—beatings, hunger, poison, vermin, numbing cold, insanity—the list is almost exhaustless, and there is worse:

> twice a day . . . there were inspections of the fixer's body; "searches" they were called. . . . Yakov had to remove his clothes . . . raise his arms and spread his legs. The deputy warden probed with his four fingers in Yakov's armpits and around his testicles. The fixer then had to open his mouth

and raise his tongue; he stretched both cheeks with his fingers as Zhitnyak peered into his mouth. At the end he had to bend over and pull apart his buttocks. . . . After his clothes were searched he was permitted to dress. It was the worst thing that happened to him and it happened twice a day.

And soon it happens six times a day, with the time in between spent in chains.

For all that it is possible to detail the causes of Yakov Bok's sufferings, the sins of commission and omission that bring him in fateful conflict with his environment, such "causes" ultimately bulk no larger than, say, Iago's realistic motivations for destroying Othello. Yakov is kin to Job, that archetypal suffering Jew, who suffers because he exists—and because he is innocent. But unlike Job he suffers also because he denies his place in Jewishness (a quality word here, the sense in which all good men are Jewish), and his place therefore in mankind. Refusing to accept the role, he dismisses both Job and Job's God:

To win a lousy bet with the devil [he tells Shmuel, who has accused him of pride in his bitterness], he killed off all the servants and innocent children of Job. For that alone I hate him, not to mention ten thousand pogroms. Ach, why do you make me talk fairy tales? Job is an invention and so is God. Let's let it go at that . . . take my word for it, it's not easy to be a freethinker in this terrible cell. . . . Still, whatever reason a man has, he's got to depend on.

Job, for all the misery he endures and all his cryings out, has always his God to depend on. Despite the clichés about "patient Job," he refuses to submit to his suffering, to accept it as valid; rather he asserts his righteousness, demands answers to his questions, and awaits with certainty the definitive response he knows must come. The answer Job gets at the end may not be the one he sought, but it satisfies him. God himself speaks, and he awes Job with the sheer fact of Creation, of order out of Chaos. And Job, properly chastened, bows down and repents. Again, we may feel that God is cheating, that Job asks legitimate questions concerning good and evil, the morality of unjust suffering, and instead of answers receives Power out of the Whirlwind and the bribe of new children and new possessions. Nonetheless, there is no doubt that Job's universe is not absurd; God is, after all, in His Heaven and, whether or not we morally approve of Him any more than we do of the Greek gods, we are convinced that He is indeed in control. Consequently, Job's losses and anguish are predicated as meaningful, for Divinity implies pattern, a larger scheme of things within which even innocent suffering can achieve validity.

Yakov's plight, in contrast with Job's, *is* existentially absurd, for his world offers no possibility of a perspective in which his plight will partake of a controlling context. Job's situation is never hopeless because it is framed by our knowledge of God's participation, His ability to call a halt at the psychologically appropriate moment. Yakov Bok's world contains no *deus ex machina,* in fact no *deus* at all; and with God dead or feeble, Yakov's situation becomes ludicrous, for against this poor schnook, this apparently will-less excuse for rational, heroic man, are arrayed all the forces of organized despotic society, with its prejudices and power, its bland indifference to the individual and its degrading and abusive violence. The contest is so utterly uneven that we are appalled, and ever more appalled as the odds against Yakov become ever more impossible, and as he curses loud and long, and curses still more when he receives in response neither freedom nor damnation, but nothing, nothing, nothing at all—and then still more injustice and meaningless suffering. And we feel ourselves desperately clinging to our own cherished verities—as Yakov Bok on the ferry clung with wavering certitude to his knowledge that his feet were *not* cloven—in order to avoid sharing the fate of a human life being crushed like an egg beneath a tank.

In contrast to his son-in-law, Shmuel is a more common Jewish stereotype; he endures all, complains stoically, and remains firmly committed to his faith because, as he would put it, after all what else has he got? Like the long-suffering father in *Fiddler on the Roof,* he asks in effect, "Would it spoil some vast eternal plan if I were a wealthy man?" But neither really expects an answer. Yakov, on the other hand, knows the answer—or thinks he does—that, yes, it *would* spoil some vast eternal plan, for Jews by the fact of their being Jews and alive in this world of shtetls and pogroms and Black Hundreds are designed to suffer, and to survive tenaciously to suffer still more. Yakov, even before his suffering had begun in earnest, had asked *his* key question, "Who invented my life?"—and now he begins to realize that he has got to invent it himself.

And so Yakov both pities himself and maintains his own ways in the face of all he is forced to endure alone. He is pressed to confess the crime, pressed by promises of freedom if he does and strident threats of pogroms if he refuses. He has his miseries to confess but nothing more: "A confession, he knew, would doom him forever. He was already doomed." His tautological resignation, his refusal to sign a confession, seems as much a negative act as a positive one; with good reason, he refuses to trust either the promises or the threats, believing he would give all and gain nothing. But later he is offered freedom *without* conditions—he need sign nothing, he need confess to no crime: "He was to be pardoned and permitted to return to his village." And Yakov Bok, long victimized by a horror and degradation that would make the strongest of men despair, and long after we who have identified with him—and to read the book *is* to identify with him—long after we have stopped hoping for a way out, have in fact asked ourselves again and again why the poor schnook doesn't simply give up this farce, this absurd parody of human life, then Yakov Bok is offered this way out—and he refuses, refuses because he is to be pardoned as a criminal rather than freed as the innocent man he is. And our shock at his absurdly magnificent refusal is intense, and it endures long after we have finished the book, and it remains with us as perhaps its supreme affirmation. No one, we feel, no one—and certainly not us—could have made such a grand refusal under such circumstances. But Yakov Bok, the littlest of little men, who began with nothing and has been going downhill ever since, he re- fuses—and his refusal shames us: for with our surpassing comfort and ad- equate faith we have complacently and condescendingly pitied "poor" Yakov whose fate, thank God, is not our own. At this climactic refusal everything changes: we learn that to the degree that our fate is not Yakov's, it is not because we are especially favored, but because we are not worthy— and because Yakov's suffering earns *him* worthiness.

What changes now is not that Yakov Bok no longer despairs; he does, over and over again, every day of his life, on every page of the book. But despair, like his cursings, no longer controls and defines him. Instead Yakov learns, he learns about people—slowly, painfully, one at a time. For example, his initial action contained among other things a rejection of Shmuel and all that that good man embodies, and later, after Schmuel at great cost and personal risk had come to see him to bring what little comfort he could, Yakov had cursed him for additional torments he received when the fact of a secret visitor was discovered. But then, after a nightmare vision of Schmuel's death, grief and guilt overwhelm him:

"Live, Shmuel," he sighs, "live. Let me die for you."

Yakov—chained, allowed to do nothing for himself, bound utterly in a life he called death because it lacked all freedom, all choice—had finally opted for suicide as the only possible escape. But now "he thinks in the dark, how can I die for [Shmuel] if I take my life? . . . He may even die for my death if they work up a pogrom in celebration of it. If so what do I get by dying, outside of release from pain? What have I earned if a single Jew dies because I did? Suffering I can gladly live without, I hate the taste of it, but if I must suffer let it be for something. Let it be for

Shmuel." And when, from the lawyer he is permitted at last, he finally learns that Schmuel is indeed dead, his new knowledge, like everything he learns, is both bitter and essential:

> Poor Shmuel, the fixer thought, now I'll never see him again. That's what happens when you say goodbye to a friend and ride out into the world.
> He covered his face with his hands and wept.
> "He was a good man, he tried to educate me."
> "The thing about life is how fast it goes," Ostrovsky [the lawyer] said.
> "Faster than that" [Yakov answered].

And now Raisl his wife comes. When she had cuckolded and deserted him, he recalls, "at first I cursed her like somebody in the Bible curses his whorish wife. 'May she keep her miscarrying womb and dry breasts.' But now I look at it like this: She had tied herself to the wrong future." For the moment they are together again; they review the bitterness of the life they had had, and he berates her with tautology: " 'So we got married,' he said bitterly. 'Still, we had a chance. Once we were married you should have been faithful. A contract is a contract. A wife is a wife. Married is married.' " Now he looks at her:

> This is where we left off, thought Yakov. The last time I saw her she was crying like this, and here she is still crying. In the meantime I've been two years in prison without cause, in solitary confinement, and chains. I've suffered freezing cold, filth, lice, the degradation of those searches, and she's still crying.
> "What are you crying for?" he asked.
> "For you, for me, for the world."

And her tears cleanse and redeem a multitude, and Yakov tells her he's sorry, he blames himself, he has learned: " 'I was out to stab myself, so I stabbed you. . . . What more can I say, Raisl? If I had my life to live over, you'd have less to cry about, so stop crying.' " And she does, and because he has spoken this way she is able to confess what she has come to reveal— that with someone else she has had the child they always prayed for. "There's no bottom to my bitterness," thinks Yakov, who now must add sexual potency to the unending list of all he lacks. But he agrees to what she asks, he acknowledges that the child is his, so that it may have a name, so that Raisl may be accepted back among her people. And this superb affirmation, this suffering for and restoring of the wife who had betrayed him, earns him much—including one of the quietest, richest, most beautiful lines in the entire book. The czar, a visionary antagonist throughout his imprisonment, appears one final time to defend himself, to say that he too suffers, to blame the fate that gave him a haemophiliac heir. He says, " 'Permit me to ask, Yakov Shepsovitch, are you a father?' " And Yakov answers the answer he has earned: " 'With all my heart.' "

First for only himself, then for Shmuel, and now for Raisl as well—Yakov, for all his initial alienation and continuing agnosticism, has at last earned the right to suffer for others, and he begins to recognize that he is responsible for all his people, that long-suffering nation without a country, alienated by birth and history, whose trials and traditions Yakov had mocked by his rejection. He realizes that "there is no way to keeping the consequences of his death to himself. To the goyim what one Jew is is what they all are. If the fixer stands accused of murdering one of their children, so does the rest of the tribe." And he now pities not himself, but all the Jews. "So what can Yakov Bok do about it?" he asks himself. "All he can do is not make things worse. . . . He will protect them to the extent that he can. This is his covenant with himself. If God's not a man he has to be. Therefore he must endure to the trial and let them confirm his innocence by their lies. He has no future but to hold on, wait it out. . . . 'I'll live,' he shouts in his cell, 'I'll wait, I'll come to my trial.' "

And finally his suffering gains perspective, a self-validating context. " 'Why me?' he asked himself for the ten thousandth time. Why did it have to happen to a poor, half-ignorant fixer? Who needed this kind of education? Education he would have been satisfied to get from books." But the education of existential man can be learned only through encountering the absurdity of experience: "Why?" he asks again.

> because no Jew was innocent in a corrupt state, the most visible sign of its corruption its fear and hatred of those it persecuted. . . . It had happened . . . because he was Yakov Bok and had an extra-ordinary amount to learn. He had learned, it wasn't easy; the experience was his; it was worse than that, it was he. . . . So I learned a little, he thought, I learned this but what good will it do me? Will it open the prison doors? Will it allow me to go out and take up my poor life again? Will it free me a little once I am free? Or have I only learned to know what my condition is—that the ocean is salty as you are drowning, and though you knew it you are drowned? Still, it was better than not knowing. A man had to learn, it was his nature.

Yakov, who now fears less and hates more, realizes too that commitment is a concomitant of existence: "One thing I've learned, he thought, there's no such thing as an unpolitical man, especially a Jew. . . . You can't sit still and see yourself destroyed."

Yakov suffers then, man suffers, as a scapegoat, so that others will suffer less: he suffers too so that he may learn, so that he may be purged, so that his innocence may be renewed; and he suffers finally because man is a creature who *can* suffer. But because he is man he can also choose, as Yakov increasingly does, to validiate his suffering, to make it meaningful. What kind of chance does Yakov ultimately have? Well, what kind of chance has any man? His lawyer tells him: " 'You have a chance. What kind of chance? A chance. A chance is a chance, it's better than no chance . . . an opposition exists, which is good and it's bad. Where there's opposition to reaction there's also repression; but better repression than public sanction of injustice. So a chance you've got.' " Should he hope? " 'If it doesn't hurt, hope.' "

It hurts, it hurts mightily, but Yakov hopes; what else can he do? Besides, who has less cause and more right? As a poor schnook, a fixer whose own fix seemed irredeemably beyond repair, he had clung to his life and suddenly discovered it had value—as if anything desired with such tenacious and stupid stubbornness must indeed be desirable. And the miracle which is Yakov's affirmation of his existence has taken its toll of his enemies; for all that they do they cannot break him and they exhaust themselves in the process—until, in the end, two of his guards sacrifice themselves for him, so that he may live, so that he may go to trial and confront whatever awaits him there, so that he will not have endured for nothing.

At the end, heading defiantly for the trial he has so long demanded, Yakov clearly has achieved the searing recognition and acceptance of self and world which is modern man's equivalent for the anagnorisis of the traditional tragic hero. As a consequence, he has already come through the trial of greatest significance, of rock-fundamental testing—and perhaps we too have come through a little, we who have created a world which denies its heroes and renders them impotent, who select as champion and scapegoat a poor schnook who, in prison, can look back on his earlier misery and ask, "How bad was bad if you were free?" and who, later still, can look back with nostalgia at his early months in prison because he did not yet have chains to bear along with all his other torments. Perhaps we too have come through a little because Yakov Bok—his past a horror, his present still worse, and his future the worst yet because unknown—can blow on the coals of the heart and discern a responding warmth that validates his suffering for him and for all. Perhaps we too may ultimately partake of his redeeming sacrifice and affirmation. As Yakov might say with a weary shrug and ironic pride, "Suffering I know intimately; I do it well. What's one or two more to suffer for?" And in such a response from such a man may lie our own last, best hope. Certainly Yakov Bok and Bernard Malamud, who create magnificently and enduringly out of negation and despair, give us cause to believe and to maintain that man who disposes may at last propose.

TONY TANNER

A New Life

We have two lives, Roy, the life we learn with and the life we live with after that. Suffering is what brings us toward happiness.

—from The Natural

Bernard Malamud's characters, like Herzog and Portnoy, are also eager to begin. And, like so many other American characters, they soon find that they are involved in a compromised environment which offers a wide variety of frustrations to their particular aspirations. What they are keen to begin is usually some form of "new life"; and one of the effects of their sufferings in the compromised environment is to make them redefine the form and content of that notional new life. At first glance Malamud might seem to be a realistic writer, deriving his topics from contemporary or historical actualities. His first novel is about a baseball hero who succumbs to corrupting influences at the height of his fame. There followed two novels, in one of which a man takes over a failing grocery store, while in the other a young college teacher takes over the wife and children of a senior but impotent colleague. Then came a novel about a poor Jew who gets caught up in the virulent anti-Semitism which was rife in Russia in the early years of this century. His most recent novel follows an American who is a "self-confessed failure as a painter" who goes to Italy to continue painting and failing. All these subjects offer occasion for studies in social realism, and indeed Malamud can register the force of historical actualities, the obdurate solidity of the

From *City of Words: American Fiction 1950–1970.* Copyright © 1971 by Tony Tanner. Harper & Row.

given world, with mordant clarity. But in fact his novels are far removed from anything we might understand by social realism. Speaking of the Jewish characters who figure in Malamud's work, Philip Roth made a relevant observation. They are not, he said, the Jews of New York City or Chicago.

> They are a kind of invention, a metaphor to stand for certain human possibilities and certain human promises . . . Malamud, as writer of fiction, has not shown specific interest in the anxieties and dilemmas and corruptions of the modern American Jew . . . rather, his people live in a timeless depression and a placeless Lower East Side; their society is not affluent, their predicament not cultural.

Roth's point was that Malamud dramatized his moral concerns in isolation from "the contemporary scene"—another example, for Roth, of an American writer who seemed not to be able to extract his fictional material from contemporary American society.

Obviously this is pertinent, but what I want to suggest in this chapter is that, while Malamud can certainly take cognizance of historical facts, he also resists history with his inventions. The pain experienced in time and place is eased by the timelessness and placelessness conferred by his own style. What Roth once saw as a possible limitation I would see as a distinctive achievement. In Malamud's apparently very different novels we can find a recurring pattern which links them closely together and reveals a profound consistency. The facts change; the pattern endures. All his novels are fables or parables of the painful process from immaturity to maturity—maturity of attitudes, not of years. This is unusual in American literature, which tends to see initiation into manhood as a trauma, a disillusioning shock, a suffocating curtailment of personal potential. Harry Angstrom in Updike's *Rabbit, Run* is a representative voice when he says, " 'If you're telling me I'm not mature, that's one thing I don't cry over since as far as I can make out it's the same thing as being dead.' " Malamud's characters discover that it is only by this "dying" into maturity that they can find the "new life" for which, in their various ways, they long.

The continuity of this vision may be suggested by the fact that all his main characters are involved in a quest. Each novel makes a point of emphasizing the searching and travelling of the central figure—characteristically we either see the central figure on a journey or just having completed one. *The Natural* (1952) starts with an account of Roy Hobbs's train ride bringing him from the Pacific Coast to Chicago where he hopes to break into big-time baseball. As Earl Wasserman has pointed out, this journey is described in such a way as to make it echo the whole birth process. And Roy Hobbs is travelling with high hopes and big demands. " 'I feel that I have got it in me—that I am due for something very big.' " Similarly Frank Alpine in *The Assistant* (1957) "had lately come from the West, looking for a better opportunity," while Sam Levin makes another exhausting trans-continental trip from New York to the West Coast searching for "a new life" in the novel of that name (1961). And Yakov Bok in *The Fixer* (1966) is moved by very similar yearnings and expectations when he leaves the *shtetl* and sets out for Kiev. " 'The truth of it is I'm a man full of wants I'll never satisfy, at least not here. It's time to get out and take a chance. Change your place, change your luck, people say.' " We may note here that for all these questers the change of luck in *material* terms is usually for the bad. After brief fame Roy Hobbs succumbs to sickness and corruption; Frank Alpine ends up running a sinking little grocery shop which is con-stantly referred to as a prison; Sam Levin gets involved in marital difficulties which terminate his tenderly cherished hopes of an academic career; while Yakov Bok is soon immured in a very real prison where he is subjected to atrocious indignities and iniquities. The quest for a better life seems always to end in some form of prison. And yet Malamud is far from being a pessimistic determinist. He shows, for one thing, how a man may help to imprison himself; for another, how an imprisoned man can forge a new self in his reaction to the imprisoning forces. In his world the bad luck which nearly breaks a man may also make a man.

Baseball being the national game, the rise and fall of Roy Hobbs readily becomes a parable concerning the fate of those youthful energies and abilities which society needs to revitalize and maintain it. As Earl Wasserman has conclusively demonstrated, while most of the incidents in the book are based on historically accurate facts (the shooting of Eddie Waitkus in 1949, Babe Ruth's stomach illness of 1925, the throwing of a crucial game by the White Sox in 1919), the novel as a whole is organized as a modern version of the Arthurian legend, an up-to-date regeneration myth. Roy Hobbs starts his career by outpitching the reigning king, the Whammer, in the process effectively killing his father figure, Sam. He is now the new champion. At the end of his career he is himself outpitched by another boy fresh from the country, Youngberry. The fertility cycle is renewed. Such transforming of history into myth and fable is an essential part of Malamud's art. But the main focus of the book is on Roy's personal moral failure. Although there are evil figures plotting round him, such as Gus the gambler (Merlin) and Memo the temptress (Morgan le Fay), Hobbs betrays *himself*. He does this by being an egotist who thinks only of what *he* wants from the world. From the start there are many indications of his infantile self-preoccupation, and when he is asked about his magic bat,

Wonderboy—so clearly phallic—he describes it as something he made "for himself." When Harriet Bird asks him what he hopes to accomplish, he says, " 'I'll break every record in the book,' " and boasts of becoming ' "the best there ever was in the game.' " When she answers, " 'Is that all? . . . Isn't there something over and above earthly things—some more glorious meaning to one's life and activities?' " he fails to understand her. In her role of the destructive mother, Harriet shoots him, thus inflicting the symbolic wound which ends his youthful, fatally solipsistic promise.

As a man (at least in years) when he returns to the game after many hardships, he is not totally selfish. For periods he does revitalize the whole team—he serves the community. But at key moments he slumps and loses form. These failures are related to his attitudes to two key women: Memo, who is barren, sick and in love with the dead; and Iris Lemon, the Lady of the Lake, who at one point restores Roy's potency so that he miraculously regains form. Memo is childless and dedicated to destruction, while Iris is so fertile she is already a grandmother and in time bears Roy's child. But Hobbs chooses to pursue Memo and ignore Iris and this reveals his central flaw. He rejects Iris because he cannot stand the thought of her being a grandmother; typically he omits to read her letter informing him of her pregnancy by him. He does not want to know anything about children. Attitude to the role of paternity is crucial in Malamud, and Roy refuses it. His fecundity, his reproductive and regenerative energies are all distorted into a sterile and self-satisfying lust. He is too narcissistic to concern himself with the continuity of generations. At one point he thinks he and Memo have run over a boy in the road—a psychological omen indicating his destruction of his own youth and innocence and also his negation of the children he might have. The self-destructive nature of his self-preoccupation is graphically dramatized by Roy's insatiable appetite for food. He develops a hunger which cannot be satisfied and it is a night of excessive gorging which brings on his crippling stomach attack. With a pump the doctors "dredged up unbelievable quantities of bile." Still hungry, in hospital he thinks he has a prime hunk of beef in his mouth, "and he found it enormously delicious only to discover it was himself he was chewing." The procreative energies turned inward become unappeasable appetites which devour the self.

Roy's disinclination to become even a nominal grandfather is allied to his attempt to deny time. On one of his good days he smashes a clock to pieces with one hit. But the image of the locomotive which he keeps hearing throughout the book indicates the inexorable movement of time which not even his energies can bash to a standstill. When he catches a sense of himself as "on a train going nowhere" he is close to the truth of the matter. He thinks he is pursuing his own impatient wants : "so much more to do, so much of the world *to win for himself*" (my italics), but as long as he has that attitude he will always experience the torment of "still wanting and not having." Time is meaningless to the man who lives only for himself. In a dream Roy has a significant conversation with his old father figure, Sam.

> "Let's go back, Sam, let's now."
>   Sam peered out of the window.
>   "I would like to, kiddo, honest, but we can't go out there now. Heck it's snowing baseballs."

Like other Malamud questers and travellers he suddenly wishes to retrace his steps, to get back to a time before time. But, of course, you can't go home again. A related discovery, in a similar image, is made by Yakov Bok. "Once you leave you're out in the open; it rains and snows. It snows history, which means what happens to somebody starts in a web of events outside the personal." (This is clearly a root metaphor for Malamud. Morris Bober's last act in *The Assistant* is the attempt to shovel away the ever-falling snow outside his failing shop. And in *A New Life* when Levin falls in love with a colleague's wife and finds his well-protected self-sufficiency shattered, Malamud adds, "It snowed heavily." Of a character in *The Magic Barrel* we read "the world had snowed on him" and so on. Snow is everything that falls on you when you leave the room, or the womb.)

But Roy Hobbs does not face up to the fact that it "snows history" and so he fails to come into possession of the meaning of his life. Iris Lemon, on the other hand, is "tied to time": although she suffers, her suffering has meaning because of the children to whom she devotes herself. It is she who gives Roy the most important lesson in the book. When, like so many of Malamud's protagonists, he is complaining of his unlucky fate she says:

> "We have two lives, Roy, the life we learn with and the life we live with after that. Suffering is what brings us toward happiness."
>   "I had it up to here." He ran a finger across his windpipe.
>   "Had what?"
>   "What I suffered—and I don't want any more."
>   "It teaches us to want the right things."
>   "All it taught me is to stay away from it. I am sick of all I have suffered."
>   She shrank away a little.

Roy is far from evil. He repents of the corrupt deal he makes with the gamblers, but it is too late. His potency has left him and his bat splits in half. He rejects the dirty money which was his reward for throwing the match and beats up the dark conspirators. It is his sentiments as he leaves his last baseball game in a mood of intense "self-hatred" that form the concluding lesson of the book. "He thought, I never did learn anything out of my past life, now I have to suffer again." Relevant here is Santayana's insight that those who ignore past history will have to live it through again. The only hope is for man to learn from his suffering, otherwise—"I have to suffer again." Roy Hobbs has at least learned that much.

Just what a man can learn from his experience and suffering, and what are the possibilities for a second life may be said to be the main preoccupation of Malamud's following three novels. In *The Assistant* Malamud seems to have moved towards realism. The economic facts of Morris Bober's fading attempts to keep his little grocer's shop running are made depressingly accurate. Morris is a poor Jew, a consistently good man who has unfailingly bad luck. History has very much happened *to* him. Even his newspaper is "yesterday's"—he is floundering and sinking in time. He is effectively "entombed" in his store, which is just one of the many dark, constricted spaces in which so many of Malamud's characters have to live out their suffering. But although the plight of the Bober family is real enough, the novel moves effortlessly towards fable. Morris Bober is the dying father who has already lost his only son. Frank Alpine, who stumbles so strangely into his life, replaces that lost son. First of all he joins in a squalid hold-up of Bober's shop in which Morris is literally felled—a ritual "killing," followed quite shortly afterwards by actual death. Out of remorse, and some more complicated feelings, Frank returns to the shop and gradually takes over all the work. In view of the fading energies of the sick old man he becomes the indispensable "assistant." When Morris is being buried, Frank accidentally slips into the grave, thus inadvertently dancing on the dead father's coffin. From now on he takes on the role and responsibility of the father—provider, protector, living for others where he had previously lived only for himself.

This transformation of Frank does not happen easily. Like Roy Hobbs he has a lot of selfish hungers in him; but he also has a quality of moral aspiration revealed by his growing desire "to change his life before the smell of it suffocated him." "He stared at the window, thinking thoughts about his past, and wanting a new life. Would he ever get what he wanted?" What kind of "new life" does he want? Is it to help himself to more of the goods of life, as he helps himself to the cash register even while working for the store, and as, in a moment of desperate frustration, he helps himself to the daughter Helen? But that would not be a "new" life, only an extension of the old. A really new life involves a radical change of attitude towards the self and other people. The painful emergence of selflessness from selfishness is the real drama of the book. We learn that he has always been attracted to St Francis of Assisi since he heard about him in the orphange where he was brought up; and since he likes to feed birds, and has a talent for carving wooden flowers, we are not surpised to find certain saintly inclinations in Francis Alpine which finally prove stronger than his merely appetitive self. In particular his attitude to the Jews changes. At first he is often disgusted with what seems to be Morris Bober's cowed resignation. "What kind of man did you have to be born to shut yourself up in an overgrown coffin? . . . The answer wasn't hard to say—you had to be a Jew. They were born prisoners." Yet he is increasingly drawn towards something in the Jewish attitude to life. He asks Morris for his definition of a Jew. Dismissing details of orthodoxy Morris says that the only important thing for a Jew is that he believes in "the Law." " 'This means to do what is right, to be honest, to be good.' " Frank complains that Jews seem to "suffer more than they have to." Morris answers, " 'If you live you suffer. Some people suffer more, but not because they want. But I think if a Jew don't suffer for the Law, he will suffer for nothing . . .' " Frank asks Morris what he suffers for and receives the answer: " 'I suffer for you.' " Asked for more clarification Morris only adds, " 'I mean you suffer for me.' "

It sounds like a simple lesson, but it is one which Malamud's characters learn only through pain and anguish, and much resistance to commitments and responsibilities which override the clamouring hungers of the self. Morris Bober is a Jew because, as the rabbi says at his funeral, " 'he lived in the Jewish experience . . . He followed the Law . . . He suffered, he endured, but with hope . . . He asked for himself little—nothing . . .' " It is this kind of Jew which Frank Alpine finally becomes. Paradoxically it is by identifying himself with these figures of imprisonment and suffering that he finds the "better life" he sought. Helen recognizes the change in him when she discovers that he works all night to keep the family fed and her at school. He is not the hungry man who once raped her. "It came to her that he had changed. It's true, he's not the same man, she said to herself . . . It was a strange thing about people—they could look the same but be different. He had been one thing, low, dirty, but because of something in himself . . . he had changed into somebody else, no longer what he had been." The main focus of the novel is not on the economic misery of the Bobers, but on the moral transformation of Frank Alpine. In taking

on the shop, replacing the father, and becoming a Jew, he is really coming
to man's estate and putting away childish things. He suffers for others now,
not simply for self: in this sense he is the "new man" he wanted to be. He
has learned what Roy Hobbs failed to learn, and he has won his "new life."
Thus realism becomes parable in Malamud's imagination and vision.

At one point in the novel Frank Alpine is reading *Anna Karenina*,
and "he was moved at the deep change that came over Levin in the woods
just after he had thought of hanging himself. At least he wanted to live."
This summarizes fairly exactly what happens to the main character in
Malamud's next novel, *A New Life*. The "woods" which provide the setting
for the great transformation are the whole Pacific North-West. Levin, an
urban Jew who has been incarcerated in New York for many alcoholic years,
moves west to teach at a small college. The fact that he brings with him
a large volume called *Western Birds, Trees and Flowers* gives some indication
both of his expectations and his "pastoral" aspirations. More specifically it
is in a forest that he encounters Pauline Gilley and they first make love.
At this point too we can talk of "the deep change that came over Levin
in the woods." Here is Levin's reaction to the vernal embrace. "He was
throughout conscious of the marvel of it—in the open forest, nothing less,
what triumph!" Inevitably there is a kind of undermining irony here which
is absent in Tolstoy, an extracting of humour from a potentially painful
sense of personal unfitness and incongruity.

Levin would not be one of Malamud's "heroes" if he did not attract
more than his share of bad luck which is both comic and incommoding—
food slopped in his lap by the nervous Pauline, a child urinating on him,
a car that breaks down as he drives feverishly towards an erotic tryst, clothes
stolen by a jealous friend during his first awkward encounter with one of
the "country copulatives," and so on. (Indeed he has trouble with his
trousers throughout, and when Pauline literally thrusts him into a pair of
her husband's trousers after the dinner accident of their first meeting, it
offers a comic adumbration of the conclusion when he steps into Gilley's
trousers more finally by taking over his role of husband.) Malamud's Levin
is a *schlemiel*—deracinated, insecure, friendless and powerless to an extent
which makes him a very remote echo of Tolstoy's powerful and authoritative
figure. And yet Malamud's point is surely that a man may yearn for a new
and better life with as much seriousness and anguish in contemporary America as in nineteenth-century Russia. Malamud refers, it is true, to Joyce's
Levin, but it is inconceivable that he did not also have Tolstoy's Levin in
mind. Malamud's Levin is not a complete *schlemiel* since he, like other
Malamud characters, finds reserves of unsuspected strength inside him

which he can bring to bear at the crucial moment. To quote some words of Malamud: "A man who can overcome circumstances and his own weakness is not, to me, a *schlemiel*." (The name Levin also means, of course, east, the light, and I have it direct from Mr Malamud that by a pun on "leaven" he is suggesting "what the marginal Jew may bring in attitude to the American scene.")

Still in relation to the name, I should like to refer to two of Malamud's short stories where it recurs. In "The Lady of the Lake" Henry Levin sets out on his travels with a view to satisfying his "adventurous appetites." He thinks he will find a new life in Europe by denying his Jewishness. "With ancient history why bother? . . . a man's past was, it could safely be said, expendable." He pretends his name is Henry Freeman. This attempt to repudiate the identity imposed on him by history, to make an Emersonian bid for the freedom and autonomy of the individual self, is of course very American. But time after time in Malamud's work it is shown to be not only an error but an impossibility; Levin-Freeman feels discontented with his new life—"he lived too much on himself." So he is delighted when he meets a mysteriously lovely girl on a slightly magical island. Sensing the possibility of an aristocratic alliance he puts forward his best new self. Thus he is much taken aback when she asks if he is Jewish and is quick and emphatic in his denials. It turns out that she is not a titled lady but a Jewish girl who suffered in Buchenwald. Levin loses the very person who could have brought fulfilment into his life because, where he attempts to deny the past, she accepts it: " 'My past is meaningful to me. I treasure what I suffered for.' " At one point in the story we read, "he felt time descend on him like an intricate trap," and one of the lessons of Malamud's tales is that the man who attempts to deny the past (which is to deny time) may find himself imprisoned and trapped in ways which are worse than the physical impositions of history. Not by any change of name can an individual transform himself into a free man. (In *A New Life* Levin first adopts the name Seymour in his attempt to create "a new Levin"; at the end he reverts to his real name—Sam.) The penalties for attempting this sort of personal leap out of history into egotistical freedom may be dire. " 'What did he do to deserve his fate?' " Freeman asks when he is shown a tapestry of a writhing leper in hell. The Lady of the Lake answers him, " ' He falsely said he could fly.' "

In "Angel Levine" Manischevitz, a poor Jewish tailor suffering Job's own tribulations, one night finds a Negro in his house who introduces himself as Alexander Levine. Manischevitz asks with a smile, " 'You are maybe Jewish?' " and receives the answer, " 'All my life I was willingly.' "

The last word is the key one. Levine is now an angel who offers vague aid, but Manischevitz dismisses him as a "faker." He now loses all faith in God as his troubles get worse, and complains about his entirely pointless suffering. But one night he does seek out Levine in a dirty Harlem bar, and above the hostile taunts of the crowd he affirms his faith. " 'I think you are an angel from God.' " When he returns home his wife has miraculously recovered her health. His final comment is: " 'A wonderful thing, Fanny . . . Believe me, there are Jews everywhere.' " Clearly Malamud is not here concerned with matters of orthodox belief, but with some more general human kind of faith which can transform a life. The miracle is partly a matter of that "luck," that quixotic turn of events, without which none of his figures would ever find their "new life." But it is also indicative, I think of a change in attitude on the part of Manischevitz. What he learns from Levine is to accept life and its sufferings positively, "willingly," instead of maintaining an attitude of personal resentment. Such a change of attitude towards the burdens of history can sometimes make those burdens miraculously lighter. Some critics complain of this kind of surrealistic fantasy in Malamud just as they suggest that his reliance on fable and myth indicates a somewhat improverished appreciation of the actual stuff of the world. It seems to me more profitable to see Malamud as a writer who has an instinctive feeling for the folk-tale, the wry fable with an only half-hidden work—his best work combines both real and "fabulous" elements.

I think that A New Life is less successful than Malamud's other novels precisely because he strains to maintain uninterrupted continuity of realistic detail. Nevertheless the fable is still clearly present, even if it does give the impression of being uneasily imposed on the close-knit, naturalistic texture of the narrative. Levin is in quest of a "new life" and wants to slough off a miserable and disastrous past. However, he soon discovers "how past-drenched present time was," and he makes a note of the discovery that "The new life hangs on an old soul." But he makes the mistake of thinking that the new life involves securing himself against all confusing emotions and relationships, just as he thinks he can shut out history by not reading the newspapers. He manifests something of the mixture of solipsism and greedy appetite which was the undoing of Roy Hobbs. However, he is not content to stay submerged in this sealed-off self-preoccupation. Still aspiring to freedom, he has learned enough to know that the crucial problem is "how to win freedom in and from self."

But it is one thing to have theories of freedom, and quite another to enact them. (The limitations involved in a purely cerebral solution to the problem of self and freedom are shown up in the figure of Fabrikant.

Fond of quoting Emerson's "Nothing at last is sacred but the integrity of your mind," he is shown up to be completely impotent—a childless bachelor who is also a coward on the campus.) Levin's test comes when he falls in love with Pauline, the wife of the very man who gave him his job, Gerald Gilley. At first Levin, fearful of any entanglement, sets out to "harden" himself and "put on armour against love." "He wanted no tying down with ropes, long or short, seen or unseen—had to have room to move so he could fruitfully use freedom." But he finally abandons this theoretic freedom for the real Pauline and her children, and in doing so he is fulfilling his part in Malamud's favourite regenerative myth—the ritual slaying of the old failing father figure. At first cringingly deferential, Levin finally challenges, eliminates and replaces the arid and by now sterile Gerald, the original father figure who effectively brought him into the western world.

Vengefully Gerald will only let him have the children if he will give up all ideas of a college career, but Levin is up to the sacrifice.

> "Goodbye to your sweet dreams," Gilley called after him . . . "An older woman than yourself and not dependable, plus two adopted kids, no choice of yours, no job or promise of one, and other assorted headaches. Why take that load on yourself?"
> "Because I can, you son of a bitch."

Levin has given up dreams for reality; and has paradoxically found his freedom by willingly taking on the load of family commitments. Suitably, after his final tourney with Gerald, Levin is informed by Pauline that she is pregnant by him. He is the new father; a mature man. Once again the quest for a new life ends in what looks like an imprisoning set of commitments and undertakings, and Levin certainly gets a trapped feeling up to the last moment. But then he realizes: "The prison was really himself, flawed edifice of failures, each locking up tight the one before." And so, perhaps with too much manifest contrivance by Malamud, the fable is concluded. Its moral is one with relevance for a large number of contemporary American heroes: the only true freedom is liberation from the prison of self. With a nice final irony Levin discovers that his earlier freedom was in part illusory because Pauline tells him that she had picked out his photograph from the heap of applicants and persuaded Gerald to offer him a job. Levin responds with appropriate Jewish irony. " 'So I was chosen.' " After much painful struggling Levin accepts his predestined role; a role ordained for him not only by Pauline, but by history and nature.

At the risk of not doing justice to the differentiating details of Malamud's novels, I have been trying to show how a certain patterning of events recurs. The pattern is roughly as follows. The hero travels somewhere in quest of a new life. He is a figure of some distinct practical ability (on the pitch, in the shop), but he has no faith in anything beyond the urgencies of his own hungers and appetites. When he arrives in the world where he is to search for this new satisfying life, despite his attempts to secure only his own interests and further his single development, he runs into all kinds of bad luck and hampering involvements. The search for a new freedom usually ends in an imprisoning tangle of relationships and commitments and responsibilities. The attempt to deny time and evade the impingements of history yields reluctantly and painfully to the discovery that when a man sets out on his travels he is involved willy-nilly in various processes and large networks of events which the individual can neither resist nor reshape. To be born is to be born into history; and various thoughts and theories concerning the freedom and invulnerability of the individual self fade before the experienced facts of involuntary involvement in the lives of other people.

This discovery is either preceded or accompanied by a ritual slaying (or replacing or dispossessing) of a symbolic father figure of failing powers (never an actual parent). This coming-of-age is signalled by the fact that the hero has to decide whether or not to take on the symbolic *role* of father (i.e. before he can have his own children he has to demonstrate that he *willingly* accepts all the ramifying responsibilities and limitations on self that the role involves, by agreeing to be the nominal father of children not his own). If he refuses, then his suffering—and they all suffer—has been for nothing, and his life remains devoid of meaning. This is the fate of Roy Hobbs who, with all the valuable energies necessary for heroic status, at the end is no hero at all. If the burden and role of nominal paternity is accepted then the *schlemiel* quester finds his true freedom, not in further gratifications of self, but in the willing undertaking to live for other people. By changing his attitude to the respective claims of self and others, he enters on his second life, the real "new life." This is what happens to Frank Alpine and Sam Levin who achieve the only true heroism in Malamud's work, the heroism of growing up. To use Bellow's phrase, this is the first *real* step. And this basic pattern is repeated down to the last detail in *The Fixer*, in which Malamud demonstrates with singular power and authority his ability to combine the intransigence of history with the resilience of fable. By transforming some particularly grim facts of Russian history into a positive parable, Malamud demonstrates his own ability to transcend the nightmare of Jewish history without forgetting it. From the sufferings imposed on one Jew, he has derived a story which is even older than the madness of anti-Semitism—the coming to maturity of a man.

It is well known by now just how closely the fate of Yakov Bok is based on the infamous Mendel Beilis case: the Black Hundred who, in an attempt to start a pogrom, helped to fabricate the charge of ritual murder against the manifestly innocent Beilis when a boy was found horribly murdered; the brick kiln in which Beilis worked; the pathological attempts of the Minister of Justice, Scheglovitov, to secure an indictment no matter how often he had to change the prosecuting officials or solicit transparently false evidence against Beilis; the two years Beilis was kept in prison without a trial—these facts appear all but unchanged in the novel. (Malamud even inserts one corroborative date. Yakov Bok signs a document on "February 27, 1913" a few months before his trial: Beilis was brought to trial in October 1913.) All this is the kind of history which gives added point to Saul Bellow's remark that history has always been singularly ambivalent for Jews: "They were divinely designated to be great and yet they were like mice. History was something which happened to them; they did not make it." And yet the book does not read like history. Despite the intense vividness of the local details it seems more like something between a folk-tale and a dream. The environment is not given full specificity; the characters are far from being fully individuated; the time, despite that one date, is any time in human history. And the impersonal tone of the narrator, telling the tale with brooding economy and drawing the various scenes with the firm, incisive contours of a woodcut, suggests that it is a tale which could be told over and over again. The blurb claims that the theme of the book is injustice and man's inhumanity to man. Both are, indeed, vividly dramatized in the book. But so much is history, though admittedly history of the direst sort. And what Malamud has always been more interested in is a man's reaction to the history he finds happening to him. This I take to be the theme of the book.

Yakov Bok comes to Kiev, "hoping for a better life than I had." When he sets out from the poverty-stricken *shtetl* he "didn't look back." As far as he is concerned "the past was a wound in the head." He is attempting to turn his back on his own history and that of his race. He resentfully dismisses the old Jewish God, and adopts instead a sort of free-thinking pragmatism. Instead of faith, he believes in his tools—he loves to fix things—and a few books, like the works of Spinoza. When, on his omen-haunted journey towards the great dark city, he is ferried across the Dnieper by a virulent anti-Semite, he silently drops his phylacteries in the river and conceals his Jewish identity. In Kiev he continues concealing it. When he helps a drunken man who turns out to be a member of the dreaded Black Hundred, he gives a non-Jewish name; and when that man in gratitude offers him a good job in a brickworks in an area which Bok knows is forbidden to Jews, he continues the deception.

And why shouldn't he? He has no faith in the Jewish God, he feels no allegiance to other people and only wants to be allowed to work and live in peace. " 'I am not a political person . . . The world's full of it but it's not for me. Politics is not in my nature.' " So he pleads. Of course he is apprehensive about getting involved with rabid anti-Semites but he has appetites crying out for satisfaction, and the anti-Semitic family offers financially rewarding work just as it puts before him great spreads of rich food. He falls on both with the same urgent hunger which was the moral undoing of Roy Hobbs. Bok rationalizes to himself, " 'After all it's only a job. I'm not selling my soul,' " but it transpires that such sophistic distinctions are not made with impunity. His punishment for trying to suppress his given identity and replace it with one of his own making is to be worse than the deprivation imposed on the Levin who wanted to be Freeman. In his office he sometimes writes essays and in one he jots down: " 'I am in history, yet not in it. In a way of speaking I'm far out, it passes me by. Is this good, or is something lacking in my character?' " When anti-Semitism rises in the area after the discovery of the murdered boy, Bok prepares for discreet and urgent flight. But he walks into a detachment of police who have come to arrest him. Yakov Bok finds himself *in* history with a vengeance. His research for a new freedom of opportunity has brought him to the most literal prison in Malamud's work. And there he stays for most of the book.

Rather than summarize the many physical things that happen to him—the interrogations, the beating up, the starvation and undoctored sicknesses, the near-madness, and so on—I want instead simply to point to a few key steps in his radical change of attitude. One influence on his mind is Spinoza, for Bok, too, sees himself as a free-thinking Jew. But just how valuable are those "free thoughts" when the unreason of human experience closes in on you? We note that, when he starts to read Spinoza, Bok also studies some books of Russian history, wincing at their accounts of indescribable cruelties. At the time he does not feel the disjunction between the theoretical serenity of free thoughts and the actual horror of accomplished facts, but he is to learn of this discrepancy through his own experience. After some time in prison we read, "the fixer's thoughts added nothing to his freedom; it was nil . . . Necessity freed Spinoza and imprisoned Yakov. Spinoza thought himself into the universe but Yakov's poor thoughts were enclosed in a cell." The philosophy of Spinoza perhaps has something of the ironic function of Emerson's creed in *A New Life.*

Philosophy alone cannot free a man from the literal impositions of history, cannot keep the brute facts at bay. Still, even if Spinoza cannot release him, the very fact that Yakov keeps constructing complex configurations of thought is a partially liberating gesture. It is a way of not totally succumbing. So Spinoza does perhaps help Yakov to tackle the burdens of history, not with applicable precepts, but by the example of resistant mental activity.

These burdens seem to Yakov, even so, monstrously unfair and incomprehensible. In particular he realizes "being born a Jew meant being vulnerable to history, including its worst errors. Accident and history had involved Yakov Bok as he had never dreamed he could be involved." He feels entirely devoid of hope. And yet a part of the meaning of the book is that such total pessimism is not finally warranted. There are some friends; there are a few who care for human justice. When Bibikov commits suicide and Bok again feels utterly abandoned, another man convinced of his innocence turns up. Even one of the prison guards, as in *King Lear*, finally rebels against the cruelty meted out by the authority he serves. Bok is indeed a victim; but he is neither as totally innocent nor as totally alone in the web of history as he thinks. (The rebellion of the guard extends the motif of adopted paternity. Kogin has lost his son in Siberia and in effect "adopts" Yakov, just as Yakov "adopts" Chaim. The found father himself finds a "father.")

The change that comes over him in prison can be seen in his transformed attitude to the authorities. At the start it is abject and conciliatory; but as the conditions get worse his resilience grows, appeasement gives way to anger, and his vigorous contempt for the imprisoning powers is revealed in his refusal to settle for less than full justice (he refuses a *pardon*, which would imply that he was guilty: he wants a free *trial*). At the same time he seems to discover something of value in the old Jewish religion; he even takes an interest in the sayings of Christ, quoting His words with cutting defiance to his Christian captors. But he refuses to take refuge in religious quietism and pious passivity. When his old father-in-law says, " 'God's justice is for the end of time,' " Bok's wry answer is, " 'I'm not so young any more, I can't wait that long.' " If he is immersed in history, then he wants a timely, not a timeless, justice. He begins to rage against injustice instead of simply trying to avoid it. While his physical freedom is diminished, until he is finally chained to the wall, his attitude to his fate becomes more positive.

At first simply nauseated by his fate and sick of Jewish history with all its suffering, he later decides, "If I must suffer let it be for something."

Offered his freedom if he will denounce the Jews, he refuses. "He is against those who are against them. He will protect them to the extent that he can. This is his convenant with himself." Not a covenant with God: Bok is not obeying an imposed rule so much as willingly creating his own responsibilities. Again we are witnessing the shift from egotistical self-concern to a sense of an involvement with others. Bok's suffering is quite disproportionate to any of his human failings (indeed it is two acts of kindness which cause most of his trouble). But that is how history can be. The important thing is that Bok makes something of all this uninvited history. He has suffered, he has learnt, he has changed. In the blackest possible circumstances he has found his new life. Unlike Roy Hobbs he has entered his human maturity.

This conclusion to the fable is emphasized by two events which are surely interpolations by Malamud. Shortly before his trial, Bok's wife Raisl, whom he had left because she was childless and unfaithful, comes to him in prison. She is allowed in because she is made to bring a confession for him to sign. The confession blames the murder on "my Jewish compatriots." On this Bok writes, "Every word is a lie." But she also tells him that she has had an illegitimate son for whom she needs a nominal father since he is suffering from being a bastard. Bok surreptitiously writes on an envelope: "I declare myself to be the father of Chaim, the infant son of my wife, Raisl Bok." This is really the key moment in the book. He refuses to betray other people in the interests of personal comfort; and he willingly takes on the role of father to a child not his own. In the Malamud world this is the heroic moment.

The decisive sequel to this moment is presented in a brilliant manner when Malamud describes a reverie Bok has when he is finally being taken to his trial. While he is being driven through the town someone throws a bomb. Bok survives, but a young Cossack's leg is now "shattered and bloody." This episode continues the subtle but insistent motif of spilt and dribbling blood which persists through the book, giving the impression that various forms of blood-letting are the very essence of history. After the incident, Bok dreams he is in a "cell or cellar" with the Tsar, Nicholas the Second. They talk first of children—and blood: they discuss the murdered boy, whose blood Bok was supposed to have drained, and the Tsar's son, a haemophiliac, liable to bleed to death any moment from natural causes. The Tsar asks Bok, " 'Are you a father?' " and Bok makes the significantly worded reply—" 'With all my heart.' " The Tsar himself is in a very enfeebled state. He is naked, "his phallus meagre," he is coughing and smoking; and he is very much on the defensive as he tries to justify his conduct in history. Yakov Bok is very much in the ascendant and refuses to accept the Tsar's insincere evasions and attempts to excuse pogroms. By way of a response to these excuses Bok takes up a revolver and shoots the Tsar.

As if to emphasize the significance of the ritual we are witnessing, Bok addresses the Tsar as "Little Father" just before he shoots him. The fact that he dreams this ritual killing of the "father" indicates only that his state of mind has changed—outside him history remains very much the same with the Tsar well out of reach. But Bok's spirit is now that of the grown man who will no longer humbly defer to the ailing and declining power of the authority which is impeding his right to a full human life. In political terms this change of mind means a new militancy on the part of Bok. "One thing I've learned, he thought, there's no such thing as an unpolitical man, especially a Jew." But the fable goes even deeper than a call to action; for it shows a representative individual coming to a mature awareness of the limitations and responsibilities of man-in-history.

Whether or not Malamud believes in the possibilities of social progress is not the main issue of the book. I think this is made clear by one last interesting point concerning Malamud's treatment of his historical data. Amazingly enough, despite anti-Semitic judges and ignorant jurymen who believed in the ritual murder legend, Mendel Beilis was acquitted. But Malamud chooses to end his novel with Yakov Bok on his way to the trial, the verdict still in doubt. Why does Malamud not show us the somewhat freakish justice of the original facts? Surely because that would shift the emphasis from the universal relevance (the growth of a man) to an account of one atypical historic moment (for the justice finally meted out to Mendel Beilis is not a justice one could rely on to recur in any repetition of the circumstances). And the inconclusiveness of the fable is surely its most important assertion of superiority over the conclusiveness of history. For any *final* verdict of innocent or guilty is out of our hands. The real trial is not a matter of sentence or acquittal but the imprisoned years which preceded it, during which a man has the chance to derive some meaning from what he is caught up in. It is in the prison, not in the courtroom, that a man must win his freedom and earn a new life. And what the "judges" will finally say is less important than man's developing attitude as he moves towards his last reckoning.

Any contemporary American writer addressing himself to the archetypal theme of the American who travels to Europe to become an artist can hardly avoid comedy. And a fine comedy is just what Malamud has produced in his most recent novel, *Pictures of Fidelman: An Exhibition*

(1969), in which Fidelman comes to Europe and tries his unlucky hand at art criticism, imitation, forgery, reproduction and original creation. It might be said that he almost shows most powers of invention when it comes to finding different ways of failing experiences of a hundred years of American artistic aspirants in Europe. It is a comedy, but not a farce. All the serious issues which have engaged Malamud in his previous fiction are present, but more implicitly, in abbreviated forms. Fidelman is the recognizable Malamud hero. He sets out on his travels with aspirations for some sort of new life. He is after something for himself ("where's mine?"), and is at first excessively protective of his own interests. Surrounded by the vast deposits of history he gets "quickly and tightly organized." When an impoverished refugee named Susskind brazenly asks Fidelman to give him a suit, Fidelman repudiates any responsibility for him. He reorganizes his routine to shut Susskind out so that he can devote himself solely to his study of Giotto. It is the first of many incidents in which he fails to make the appropriate adjustments and adjudications between the claims of art and the needs of life. As happens to most of Malamud's heroes, his egotism is chastened the hard way. His tight organization proves to be hopelessly porous to disintegrating and distracting contingencies. He is incarcerated and beaten up by some crooks who make him forge a painting; he is humiliated and rejected for months by a frigid woman; he comes close to starvation. Unlucky in love, he becomes a pimp; insufficiently talented in art, he falls into derivative pastiche. In a dream he is buried alive. As who should say—there's yours.

Yet, the book is a comedy. For one thing, Fidelman does have his resiliences and triumphs. For another, in the last chapter Fidelman finds love (with both sexes), and abandons his pretensions to art for the more modest role of apprentice craftsman. Recognizing that his previous attempts to teach himself have been another aspect of his doomed egotism, he is now happy to be "instructed." He becomes an "assistant" and we recognize the term as honorific in Malamud's moral universe. More than that, he reverses the whole myth and shows that you can go home again. He returns to America where "he worked as a craftsman in glass and loved men and women." To Yeats's poetic statement that man is forced to choose "Perfection of the life, or of the work," Fidelman before setting out on his travels had added his comment—"Both." To this somewhat greedy demand, his experiences would seem to offer the harsh rejoinder—"Neither." Yet Malamud bestows on him the happy ending he seems to have earned at last. We leave Fidelman with his dream of inclusive satisfactions realized (albeit on a humbler level than he initially expected), the life and the work improbably, felicitously, at one. It is worth noting that this comic resolution and happiness is achieved only after Fidelman has finally put behind him his various attempts at art. His manuscript on Giotto is burned by Susskind, who recognizes that "the spirit was missing." The one original work he completes he himself effectively destroys. In the last chapter Beppo, Fidelman's lover and instructor in glass-blowing, persuades him to burn all his derivative attempts to emulate contemporary styles. " 'Show who's master of your fate—bad art or you.' " Fidelman thus finds release from all those formings and framings of the past and present which have effectively imprisoned him. His return from an inhospitable Europe is at the same time an escape from unsuitable artistic ambitions and alien orderings.

The book is also a comedy because all the incidents are suspended in a medium of lyricism and humour which invites us to respond to those intimations of reconciliation and hints of magic which take us beyond the tragic moment. In Malamud's vision, there *is* magic in the web of it—and for "it" you can read art and/or life, sometimes one, sometimes the other, sometimes both. If *The Fixer* has some of the grimness of Rouault, this book has some of the life of Chagall. Comparisons with paintings are apt in connection with this novel. It is an exhibition, and one which is mounted with unobtrusive mastery. When you come out you do not at first realize how much you have seen. Although the first three chapters have been published previously as short stories (in *The Magic Barrel* [1958] and *Idiots First* [1963]), the whole novel is beautifully organized. Most of the chapters are set in a specific city—Rome, Milan, Florence, Naples, and finally of course, Venice. Each one has some subtle connections with particular painters or paintings—Giotto, Rembrandt, Titian, Picasso, Modigliani, Tintoretto. References to art works ranging from Sicilian mosaics to the productions of Pop Art contribute to the overall texture, and also help to make us realize the hopeless plethora of styles Fidelman as artistic aspirant is confronted with. Faced with such a gallery, what can originality mean, what indeed can creation mean? Fidelman works in turn from other works, from imagination, from devious sexual aspiration, from sheer financial desperation.

He runs the gamut of the problematics of "invention" and it is hardly surprising that at one point he should declare, " 'I reject originality,' " thus echoing the artist hero of William Gaddis's *The Recognitions*, and, more curiously, Hilda in *The Marble Faun*. Forced to forge an imitation of a Titian Venus, he falls in love with his own copy, a poor thing but his own. As long as he is struggling to become an artist, with insufficient genius to move beyond all extant formulations, such solipsism is understandable

and perhaps inevitable. One of Fidelman's failures in art, his most protracted, is his inability to recapture, evoke or invent the image of his
mother. At the same time, he can, for much needed money, turn out any
number of highly competent and acceptable carvings of the Madonna. One
of the first objects that Fidelman notices on his arrival in Italy is a statue
of "the heavy-dugged Etruscan wolf suckling the infants Romulus and Re-
mus." At the end, Beppo, his instructor, reminds him of his mother. One
could say that Fidelman has to find out just which is his real mother, or
where the source of true nourishment is to be found. He has to learn to
distinguish between what suckles life and what negates it.

While Fidelman fails in different modes, Malamud succeeds. As he
modulates his style, changes the pace, brightens his colours or works in
chiaroscuro, we have the sensation of watching different pictorial representations. As we have seen, Malamud has always been able to move from
economic realistic notations to fable, folk-tale, surrealism and fantasy, and
his manifest ability in this book to produce so many different canvases
conveys an exhilarating sense of a man in assured control of the resources
of his medium. While Fidelman's life is disintegrating, Malamud's style is
reorganizing it on a verbal level. I will point to one example of the way in
which the different pictures are related to each other. In the comparatively
realistic first chapter where Fidelman repudiates Susskind, we have a long
account of Fidelman's attempt to trace Susskind after the latter has stolen
his manuscript. By the end of his search Fidelman finds himself in a graveyard. He notices an empty grave which commemorates an unretrieved
victim of the Nazis. Fidelman also has dreams of catacombs, of cemeterial
darkness, of Susskind rising up from a grave. When he does find where
Susskind lives, it proves to be no more than a wretched cave. In the strange
surrealistic dream which makes up the fifth chapter, or picture, many of
these details reappear, having been subjected to the metamorphoses of
Malamud's art and Fidelman's life. In very reduced circumstances Fidelman
is now concentrating on sculpting perfect holes (as, indeed, Claes Old-
enburg has done). He justifies these empty holes as studies in pure form,
and charges admission to anyone who wants to see them. A poor young
man is tempted into one of these shows, paying with money which should
have been used to buy his children bread. Finding nothing nutritious to
the spirit in the exhibition (" 'Holes are of no use to me, my life being so
full of them' "), he asks for his money back so that he can at least provide
bodily nourishment for his children. Fidelman sends him away penniless,
and in remorse the man commits suicide. As the dream gathers pace a
threatening figure appears at Fidelman's exhibition to revenge the poor
young man. He knocks Fidelman into one of his own empty holes (which,

unlike the empty grave in Chapter One, has no human significance), and covers him up with earth, adding mordantly—" 'So now we got form but we also got content.' " With his arid aesthetics and indifference to humanity Fidelman has indeed been digging his own grave.

The dream continues with a sermon by Susskind transformed into a Christ figure; and it concludes with an account of a surviving engraving by Fidelman called "The Cave" from a series entitled "A Painter's Progress." It depicts Fidelman working away in a cave, covering its surface wth colours and designs, while upstairs his sister is dying alone. Advice can come from strange sources in Malamud, and in this case a light bulb tells Fidelman to go upstairs. That he does finally manage to leave the cave of art for the house of life-and-death perhaps prefigures his success in the next chapter when, in the Venetian daylight, he becomes an assistant and a lover. From the house of his lover(s) he can look out over the island cemetery. Life and death are still close together, but now at last they are in their proper places. And so the theme of the differing claims of art and life is refracted through many different scenes and styles, the spirit being absent or present in unpredictable ways.

Beppo, who initiates Fidelman into homosexual love when he finds Fidelman sleeping with his wife ("Both"), also teaches Fidelman to blow glass. He tells him that it is a wonderfully flexible medium—" 'you can make a form or change it into its opposite.' " Fidelman finds that its plasticity helps you to understand "the possibilities of life." From the little hole which you first introduce into the molten glass—"a sculptured womb"—you can, if you know how, "blow anything." This craft has its own mothering powers and can generate "unexpected forms," new worlds. Fidelman as apprentice is not sufficiently the artist to be in control of the medium. He "blew forms he had never blown before, or seen blown," evoking huge complicated monstrosities which sometimes crack in mid-air, or fail to stand upright when completed. Free form can lead to mal-form, and the assistant still needs to be instructed. But in the hands of a master, like Malamud, this freedom to produce new unexpected forms in the flexible medium of the novel/fable does serve to increase our sense of the possibilities both of art and life.

Just before he leaves Italy for America, Fidelman does manage to produce one perfect and pure red glass bowl. After the golden bowl, the glass one: and unlike the bowl in Henry James's last created work, Fidelman's has no crack in it. Instead of being broken and reassembled it simply vanishes, leaving Fidelman free to go home, and leaving us with Malamud's flawless fable clear before us.

ALLEN GUTTMANN

"All Men Are Jews"

Although he is not in any important sense a Zionist, Bernard Malamud is almost certain to be mentioned in any discussion of the post-war reaffirmation of Jewishness. He has been acclaimed, in *Judaism*, as "the most Jewish of American Jewish writers." There is, however, a very problematic quality to his fiction. His conception of what it means to be a Jew seems at times to resemble that of Ludwig Lewisohn, at other times that of Philip Roth. His work has been related to that of Sholom Aleichem and the tradition of Yiddish literature; it has also been described as "distinctly in the American grain." Each new publication complicates matters and increases the difficulty of assessing the purport of his career.

Malamud's first book, *The Natural* (1952), had no Jewish characters of any importance. As many critics have noted, the novel combined the myths of the Grail Knight and the Fisher King with the national mystique of professional baseball. The result was a comic hero named Roy Hobbs (the common man as king?), armed with a magic bat named Wonder Boy. The novel is divided into two unequal parts, the first of which is "Pre-Game." In "Pre-Game," the young hero is tested. In an impromptu contest staged by the side of a halted train on which both were travelling, Roy strikes out the "Whammer," the best batter of the day. For his *hubris*, Roy is struck down by a mysterious woman, curiously ornithic Harriet Bird, "a snappy goddess" who tempts him and then shoots him in the stomach (as, in actuality, Eddie Waitkus was shot in 1949 by a temptress in Chicago's Edgewater Beach Hotel). Lucky Roy has a second chance. In "Batter Up!"

From *The Jewish Writer in America: Assimilation and the Crisis of Identity.* Copyright © 1971 by Oxford University Press, Inc.

(much the longer of the two parts), he finds employment with the New York Knights, under Pop Fisher.

Allusions to the medieval myth used by T. S. Eliot are many—Pop Fisher wants rain and gets it when Roy bats. Elements of the psychoanalytic theories of Carl Jung are also part of the composition. Roy lusts for wicked Memo Paris and loses his chance for Iris Lemon, takes a bribe to throw the game and changes his mind when it is too late. Malamud's moral is, therefore, conventional enough—selfishness and dishonesty are deplorable. At the very end, a child asks Roy what a child is alleged to have asked Shoeless Joe Jackson at the time of the Black Sox scandal of 1919: "Say it ain't true, Roy." On the basis of this oddly mythical novel, there was no reason to expect that Malamud was soon to be categorized among "Jewish novelists of the postwar period."

He had, however, already begun to publish the short stories later collected in *The Magic Barrel* (1958). Many of these stories resemble the Yiddish literature of Sholom Aleichem and Mendele Mocher Sforim or tales written in the older conventions of Chassidism. Poor Jews survive by hook, crook, and the grace of God. Two of the stories relate directly to the theme of peoplehood. "The Lady of the Lake" is a parable in the sense that the shorter stories of *Goodbye, Columbus* are parables, but Malamud's moral is very different from Roth's. Henry Levin, "an ambitious, handsome thirty, who walked the floors in Macy's book department wearing a white flower in his lapel," inherits money and heads for Europe. He changes his name to Henry R. Freeman, in an obvious effort to shed his Jewish identity for that of a free man. At Isola del Dongo he meets a girl who rises from the water like Botticelli's Venus, or like Roth's Brenda Patimkin:

> Freeman stared as she sloshed up the shore, her wet skin glistening in bright sunlight. She had seen him and quickly bent for a towel she had left on a blanket, draped it over her shoulders and modestly held the ends together over her high-arched breast.

When the girl asks if he's Jewish, Freeman suppresses a groan and denies the truth. She claims to be Isabella del Dongo, a princess; she takes him on a tour of the palazzo, which has the old-world equivalent of the Patimkins' suburban splendor—works of art. It turns out that the Titians are copies and that Isabella is the daughter of a caretaker. Despite the deception, "Freeman" decides to propose to her, only to be queried again about his identity, only to deny again (like St. Peter) the truth. Then, the irony. She is a Jewess whom the Nazis had placed in Buchenwald:

> Slowly she unbuttoned her bodice. . . . When she revealed her breasts—
> he could have wept at their beauty (now recalling a former invitation to

gaze at them, but he had arrived too late on the raft)—to his horror he discerned tatooed on the soft and tender flesh a bluish line of distorted numbers.

She will not marry him because she treasures the past she suffered for. Before he can explain, she steps among the statues of the palazzo garden. "Freeman" embraces the moonlit stone of a faked masterpiece, which is just what he deserves. The point of the story is almost too plain. Isabella had shown him a tapestry from Dante in which a tormented leper suffers punishment for mendacity; she had asked him if seven mountain peaks did not resemble the Menorah. Still, the story is well told.

"The Last Mohican," another story collected in *The Magic Barrel*, stresses the claim that every Jew has on every other Jew and is, therefore, the counterpart to Roth's "Defender of the Faith" and "Eli, the Fanatic." This story too is set in Italy, where Fidelman, "Self-confessed failure as a painter," proves finally to be the man of faith his name proclaims him to be. Greeted in Rome with a cheery "Shalom" from a cicerone-schnorrer named Susskind, Fidelman's heart sinks. But Susskind reveals strange facets. He refuses, for instance, to accept a Jewish organization's offer of a ticket to Israel because he likes the freedom of his hand-to-mouth existence in Rome. He enjoys his precarious autonomy but makes sure that Fidelman feels a sense of responsibility. He demands one of Fidelman's suits. When Fidelman refuses ("I am a single individual and can't take on everybody's personal burden"), Susskind steals his manuscript on the work of Giotto. In pursuit of the bandy-legged thief, Fidelman comes to know the Jews of Rome and even the cemetery where six-pointed stars commemorate those who were murdered at Auschwitz. Eventually, he finds Susskind (selling rosaries), gives him the suit, and recovers the briefcase. Enraged that Susskind has burned the manuscript, Fidelman pursues him through the streets of the ghetto until he is suddenly transfigured by "a triumphant insight." He recognizes his responsibility to Susskind and cries out that all is forgiven.

Does Fidelman's faith matter? His further adventures, told in *Idiots First* (1963), lead one to wonder. In "Still Life," Fidelman appears again, in love with Annamaria Oliovino, whose name seems to suggest the fruitfulness of olives and grapes (i.e. oil and wine). He paints her as the Virgin Mary and is sexually aroused. His attempts to fornicate with the more than ready *shikse* come to naught when she shouts, "Enough of antipasto," grabs his penis, and brings him to premature ejaculation. She kicks him out, shouting, "Pig, beast, onanist." Eventually, Fidelman dresses as a priest and paints a portrait of himself with a cross. Annamaria Oliovino changes her mind and offers herself once again. "She clasped his buttocks, he cupped hers. Pumping slowly he nailed her to her cross." This is a memorable conclusion but one is puzzled about what to conclude from it. Is metaphoric conversion necessary before Fidelman can enjoy forbidden fruit? Had he donned caftan and yarmulka before coitus, critics would surely have discovered a return to Jewishness. Fidelman's later appearance in "Naked Nude" leaves one equally doubtful. Malamud subsequently wrote three more stories about Fidelman and collected all six in *Pictures of Fidelman: An Exhibition* (1969). In his later treatment of Fidelman's unusual erotic and artistic escapades, the theme of Jewishness is of negligible importance.

A New Life (1961), which appeared while Malamud was working on the various stories of *Idiots First,* is a more conventional work in the pastoral mode. S. Levin goes west to teach at Pacifica College and runs into rather tedious difficulties with foolish colleagues, incompetent administrators, and a coed who questions his masculinity because the unanticipated arrival of her boyfriend cooled instructor Levin's animal ardor. By the end of the novel, Levin accepts the responsibilities incurred by an affair with a colleague's wife, whom he has made pregnant. He drives off with her and her children while her husband gleefully takes pictures. It looks to be one of the most mixed-up of mixed marriages. *A New Life* is not Malamud's "best effort," although some have called it so.

The ambiguities recurrent when Malamud writes of Jews, which he does most of the time, occur even in the two novels that seem at first unambivalently to affirm the responsibility of all Jews to each other. *The Assistant,* published in 1957, represents a turnabout in the fictional treatment of conversion. Now the Gentile gives up the faith of his fathers in order to become a Jew. The significance of the conversion remains somewhat unclear because Malamud's implication is that the Jew can be defined as the man who suffers. The first scene presents the Jew as the much put-upon bearer of burdens:

> The early November street was dark though night had ended, but the wind, to the grocer's surprise, already clawed. It flung his apron into his face as he bent for the two milk cases at the curb. Morris Bober dragged the heavy boxes to the door, panting. A large brown bag of hard rolls stood in the doorway along with the sour-faced, gray-haired Polisheh huddled there, who wanted one.
> "What's the matter so late?"
> "Ten after six," said the grocer.
> "Is cold," she complained.

Morris Bober's assistant is a petty thief, Frank Alpine, who becomes increasingly involved in Morris Bober's affairs. Frank is fascinated by what one critic has cleverly referred to as the "Cartesian minimum": I suffer, therefore I am. For Morris Bober, the statement seems to have an implied predicate nominative: "I suffer, therefore I am [a Jew]." Frank asks him why Jews suffer "so damn much," and Morris answers that they suffer because they are Jews.

> "If you live, you suffer. Some people suffer more, but not because they want. But I think if a Jew don't suffer for the Law, he will suffer for nothing."
> "What do you suffer for, Morris?" Frank said.
> "I suffer for you," Morris said calmly.
> Frank laid his knife down on the table. His mouth ached.
> "What do you mean?"
> "I mean you suffer for me."

Frank's involvement is in large part motivated by his love of Morris Bober's daughter, who bears the rather classical name Helen. Like the elders who spied on Susanna, like David who caught sight of bathing Bathsheba (the prototype, perhaps, of Brenda Patimkin and Isabella del Dongo), Frank Alpine hides in a dumbwaiter to catch a sight of Helen Bober: "Her body was young, soft, lovely, the breasts like small birds in flight, her ass like a flower." She returns his love but refuses his sexual advances; eventually, she is saved *from* rape by his intervention, is then raped *by* him, and curses him as an uncircumcised dog. Frank continues his unorthodox courtship, returns to the store despite the fact that Morris had fired him for dishonesty, and—after Morris dies—takes over completely. At the funeral, Frank tumbles awkwardly into the grave and climbs out again, symbolically reborn. Madly in love with Helen, he runs the store.

His religious decision comes when he imagines St. Francis going to the garbage can into which Helen has thrown his gift of a carved rose and presenting it to her. The image of St. Francis has appeared earlier. At a candy store, Frank Alpine thumbed through a magazine and discovered the picture of a monk raising his skinny arms to a flock of birds. Frank identifies with the saint, for whom, after all, he may well have been named. He undergoes circumcision and becomes one of the sufferers whom he had earlier wondered at, a Jew.

But what is this strange identity that Frank Alpine has assumed? In their discussion of the famous dialogue on suffering, critics rarely point to what comes before and after Morris Bober's remark that Frank suffers for him. Earlier Frank asks why Morris keeps his store open on Jewish holidays, why he eats ham. Morris responds as follows:

> "This is not important to me if I taste pig or if I don't. To some Jews is this important but not to me. Nobody will tell me that I am not Jewish

because I put in my mouth once in a while, when my tongue is dry, a piece ham. But they will tell me, and I will believe them if I forget the Law. This means to do what is right, to be honest, to be good."

After Frank's query and Morris Bober's assertion that Frank suffers for him, Morris goes on: "If a Jew forgets the Law, he is not a good Jew, and not a good man." There can be no doubt about the seriousness of this redefinition. At the funeral of Morris Bober, the rabbi preaches on Jewishness:

"When a Jew dies, who asks if he is a Jew? He is a Jew, we don't ask. There are many ways to be a Jew. So if somebody comes to me and says, 'Rabbi, shall we call such a man Jewish who lived and worked among the gentiles and sold them pig meat, trayfe, that we don't eat, and not once in twenty years comes inside a synagogue, is such a man a Jew, rabbi?' To him I will say, 'Yes, Morris Bober was to me a true Jew because he lived in the Jewish experience, which he remembered, and with the Jewish heart.' Maybe not to our formal tradition—for this I don't excuse him—but he was true to the spirit of our life—to want for others that which he wants also for himself. He followed the Law which God gave to Moses on Sinai and told him to bring to the people. He suffered. He endu-red [sic] but with hope."

The rabbi's comments are crucial. Although the rabbi refers to the Law that God gave Moses on Sinai, he has already insisted that Morris Bober is a true Jew despite his numerous infractions of what Orthodox Jews have taken to be the essence of that law. The letter of the Law is less important than the spirit, which turns out to be remarkably like Immanuel Kant's categorical imperative: to want for others what you want for yourself. One critic, disturbed by the implications of the rabbi's speech, has called it "clearly ironic," but this attempt to whisk away the difficulties is too simple. What Malamud has done explicitly throughout his work is widen the definition of "Jew" to the point of meaninglessness. If any good man, measured by Kant's categorical imperative or the Golden Rule or the rabbi's formulation, is doomed to suffer and, therefore, to be a Jew, then the concept has been permanently replaced by its own metaphoric extensions. Frank Alpine's conversion was merely the painful ratification of a prior change of heart. No wonder, then, that Malamud's most famous epigram is the orphic statement: "All men are Jews."

The difficulty, for those anxious to insure the survival of the Jews as a distinct people, is that Malamud's conclusions are too much of a good thing. If all men are Jews, then the divinely drawn line between the Chosen People and the goyim has been erased. Robert Alter's comments on Malamud are shrewd and to the point: "Although his protagonists are avowedly

Jewish, he has never really written *about* Jews, in the manner of other American Jewish novelists." To Alter, *The Fixer* (1966) is Malamud's finest achievement because the central metaphor of imprisonment is derived from the social facts of Czarist Russia and from the actual details of the career of Mendel Beilis. The novel is certainly Malamud's most intense and sustained dramatization of the responsibilities of peoplehood. The novel tells the story of Yakov Bok, the fictional correlative of the Russian martyr Mendel Beilis. Like "Henry Freeman," Yakov Bok attempts to evade the responsibilities of his identity. He discovers as a child that the life of a Russian Jew is a dangerous one:

> On the third morning when the houses were still smoldering and he was led, with a half dozen other children, out of a cellar where they had been hiding he saw a black-bearded Jew with a white sausage stuffed into his mouth, lying in the road on a pile of bloody feathers, a peasant's pig devouring his arm.

He decides, therefore, to flee, Jonah-like. He drops his bag of prayer articles in the Dnieper River and goes to Kiev and takes the name of Yakov Ivanovitch Dologushev. The name Bok, which signifies scapegoat, was the truer sign. A boy is murdered and Yakov is accused. Under pressure, he admits that he is a Jew. Most of the book is filled with the anguish of his imprisonment and trial, with his terrible disappointments (such as, for instance, the suicide of his sympathetic lawyer), with the dishonest machinations of anti-Semitic officials. Although Yakov Bok is doomed to die because he is a Jew, he rejects the God of his people: "Don't talk to me about God," he answers bitterly when soothed by a friend, "I want no part of God. When you need him most he's farthest away." Advised that "God's justice is for the end of time," he cries out, "I'm not so young any more, I can't wait that long. . . . God counts in astronomy but where men are concerned all I know is one plus one." No more than the Jews of Philip Roth's Woodenton is he impressed by the Biblical myths. How can one respect a God who plays games with men? "To win a lousy bet with the devil he killed off all the servants and innocent children of Job." Although Malamud ends the novel before the execution of the hero-victim, it is clear that Yakov will be sacrificed because the world insists that he is what he has no desire to be.

But Malamud's portrayal of Yakov Bok, whose distinctness was insisted upon by friend and foe alike, suggests that the flamboyant, quotable assertion of the universality of Jewishness is hyperbole. Jews are Jews, in Malamud's fiction as in the popular mind, because their parents or grandparents were believers in the God of Abraham and Isaac and keepers of

His Law. Fidelman gives up his suit because he and Susskind share a common fate. Henry Freeman loses Isabella del Dongo because he denies his share in their particular *Schicksalsgemeinschaft*. Malamud sometimes sounds like the contemporary of Philip Roth, but he seems in his heart of hearts to be, like Ludwig Lewisohn, a believer in peoplehood.

RUTH R. WISSE

Requiem for the Schlemiel

Ours is not a hero for all seasons. By
the end of the 1960s the Jewish fool began to falter: his ironic balance
teetered dangerously between self-indulgence and self-hatred. The writers
still drawing on the resources of Jewishness found that the supply lines of
the East European culture had been stretched so far in space and time that
no rich nourishment remained. To Alexander Portnoy, *Jewish* is a system
of repressions with two allowable passions—hatred of the goyim and love
of the male child. All the inner stuff of life and ritual, as he perceives it,
has been gouged out leaving an empty frame of observance and a feigning
of identification or emotion. The traditional culture once insisted that its
men got something in return for the sacrifice of their pride and prowess.
This claim could have no worth once it appeared that the entire culture
had pitiably betrayed itself. A Sunday baseball game played "when the
weather is warm enough" does not have the same power to bind and exalt
a community as the network of observance that included three daily *min-
yanim*, assembled in honor of a God who was not known to wait.

Besides, a literature feeds on itself as much as on the living environment. Once the homey and holy uses of Jewish tradition seemed ex-
hausted in modern American writing, writers felt compelled to state the
case anew, or to move on to fresh material. One Herzog alone can saturate
a theme.

The progress of the schlemiel as a literary hero was more seriously
deflected by mounting opposition in the dominant culture, beginning in
the mid-1960s, to liberal resignation. Ironic accommodationism, which was
intellectually respectable a decade earlier, was denounced as a liberal plot

to speed the advent of a fascist state. The Vietnam war, the most persistent war in American history, could not be stopped or contained by those who called it stupid, nor by those who called it tragic, nor even by those who called it genocide. Noam Chomsky and Arthur Schlesinger arguing in the editorial columns of *Commentary* over the meaning of the war seemed, for all their obvious sincerity and information, to be merely an updated version of the Tuneyadevke bathhouse philosophers. As debates lengthened and the war with them, impotence no longer served as proper comic material. The concomitant polarization of left and right in politics and the righteous anger of formerly pacific groups like the blacks and high school students and women, brought on a period of alignment, even a return to ideology. And all activism dismisses the schlemiel. Single-minded—not to say simple-minded—dedication to a particular cause or specific goal cannot tolerate a character whose perception of reality is essentially dualistic. The schlemiel, on his part, is too skeptical of visionary schemes to follow a messianic movement like Marxism and too wary of gloom to accept a fatalistic call like that of the black extremists who declare it is better to die on your feet than live on your knees. One European rabbi is said to have worn a coat with contradictory quotations sewn into the lining of his two pockets. On one side the quotation read: "The world was created for your sake"; on the other, "You are but dust and ashes." Out of the ability to sustain this paradoxical position and to wear such a coat, the irony of East European Jewry grew. But the lifeblood of irony coagulates when a society becomes either wholly optimistic or wholly pessimistic about human potential or God's.

We see the demise of irony reflected in the very literature that gave it such forceful expression. Consciously, or despite their actual intentions, American Jewish writers recreate the familiar character only to prove that he no longer serves.

One sad requiem for the schlemiel is composed by Bernard Malamud, in the six episodes that comprise *Pictures of Fidelman.* In much of his writing, Malamud has been attracted to the weak character for both his comic and tragic qualities. Levin begins *A New Life* when he is pissed on by an aggressive child, and his first lecture is marked by the unusual attention accorded to one who has forgotten to zip up his fly. Yakov Bok, whose surname means goat, is the tragic equivalent of Levin. In *The Fixer,* Malamud has dramatized the most classic case of victimization in recent Jewish history to prove the liberating effects of imprisonment.

Malamud's interest in the Jewish character has not been sociologically determined. Alone among American writers he has fixed on the Jew as representative man—and on the schlemiel as representative Jew. His Jewish Everyman is an isolated, displaced loner, American in Italy, Easterner in the West, German refugee in America, bird among bipeds. Though they sometimes speak with a Yiddish intonation, his heroes bear little actual resemblance to their coreligionists. Malamud's failing shopkeepers and starving boarders appear in contemporary fiction as a kind of anachronism; in the works of his contemporaries, like Wallace Markfield, Mordecai Richler, Herbert Gold, such characters are already subjects of nostalgia.

Malamud sees the schlemiel condition as the clearest alternative to the still-dominant religion of success. "The Morris Bobers and S. Levins in Malamud's fictional world succeed as men only by virtue of their failures in society." There is, of course, nothing new about this opposition to success in American fiction. Anti-heroes from the pens of Henry James through James T. Farrell have reached the point of no return by climbing to the doom at the top. But some moderns, Malamud especially, have stated the case positively, for the failures, rather than negatively, against the successes. In Malamud's stories, the protagonist usually has the raw potential for becoming a schlemiel, that is, the potential for suffering, submitting to loss, pain, humiliation, for recognizing himself as, alas, only himself. This potential is sometimes realized, sometimes not. The hero of A New Life, S. Levin, wins what the title promises because he takes burdens on himself and follows the bungling path of the loser. A relative, H. Levin, in a story called "The Lady of the Lake," changes his name and, as he hopes, his status to Freeman, but ends as a slave to his own deception, embracing "only moonlit stone," the symbol of deception. The character courageous enough to accept his ignominy without being crushed by it is the true hero of Malamud's opus, while the man playing the Western hero without admitting to his real identity—Jewish, fearful, suffering, loving, unheroic—is the absolute loser.

Pictures of Fidelman, studies of one more such protagonist, appeared between 1958 and 1969, a span of eleven years. At the beginning of the series of stories, the main character is another of Malamud's protests against what he calls "the colossally deceitful devaluation of man in this day." By the end, both character and author are dispirited, possibly because of an overly lengthy association, but more probably as a result of the growing difficulties in the culture of keeping such a character alive.

In the first episode, which reads like a Jewish parody of The Aspern Papers, one Arthur Fidelman, "self-confessed failure as a painter," turns up in Rome on a carefully planned and budgeted trip to prepare a study of Giotto. Fidelman has the good fortune to meet his "Vergil," a moral guide in the form of Shimon Susskind, who is "a Jewish refugee from Israel no less." The author's selectivity is nowhere more apparent than in this deliberate distinction between the Jewish type that interests him ("I'm always running") and the Israeli heroism which does not ("the desert air makes me constipated").

Susskind leads Fidelman to a true understanding of his own schlemielhood, which is also the process whereby a man becomes a *mensch*, as Hassan has so quotably put it. The unredeemed Fidelman's crime is his refusal to part with his suit. As he justifiably explains to the schnorrer, Susskind, "All I have is a change from the one you now see me wearing." Though Fidelman's crime is mere parsimony, and though he does give up five banknotes in his eagerness to rid himself of Susskind, the acts of withholding and of giving only under duress confirm that Fidelman is unsatisfactory in human responses. He is too measured, both in taking and giving. He is even afraid of his passion for history: "This kind of excitement was all right up to a point, perfect maybe for a creative artist, but less so for a critic. A critic, he thought, should live on beans." Susskind takes it upon himself to be the visiting American's "guide."

Cruel to be kind, Susskind steals the budding scholar's opening chapter on Giotto, and as we later learn, consigns it to the flames. The disorientation Fidelman experiences after the loss of his chapter is the first hopeful sign of his development; his quest for the manuscript, orderly at first, then increasingly frantic, is accompanied by the disintegration of his former self. He cannot go on with the meticulous notetaking; he rearranges his studied schedule of travel, this time improvising; he frequents movie houses instead of museums, sees the prostitutes in the street, not merely those on canvas; and, eventually, tracking Susskind down, he is exposed to misery in a form and degree unknown to him before. Slowly, he learns.

The redemption is not complete until after a visit to Susskind's room, a visit from which "he never fully recovered." Fidelman brings Susskind the suit he has so consistently denied him. But Fidelman has yet to grasp the full interconnection between life and art. In return for his suit, Susskind returns the empty briefcase, revealing that its content, the Giotto chapter, has been destroyed.

"I did you a favor," says Susskind, "The words were there but the spirit was missing."

Vergilio Susskind thus leads Fidelman into the final humiliating perception of the failure of all he had previously aspired to as success. The acceptance of failure is the crucial moment of initiation, as when Yakov Bok accepts his imprisonment, or when Frankie Alpine accepts himself as

Jew. Now, reconciled to failure, Fidelman can proceed to live out his comic humanity.

This first episode, called "The Last Mohican," tells a fairly standard story, and we are all antipriggish enough to appreciate a bit of *Pull Down Vanity*. A repressed American critic in oxblood shoes with a neat schedule of inquiry is itching to be reformed, and nothing in the denouement is surprising or displeasing. But when Fidelman next turns up as an inferior painter, paying, like Gimpel the Fool, far more than he should for the privilege of loving an Italian *pittrice*, the theme of failure intensifies. Malamud challenges the last remnant of the hero-myth in Western culture, the myth of the artist as the final embodiment of that noble quest for purity and truth. Fidelman is not fearlessly independent but the enslaved toilet cleaner and copyist for a pair of small-time art thieves. Fidelman is not perfect in his moral radiance but a cheap procurer, and a not-too-successful one at that. Above all, Fidelman is a bad artist, as inferior a craftsman as the Bratslaver's simple man was a bad shoemaker. No matter how intimate his knowledge of life or how edifying his many adventures of body and soul, his art never improves. He works among compromises, with dictated subjects, tools, circumstances. This is a generalized portrait of the artist as schlemiel, a man drawn on the same scale as other men, small and silly, but involved in a recognizably human enterprise.

The adventures of Fidelman become increasingly zany, keeping pace with the subject's experiments in painting and the author's growing ambivalence about his character. By the penultimate episode, from which the book's title is taken, the frenetic, staccato pace gives the uncomfortable impression that Fidelman's time has run out, like a wound-up doll that is stumbling to a halt after a lengthy dance. The "pictures" are hurried impressions of the subject in real and imagined poses. While Fidelman does not seem appreciably different, the cost of his style of living has risen so sharply that the gentle ironies have worn thin, revealing much harsher ones: "Fidelman pissing in muddy waters discovers water over his head." Language, imagery, and the hero, have lost the innocence of earlier episodes. The quick impression of church art, as summarized by Fidelman, is a house of horrors:

> Lives of the Saints. S. Sebastian, arrow collector, swimming in bloody sewer. Pictured transfixed with arrows. S. Denis, decapitated. Pictured holding his head. S. Agatha, breasts shorn clean running enflamed. Painted carrying both bloody breasts in white salver. S. Stephen crowned with rocks. Shown stoned. S. Lucy tearing out eyes for suitor smitten by same. Portrayed bearing two-eyed omelet on dish . . .

The artist's vision runs amok. Withdrawing completely from representational art, and from human life, Fidelman tries digging perfect holes, travelling from place to place with his mobile exhibition. The holes are graves, the death of expression. Fidelman's soul is in obvious danger, and as in the opening story, Susskind appears as savior. There, events were plotted realistically, and if certain images rose to the level of symbols, they were still embedded in the actual events of the story. But by this point the lines between realism and symbolism have disappeared, as in the mind of one who can no longer accurately distinguish between fact and fancy. Susskind is Sussking, the reincarnated Christ, preaching the new gospel. "Tell the truth. Don't cheat. If its easy it don't mean its good. Be kind, specially to those that they got less than you." Fidelman in this frame is the guilt-ridden Judas who sells his redeemer for thirty-nine pieces of silver and "runneth out to buy paints, brushes, canvas." The morality of the artist is the betrayal of goodness. The final "picture" has Fidelman as "the painter in the cave," an artistic Plato, trying to capture pure ideas in pure geometric designs. Susskind reappears in the cave of shadows as the source of light—a one-hundred-watt light bulb. The bulb is the Hebraic light giving out its moral message to the Hellenized painter, telling him to go upstairs to "say hello to your poor sister who hasn't seen you in years." Bessie, his source of support over the years, is dying, and it would make her so happy to see her brother Arthur again. At first Fidelman insists on staying put and painting out his perfect truths on the walls of the cave, but eventually he gives up his "graven images" long enough to fulfill his obligation, to go upstairs and say his last goodbye. "Bessie died and rose to heaven, holding in her heart her brother's hello." The standard bedside leave-taking, although here in a parodistic form, does not entirely cancel out the underlying seriousness of Fidelman's decision. The closing line is "natura, morta. Still life," echo of a previous motif, the counterpoint of dead nature, yet still, life.

Because he is a human animal, the artist dare not deal in Platonic purities; there is someone dying in the room upstairs to whom he is accountable and whose imperfections he shares. To live within the comedy of human limitation, while striving to create the aesthetic verities in some eternal form—that is the artistic equivalent to the schlemiel's suspension between despair and hope. Between the house of horrors that opens the story—art like Francis Bacon's that lingers over the brutal and the grotesque—and the escape from reality, represented by the empty holes and geometric forms to which Fidelman turns for solace, lies the real task of art, the confrontation with Bessie. From her Fidelman first escaped to Rome, and it is to her, to the "too complicated" (repeated three times) past that she represents that he returns. But the prolonged unwillingness of Fidelman to leave his purities, and the tortured difficulties of the style, point strongly to the increasing difficulty of maintaining schlemiel irony. In fact, the concluding episode called "Glass Blower of Venice," is a labored story, dragging its sad weight along much as its hero drags his customers piggyback across the flooded piazza.

Fidelman enters his final metamorphosis, as craftsman and bisexual lover. Not finding everything he seeks in the mythical Margherita, he is taken over by her husband, Beppo. "Fidelman had never in his life said 'I love you' without reservation to anyone. He said it to Beppo. If that's the way it works, that's the way it works. Better love than no love. If you sneeze at life it backs off and instead of fruits you're holding a bone." A homosexual with hemorrhoids is the contemporary candidate for the role of victimized male, seeing that representations of the cuckold and rejected suitor are outworn. By taking upon himself the burden of this unsanctioned love, Fidelman becomes a still more faithful human adventurer, for only the man with the heaviest load is, according to Malamud's perception, the realized being.

What distinguishes this story from earlier ones is its utterly cheerless tone, and its fatal self-consciousness. As if holding the bone were insufficient, Fidelman learns to love his man as he learns to blow glass. The two are one, and the paragraph describing this double education ends with the prescription: "If you knew how, you could blow anything," the author blowing up his own metaphor with a rude bray. Beppo slashes up all Fidelman's canvases on the theory that no art is better than bad art, and by accepting this harsh judgment the painter is supposed to prove his mastery over a bad fate. Beppo, like Susskind, teaches the gospel of failure as the beginning of wisdom.

Fidelman, now the wiser adventurer, returns home where, we are told, "he worked as a craftsman in glass and loved men and women." Yet this time the internal evidence of the story is unconvincing, and it contains nothing to warrant our faith in the upbeat conclusion. The life of Fidelman has grown as heavy as the punning. Humor has descended to scatology, from heart to rectum. The author repeats a process he has already described, but without conviction. Final pictures of Fidelman are of a comic strip caricature, a poor stumblebum whose failures remain unmitigated. The price of failure hardly seems worth the prize.

ROBERT DUCHARME

The Artist in Hell

Critical response to the Fidelman
stories when they appeared in Malamud's earlier collections was not notably
favorable. Sidney Richman has singled out "Still Life" and "Naked Nude"
as among Malamud's worst stories. The Italian setting was thought by some
critics to be uncongenial to Malamud, who, as an urban Jew, was supposed
to stick to his familiar terrain—the lower east side of New York City. When
the five Fidelman stories (with a previously unpublished sixth) were issued
as one book in 1969 under the title *Pictures of Fidelman: An Exhibition*,
critical opinion clearly had not changed much. Katherine Jackson, reviewing for *Harper's*, found that Fidelman invited comparison with Gully Jimson
of *The Horse's Mouth*, but she thought Fidelman less interesting and less
credible than Joyce Cary's picaro-artist. "His [Fidelman's] insatiable dedication to his art, his inability to say No to life, are interesting and no doubt
in some sense admirable, but devoid as they are of any common sense
judgment one tires of the endless troubles they get him into." Anatole
Broyard's review in *New York Times Book Review* and the reviews in *Time*
and *Newsweek* were also largely negative. Only Robert Scholes' review-
criticism in *Saturday Review* offered unqualified praise with a persuasive
analysis to support it. The following discussion of the book will be undertaken in two sections: the first devoted to an analysis of its form, the second
to its central character and dominant themes.

From *Art and Idea in the Novels of Bernard Malamud*. Copyright © 1974 by Mouton &
Company.

I

The form of *Pictures of Fidelman* is a departure for Malamud, although it is by no means a literary innovation. Books of interrelated short stories have been published by several authors within the last half-century or so. Yet *Pictures of Fidelman* seems to be more than a collection of loosely related fragments like Joyce's *Dubliners,* for example, or Eudora Welty's *The Golden Apples.* It bears a remarkable resemblance in form to John Updike's recent collection of related stories, *Bech: A Book.* One might describe *Pictures of Fidelman* as a picaresque chronicle of the misadventures of an American artist manqué who comes to Italy in quest of his vocation and in search of love. In my opinion *Pictures of Fidelman* may be considered a novel in the broad sense that Sherwood Anderson's *Winesburg, Ohio* or William Faulkner's *The Unvanquished* have been called novels. The parts of these books may stand as independent short stories, but there is a definite sense in which they belong together, between the covers of the same book, to form "a self-contained narrative."

Pictures of Fidelman: An Exhibition is an apt title for the book and offers a clue to determining its form. The book is like an exhibition of pictures, each story an image of Arthur Fidelman, "frozen in some crucial posture, on his way to an esthetic Calvary. The stories are, in a sense, six comic Stations of the Cross"—another set of graphic illustrations of a hero's defeat. Malamud himself considered the book to be a novel in a loosely picaresque fashion: "a loose novel, a novel of episodes, like a picaresque piece." Malamud specifically approved of Robert Scholes' review of *Pictures* (though Scholes never calls it a novel) in which Scholes describes the book as a "panel of pictures reminiscent of Hogarth" which sets forth Fidelman's progress "down and out—to salvation."

Nevertheless, *Pictures of Fidelman* is a unique kind of novel. Its loosely episodic structure, the variety of its narrative styles, the "set piece" quality of the first two stories especially—all serve to set it apart from Malamud's four other single-unit prose narrative books. I have it from Malamud himself that the Fidelman stories were not originally conceived of as a novelistic whole (as, for example, Faulkner's *The Unvanquished* surely was). After "Last Mohican" was first written, Malamud considered extending the saga of Fidelman "writing stories from time to time." He roughly sketched in outline form Fidelman's further adventures, complete with resolution and denouement. Sometime early, probably while he was composing "Naked Nude," Malamud began thinking of publishing additional stories (as yet uncomposed), along with the earlier Fidelman pieces, as a single work. With this purpose in mind, he did not issue the last story, "Glass Blower of Venice," first in a journal publication because he did not want to reveal the book's ending.

This description of the origin and growth of the Fidelman stories accounts in part for the fragmentary nature of the early stories. "Last Mohican" has a finality about it that detracts from the cohesiveness of the entire sequence. The story ends in a kind of tableau on which Fidelman, while chasing Susskind, has "a triumphant insight." Whatever that triumphant insight was is not explicitly stated; but there is the suggestion of a reversal of attitude in Fidelman. When "Last Mohican" stood apart as a separate story, it was possible to conclude that Fidelman's insight was that he was in some sense responsible for Susskind (the *schnorrer* being Malamud's familiar Jew-as-Everyman figure), that Fidelman would abandon his selfishness and approach life with a different attitude. The appearance of "Still Life" a few years later need not have altered such a conclusion toward the first story. "Still Life" seemed to be a wholly different story about the same character, but there was no reason to conclude that it somehow "grew out" of the earlier story. Yet when the two stories are read as parts of·a related sequence, one discovers in retrospect that Fidelman's triumphant insight had more to do with art than with life and that it was no triumph but a mistake. It becomes clear that Fidelman had apparently learned that being an art critic was all wrong for him; but, instead of taking up a profession for which he was suited, Fidelman returned, in "Still Life," to his previously abandoned attempt to be a painter. The total futility of this enterprise does not emerge unmistakably, however, until "A Pimp's Revenge," although Fidelman's comically lustful pursuit of his landlady in "Still Life" showed that he had not learned the lesson of unselfishness that one might have concluded was his triumphant insight at the end of "Last Mohican."

Whatever confusion may have arisen from reading "Last Mohican" when it first appeared can be attributed to its publication as a self-contained piece. If it still retains some ambiguity within the present sequence, this probably arises as much from the nature of the conception as from a reader's earlier experience of it.

Variety in style does not necessarily fragment a work; after all, one section of *Ulysses* is written in a spectrum of styles that covers most of the changes in narrative diction in the history of the English language. Yet style is one element of unity in a long prose narrative; it lends cohesiveness to a book. A novel seems to demand a consistent style. An interrelated sequence of stories should forgo consistency of diction only for indispensable artistic effect; otherwise, the unity of the work is imperiled and its claims to the status of a novel are compromised. The first two stories of *Pictures of Fidelman* are written in the past tense, in the narrative manner of Malamud's other short stories—a combination of lyric symbolism and a slangy realism of diction. "Naked Nude," however, shifts into the present tense, and the diction becomes terse, more sinewy. "A Pimp's Revenge" returns to the past tense, and Fidelman is referred to, throughout the story, as merely "F." In this story, for the first time in the sequence, there is a sense of place. Fidelman goes to the marketplace, he accompanies his whore to the public square, he visits a woodcraft shop and picture galleries; all these scenes are reported with some vividness of detail. Though the book is called an exhibition of pictures, visual elements have been barely detectable in the first three stories. Voice has been the really distinguishing element of character; there has been little attempt to create a recognizably Italian setting. Though Fidelman has responded to the historical panorama of Rome, the reader has not been given much help in visualizing just what Fidelman is responding to. Toward the end of "A Pimp's Revenge," the narrative switches from the past to the present tense, for no discernible reason and returns to the past tense once more after three and a half pages.

"Pictures of the Artist," the fifth part of the book, is Fidelman's journey through the underworld. The style is surrealistic and highly comic. Past and present tenses mix freely. A mock Biblical diction is employed to narrate a Hawthorne-like exemplary parable: Fidelman as fabled earth-sculptor. Disconnected sections present wildly improbable scenes of Susskind as Savior and Fidelman as Judas; dream-like evocations of Fidelman's subconscious hopes and fears, all grotesquely twisted, are juxtaposed to ridiculous images of outlandish paintings: "Oil on wood. Bottle fucking guitar? Bull impaled on pole? One-eyed carp stuffed in staring green bottle? Clown spooning dog dung out of sawdust? Staircase ascending a nude?" This story climaxes in Fidelman's hearing Susskind's voice speak to him from a lightbulb as Fidelman in a loincloth (a latter-day Michaelangelo) paints geometrical designs on the ceiling and walls of a subterranean cave. The distinct style of this fifth story—reminiscent of the night-town section of *Ulysses*—effectively communicates the quality of Fidelman's nightmare journey through his subconscious. The comic surrealism is liberating and appropriate; the stylistic pecularities in "Naked Nude" and "A Pimp's Revenge," however, do not seem to serve as obviously useful a purpose and are, therefore, open to the charge of being idiosyncratic. The sixth story, "Glass Blower of Venice," returns to a straight narrative approach, the past tense used throughout. As this story moves to a climax, a warm lyricism—that occasionally relieved the stark realism of the *Assistant*—returns to Malamud's style.

To summarize, *Pictures of Fidelman* gets off to a jerky start with "Last Mohican." The fragmentary quality diminishes in the next story and virtually disappears in the third. The last three stories, which were composed closely together, have an unmistakable cohesiveness of tone and a smooth narrative line that flows naturally from story to story.

Though an inconsistency of style among the six stories detracts somewhat from the unity of *Pictures of Fidelman,* the book is held together by its focus on the same main character, Arthur Fidelman, by the Italian setting, and the recurrent appearance of Susskind both as a real character and as a moral image in Fidelman's imagination. The book's unity of theme will be discussed below. The elements of character, setting, and theme that serve to unify *Pictures of Fidelman* may be used as arguments to support the position that the book is indeed a novel. It is clear, however, that *Pictures of Fidelman* is not the same kind of novel as *The Assistant* is, for example. It does not have the mythic undergirding employed by Malamud as a characteristic element of form in his four previous novels. *Pictures of Fidelman* may represent only a single departure in technique for Malamud; future publications must decide that question.

All novels, of course, are made up, more or less, of episodic parts. But in the conventional, extended prose narrative verbal devices and structural strategies are used to weld those parts together; in the best novels the literary glue does not show. When a writer chooses not to unify the parts of a book with connectives, to leave them as it were sitting together side by side but not touching, he must rely on theme, character, style, and setting to make his work cohesive. As I have shown, Malamud does not use style to any great extent as a unifying device; he seems purposely to avoid doing so, preferring to employ an unfettered mixture of styles for local effects. It has also been remarked by critics of Malamud's short fiction that the Fidelman stories lack a sense of place, have no vivid quality in their Italian setting. Perhaps necessarily because of the way *Pictures of Fidelman* grew from one or two stories with a common hero to a related sequence with novelistic aspirations, the mythic method did not suggest itself as an appropriate unifying structural device. All this leaves only theme and character as possibly strong unifying elements; in the ensuing discussion of the individual stories in *Pictures of Fidelman,* I hope to show that these two elements do have a strong unifying effect.

II

The themes of *Pictures of Fidelman* are Malamud's familiar themes of suffering and responsibility; related to both of these are the quest for a meaningful life and the search for love. Fidelman is a quintessential Malamud hero, the irrepressible *schlemiel*. "There is in him something of both Alpine and Bober, but he is in his vulnerable good will and poverty closer perhaps to Bober." If his vulnerable good will suggests Morris Bober, his experience closely parallels Frank Alpine's: "The curve of Frank's experience is paralleled by that of Arthur Fidelman—from the frustrations of a bungler ("The Last Mohican") through the captivity of sexual bewitchment ("Still Life") to the iron jaws of imprisonment ("Naked Nude") where Fidelman is held prisoner by gangsters in a whorehouse. . . ."

As "Last Mohican" begins, Fidelman has just arrived in Rome with the announced purpose of beginning a year of research and writing for a work of art criticism devoted to the paintings of Giotto. The reader soon suspects that Fidelman's change of locale has other motivations. Like so many of Malamud's heroes, Fidelman's search for a meaningful life is symbolized in a journey motif; this journey will be continued figuratively and literally as Fidelman wanders from town to town in Italy, from story to story in the book. Fidelman is met upon his arrival in Rome by one Shimon Susskind, a *schnorrer* (artful beggar) who pesters the art critic for a suit. Susskind is the title character of this story, "the last honest man, honest to art and to conscience." When Fidelman refuses to give Susskind a suit, the *schnorrer* steals the art critic's brief case which contains the first chapter of his book on Giotto. Now the pursuer becomes the pursued, and in a curious reversal of roles Fidelman seeks an elusive Susskind. The *schnorrer* had earlier followed "the pedantic art critic through Rome like the shadow of a history he hardly understands." But when he cannot find Susskind, Fidelman's earlier sense of history ("It was an inspiring business, he, Arthur Fidelman, after all, born a Bronx boy, wallowing around in all this history") undergoes an important change. As he wanders through the Jewish ghetto, in and out of synagogues, through a cemetery (with stones commemorating the deaths of Jews killed by the Nazis), Fidelman is no longer exhilarated but "oppressed by history." He finally discovers Susskind selling rosaries on the steps of St. Peter's, an ironic parallel to Fidelman's earlier activity as an art critic searching into an alien past; in his pursuit of Susskind (the European Jew, refugee even from Israel), Fidelman is seeking the "real missing chapter of his own past self."

Earlier in the story when Susskind was importuning him for some capital to start a small business, Fidelman had refused with this question:

"Am I responsible for you then, Susskind?"

"Who else?" Susskind loudly replied.

"Lower your voice please, people are sleeping around here," said Fidelman, beginning to perspire. "Why should I be?"

"You know what responsibility means?"

"I think so."

"Then you are responsible. Because you are a man. Because you are a Jew, aren't you?"

This exchange comes immediately to the reader's mind at the end of the story when Fidelman spontaneously gives his suit to Susskind with no request for his missing chapter, declaring "all is forgiven." When Malamud declares in the final paragraph that Fidelman "moved by all he had lately learned, had a triumphant insight," the reader is prepared to conclude that Fidelman has at last understood his responsibility for Susskind as a repre-sentative figure of suffering mankind. Marc Ratner points out that, while studying Giotto's painting, Fidelman had overlooked its meaning; but, after a search for Susskind has resulted in an apparent change in attitude toward the historical catalogue of human suffering, Fidelman thinks of Giotto's painting of St. Francis giving his clothes to a poor man and immediately stuffs his suit into a bag and runs out to find Susskind. From all this the critic Samuel Bluefarb concludes that "Susskind the poor *schnorrer* proves to be the means by which Fidelman finds his own awakening; from Esthete . . ., Fidelman finally comes to see in the suffering of a Susskind Beggar, the root of all suffering, including his own perhaps."

But that does not prove to be the case in the ensuing two stories. In "Still Life" Fidelman, abandoning the role of critic, has undertaken again the profession of painter. He is lodging with Annamaria Oliovino, also a painter, after whom he lusts mightily. But Fidelman is an ineffectual Prufrock figure for the most part; he approaches his old career with "many indecisions, enunciations and renunciations." He is capable of a kind of love, "but his tragedy is that he bestows it on an unworthy object." But Fidelman's love is selfish too, a gnawing lust that "blocks his creative energy as an artist."

When it occurs to Fidelman to paint Annamaria as Virgin with Child, her sentimental vanity is so touched that she agrees to go to bed with him; but the scene ends in a comic premature emission of Fidelman's seed and with the pittrice's enraged cry "Pig, beast, onanist!" "In the final scene, dressed as a priest, [Fidelman] . . . gives the guilt-ridden Annamaria [She had once drowned a bastard child; thence arises one of the title's ironies] absolution, penance, and expiation" through sexual intercourse. Though the comic quality of this final tableau (with Fidelman in priestly biretta pumping the ecstatic penitent) is undeniable, it is clear that the moral curve of Fidelman's progress in these fictional pictures is downward. Susskind—whose recurrent image functions symbolically to remind Fidelman of his moral responsibility—appears but briefly in "Still Life": "Almost in panic he [Fidelman] sketched in charcoal a coattailed 'Figure of a Jew Fleeing' and quickly hid it away." Again in the next story, Susskind is briefly glimpsed as a "long-coated figure loosely dangling from a gallows rope amid Fidelman's other doodles. Who but Susskind, surely. A dim figure out of the past."

In "Naked Nude," the third story of the sequence, Fidelman is held captive by the keepers of a brothel. When it is discovered that he is an artist, the padrone and his male lover persuade Fidelman to fake a painting of the Venus Urbino, to be left in a nearby gallery in place of the authentic painting which they plan to steal. Though Fidelman has misgivings because he considers the enterprise artistically dishonest, he is persuaded to co-operate when promised his freedom if he succeeds in producing a good likeness. To help him in this undertaking, Fidelman is allowed to visit the gallery where the original hangs. He falls in love with the image of the Venus and returns to his prison to make a copy of the Urbino painting. The painting is a success and Fidelman falls in love with it. He persuades his captors to allow him to be one of the two persons sent on the expedition to steal the original; he contrives to have his own copy confused with it and carried off as the authentic Venus. Fidelman then eludes his accomplice and rows off in the night stopping periodically to adore his handiwork by the light of numerous matches.

Fidelman's refusal to steal may be seen as an implicit rejection of the shoddy morality of the brothel keeper, who casuistically argued that "Art steals and so does everybody." Marc Ratner sees Fidelman's painting of the Venus as "representative of his spirit, which heroically survives the brutal oppression of the two gangsters . . . [and] also, perhaps the ultimate symbol of Fidelman's spiritual progress through these stories." Ratner made this remark without benefit of the latter three stories, and his conclusion, because premature, is inaccurate. It should be remembered that Fidelman's theft of his own work has been motivated by self-love as much as anything; and it is selflessness that Fidelman—like Roy Hobbs, Frank Alpine, S. Levin and Yakov Bok before him—needs most to learn.

"A Pimp's Revenge" finds Fidelman in Florence, nearly starving in a garret and trying to paint a picture of his mother from an old photograph. By chance one day, Fidelman meets a young whore named Esmeralda on his way to the market, and he is attracted to her. She comes to live with him, mainly to escape Ludovico her pimp, and becomes a virtual servant in Fidelman's shabby apartment. Explaining to Esmeralda why he feels obsessed with painting a picture of his mother, Fidelman says, "I sometimes think that if I could paint such a picture much that was wrong in my life would rearrange itself and add up to more, if you know what I mean." Esmeralda observes that Fidelman's efforts look as though he is trying to paint himself into his mother's arms. To a large extent this is true. Besides the Oedipal implications in this enterprise, Fidelman is trying to recapture an idealized past, perhaps one that never existed. Like Roy Hobbs he is attracted to an image of past innocence, but, also like Roy, Fidelman has failed to learn from his experience. In his efforts to paint his mother's likeness, Fidelman produces images that sometimes resemble Susskind; he has failed to learn that he is neither critic nor painter.

In "Still Life" Fidelman's fear of painting Susskind leads him to paint abstractions until he reaches the ultimate, a blank canvas. In "A Pimp's Revenge," his obsession with an idyllic image of his innocent past drives him to paint his mother with himself, as "Madonna and Child." Then Fidelman paints Esmeralda and himself, first as "Brother and Sister," then honestly as "Prostitute and Procurer." This last painting proves successful; Fidelman proclaims it his "most honest piece of work." But Ludovico, Esmeralda's former pimp, has his revenge on Fidelman for subverting his source of income by depriving him of his whore; he tricks the artist into touching up the picture a bit. But in his attempt to make the picture "truer to life," Fidelman ruins it. Esmeralda, enraged, runs at Ludovico with a bread knife. Fidelman twists it out of her hand "and in anguish lifted the blade into his gut."

In the fifth story, "Pictures of the Artist," it is obvious that Fidelman's moral descent has now led him to the underworld of his own subconscious. Like Prufrock, Fidelman intones, "If we wake we drown" and plunges into the nightmare world of an outlandish artist's hell. Part of this story is devoted to a quaintly indirect recounting of Fidelman's legendary progress through various Italian towns digging holes in the ground—symbolic graves of his failure as an artist—and passing them off as modern sculpture. From artist as panderer in the previous story, Fidelman has descended to the role of artist as huckster of graveplots. In one dream-like sequence Susskind appears as Christ preaching from a mountaintop, exhorting the practice of love, mercy, and charity. He advises Fidelman "to give up your paints and your brushes and follow me where I go, and we will see what we will see." In a mock sequence of the Last Supper, Fidelman plays the role of Judas and blushes red when Christ/Susskind predicts that one of those seated at table will betray him. A subsequent paragraph bears out the prediction as Fidelman kisses Susskind to identify him for a crowd that has come to take him prisoner. With the pieces of silver that are his reward, Fidelman rushes out to buy paints, brushes, canvas. This betrayal is Fidelman's betrayal of himself. His obsession with being a painter, a role for which he has little talent, has not only led him through a personal hell of degradation but has impelled him to treat people as objects, to exploit the guilt feelings of Annamaria in order to satisfy his lust, to take advantage of the generosity of Esmeralda so that his self-indulgent efforts at painting will not be distracted by the petty concerns of everyday life.

The father-son motif, a favorite device of Malamud's, also appears in this story. In an imaginary sequence, a voice (Susskind's) from a lightbulb is heard (an ironic parallel to the divine voice from a cloud) and it urges Fidelman to abandon his obsessive painting in a subterranean cave and go upstairs to say hello to his sister Bessie before she dies. Fidelman remarks, "It's no fault of mine if people die." The lightbulb replies with a warning to remember the pride of the Greeks. When Fidelman asks which Greek, this answer is heard: "the one that he tore out his eyes." It seems evident now that Susskind is a kind of spiritual father who had instructed Fidelman earlier on the nature of moral responsibility. Fidelman's spurning of Susskind's advice and his blindly willful resumption of the artist's role amount to a rejection of his spiritual father, a symbolic Oedipal murder (cf. the doodle images in "Naked Nude" of Susskind hanging from a gallows). Likewise, Fidelman's desire to paint himself into his mother's arms reveals an oedipally-oriented flight from life. Susskind is not rejected now as he speaks to Fidelman from the lightbulb. Fidelman's declaration "Be my Virgil" indicates his acceptance of Susskind's spiritual guidance and his willingness to be led, like Dante, out of hell, this one a hell of his own creating. As Fidelman goes upstairs to say hello to his dying sister, he earns, by his act of self-denial, the curious redemption that comes to him in the book's final story.

"Glass Blower of Venice" finds Fidelman in Venice, "floating city of green and gold canals." Though emerged from the underworld of the tortured self, Fidelman carries on a Charon-like profession as he ferries passengers across the Grand Canal in this symbolic city of the dead. When the floods in January cover the campos adjacent to the canals, Fidelman—in a symbolic St. Christopher role—does his ferrying piggyback. While carrying one "attractive, long-nosed, almost oriental-eyed young Venetian woman," Fidelman finds himself with a throbbing groin and an erect penis. Sure that he is in love, he begins a search for the elusive lady in the shops and streets of Venice (echoing his search for Susskind in the first story). One day they meet by chance in a glass trinket shop; both are impassioned, eager for bed. She, Margherita Fassoli, is nevertheless anxious to have Fidelman meet her husband, Beppo, a glass blower, who is very "wise about life." Margherita and Fidelman make love during the daytime when her husband is away at work. Fidelman usually stays on for supper with Beppo with whom he soon becomes fast friends. Fidelman invites the glass blower to his room to see some of his paintings; he had "destroyed most but kept a dozen perhaps justificatory pictures, and a few pieces of sculpture." After thoughtful observation of Fidelman's art, Beppo says, "Your work lacks authority and originality. . . . Burn them all." At first angry, Fidelman eventually helps Beppo slash the canvases and dump them in the trash.

With Beppo's advice still ringing in his ears ("Don't waste your life doing what you can't do"), Fidelman, after a few days, goes to Margherita's bed for comfort. While they are engaged in "violent intercourse," Beppo enters the room naked and aroused; he assaults Fidelman from behind as Margherita slips out from under them and flees. Though salvation through sodomy is an unlikely dénouement to the progress of the artist, that is exactly what Malamud asks the reader to accept here. Even in this wildly improbable scene, the glass blower utters wise words as he impales the terrified Fidelman: "Think of love. . . . You've run from it all your life." Robert Scholes remarks that in his willingness to accept love even from this queer glass blower of Venice, Fidelman accepts the entire flawed universe of his past and of himself. "In the iconography of these pictures, Fidelman's submission to Beppo symbolizes his acceptance of imperfection in existence."

Beppo's advice to Fidelman is simply, "If you can't invent art, invent life." At this point the book's epigraphs leap into the mind. Yeats is quoted as affirming that "The intellect of man is forced to choose / Perfection of the life, or of the work . . ." Fidelman contradicts with a curt "Both." But Fidelman ultimately discovers that he can have neither as long as he persists in a profession for which he has little talent. He manages to get both by learning the crafts of love and glass blowing from Beppo, to whom he quickly apprentices himself.

III

The sufferings of most Malamud characters seem like a combination of fate and their own mistakes. Roy Hobbs and S. Levin increase the pain of their misfortunes by failing to learn from past experience and by resisting a responsible form of unselfish love. Morris Bober seems to suffer for no reason other than because he cannot avoid doing so. But he accepts the inevitable and struggles to wrest a meaning from it, passing both the role of sufferer and his own hard-won meaning on to his assistant Frank Alpine. Yakov Bok's suffering is largely imposed from without and the fixer resists it with all his soul. Fidelman's fate, however, seems largely self-created; all his suffering appears to derive from his wrong choices and his blind and selfish behavior. Thus the amelioration of his fate, though it comes in the form of another's love, is likewise the result of Fidelman's own decision. "Fidelman had never in his life said 'I love you' without reservation to anyone. He said it to Beppo. . . . Better love than no love." This surrender to love leads Fidelman to a totally unselfish act. When Margherita comes to Fidelman begging him not to destroy her marriage with Beppo, the apprentice glass blower agrees to leave his lover and the country; he returns to America and works as a craftsman in glass. Fidelman's denial of self can be seen as an act of higher love that flows out of a broad sense of responsibility for others—although there is no indication in Fidelman of the kind of political consciousness Yakov Bok develops in *The Fixer*. Like Frank Alpine, Fidelman is an assistant, "assisting for love's sake," and he learns both wisdom and craft from Beppo. Having discovered the limits of his own capabilities, Fidelman now finds perfection both of the life and the work. "In America he worked as a craftsman in glass and loved men and women."

The ideas of suffering and responsibility have played a subtle and important thematic counterpoint, throughout *Pictures of Fidelman*, to the central character's overriding quest for success in life and art. These themes and the character of Fidelman himself have drawn these stories together into a loose novelistic unity they would not otherwise have. When the Fidelman stories first began to appear, Samuel Bellman recognized the dynamic possibilities of the bumbling artist when he called him a character "constantly growing, realizing himself, transforming his unsatisfactory old life into a more satisfactory new one." By finally "abandoning the pretenses of art for the honesty of craftsmanship," and transcending his own selfishness by accepting love, Fidelman manages to reconcile the claims of the head and the heart which were so sorely at variance in "Last Mohican." If some degree of suffering is inescapable in every man's fate, Fidelman has at least learned that it need not be aggravated by foolish behavior and selfish choices. He has also shown that the denial of destructive lust, for the sake of a selfless and responsible love, can in the end lead to a new and better life.

MARK SHECHNER

The Return of the Repressed

Our image of Bernard Malamud is so bound up with certain familiar sentiments concerning conscience and moral accountability that scarcely anyone writes about him without paying tribute to them. Malamud's books, we are repeatedly told, speak for "the possibility of man's redemption through purgative suffering and selfless love," or betray a concern with "Love, Mercy (*Rachmones*), *Menschlechkeit*," or "probe the animal nature of man, reveal a fearful mistrust of instinctual behavior, and struggle toward an answer in discipline and love." With the prevailing consensus thus in favor of Malamud's mission of moral improvement, readers might well wonder whether it would not be more direct to bypass him altogether and proceed directly to the original teachings, whatever they may be. Not everyone would rush off to the library for a writer's books after being told that, as one critic has put it, he "follows in the ancient tradition of the prophets, Amos, Jeremiah, the Second Isaiah, who announce suffering to be the Jew's special destiny, evidence of his unique covenant with God. . . ." Indeed, some might sensibly conclude from such praise that the writer in question was altogether too morally accomplished for them, or too gloomy, and decide to stick with Dr. Brothers, who at least is cheerful, and reassures us that we can get what we want out of life.

This state of affairs has not exactly been imposed upon Malamud. If anything, he has encouraged this view of himself as a champion of humanism and spokesman for the special moral insight of the Jews by announcing on various occasions that "the purpose of the writer . . . is to keep civilization from destroying itself" and that "what has made the Jewish

From *The Nation* 10, vol. 228 (March 17, 1979). Copyright © 1979 by The Nation Associates, Inc.

writers conspicuous in American literature is their sensitivity to the value of man." The books themselves, with their parables of affliction and endurance and their quasi-symbolic Jews, standing for all mankind in their existential *Angst* while remaining Jews in their historical particularity, give body to such intentions. In all of contemporary literature, there is scarcely a compact, nay, covenant, between an author and critics more binding than that between Malamud and his. The latter have agreed in the main not to ask questions about Malamud's work that fall outside the domain of humanist morality and Jewish suffering that he has staked out as his territory.

What has gone unnoticed in the rush to sanctify Malamud is that the very system of values for which he is acclaimed has been, from the start, marked by discrepancies—contradictions between his celebrated pleas for restraint and certain powerful emotional promptings—and that those contradictions have been steadily growing sharper. In early books they appeared as mere matters of dramatic conflict, so that in *The Assistant*, Frank Alpine's "redemption" and his education in Jewish sexual taboos and rites, culminating in his circumcision, could be made to seem dimensions of the same moral development. But more recently those discrepancies between the emotional tenor of his book and their instructional premises have become too extreme for patching up, and have threatened to fracture the Malamudian universe altogether. We seem not to have been noticing that Malamud is changing on us, becoming more extravagant, and that in abandoning his early manner, with its special ethical coloration—its balance of longing and caution, irony and Talmudic strictness, Yiddish folklore and depression realism—he has not merely been losing touch with his original talent but trying strenuously to get around its limitations.

It now appears that Malamud, like many another Jewish writer who has grown weary of ethical or literary circumspection, has been trying to cut through to something else. How else are we to account for the heightened sexuality of recent books or the frightening bursts of mayhem that appear when his meticulously applied irony wears thin? What can the conventional formulas about Malamud tell us about the end of *The Tenants*, where Willie Spearmint slices off Harry Lesser's balls with a razor, just as Lesser is sinking an ax into Spearmint's head, while the hapless landlord, Levenspiel, looks on in horror and cries out the ostensible moral of the book: "Mercy, mercy, mercy. . . ," as if that could dampen any of the accumulated rage? And how might they account for the raunchy conclusion to *Pictures of Fidelman*, in which Fidelman submits to the advances of Beppo, the Venetian glass blower, who knows the ins and outs of love, and assures his neophyte Jewish lover that they don't hurt a bit: "It'll be a cool job, I'm wearing mentholated vaseline. You'll be surprised at the pleasure." Is this *our* Malamud? Is this just a new twist on redemption through purgative suffering and selfless love or on Morris Bober's "I suffer for you, you suffer for me"? After such knowledge, what forgiveness?

Dubin's Lives would appear to be the last nail in the coffin of the old Malamud, since this novel of middle-aged yearning and marital infidelity is certainly his most thoroughgoing adventure into the erotic. William Dubin, biographer, who has written a life of Thoreau and is currently, and painfully, at work on a life of D.H. Lawrence, begins, at age 56, to feel the itch of Lawrencian blood consciousness when his wife, Kitty, hires the nubile Fanny Bick as housekeeper, and Fanny, whose nipples are usually on show beneath her blouse, begins to hang around the biographer's study. Like many of Malamud's heroes, Dubin is teased to distraction by this peep show, which culminates at the stunning moment when Fanny, bent on calling Dubin's bluff—he has been lecturing her on the morality of living life "to the hilt"—barges into his study and removes her clothes. "Fanny tossed her yellow underpants at him. He caught them and tossed them back. They struck her breasts and fell to the floor."

" 'Whatever you're offering,' " he apologizes, " 'I regret I can't accept.' "

But such resolve is only whistling in the dark. Dubin has taken the bait—those fatal yellow underpants—and he's hooked. Thus begins a furtive chase that takes him to New York, where he is miserably stood up in a hotel bar, and then to Venice with Fanny (telling his wife he needs to do research) in order to redeem at last the promise of those undies.

But readers who are familiar with the ground rules of the Malamudian erotic will anticipate what comes next—The Putdown—though they may not be ready for the way it is done here. Malamud is a specialist in disappointment, the contemporary master of blueballs, and ever since Roy Hobbs in *The Natural* was shot down in that hotel room by the woman who lured him there, and Frank Alpine in *The Assistant* was spurned by Helen Bober for being "an uncircumcised dog," Malamud has been contriving newer and more spectacular ways to liven up the scenario of male shame. After drinks, wine, a sumptuous dinner (Fanny orders brains), and hours of slow teasing ("She had removed her shoe and was caressing him under the table"), they retire to the hotel room where Fanny is suddenly beset by the effects of those brains. Losing control of her bowels she rushes to the bathroom, and when Dubin checks in on her after several minutes of impatient waiting, he is greeted by this Swiftian vision of the nymph:

"She was standing at the toilet bowl, retching, a blob of diarrhea dribbling down her leg." Purgative suffering indeed. That Fanny remains ill and indisposed for the remainder of their stay, and then betrays Dubin with a gondolier and a motorboat operator, is strictly literary afterplay. That blob of diarrhea is the touch of a master and the irrepressible comedy of the unconscious. Dubin tries to salvage some dignity from his predicament by recalling Yeats's line: "Love has pitched its mansion in the place of excrement," but is neither comforted nor enlightened by so lofty a point of view.

That scene might mark the climax of a Malamud short story or point the moral of an early novel on the rewards of appetite, but Malamud is no longer content with comic catastrophes and moral epiphanies, no matter what psychic depths they may divulge. What makes *Dubin's Lives* different is that Malamud rejects the customary conservative moral—that Dubin should act his age and patch up his marriage—in favor of something more problematic and more interesting. Like any Malamud character, Dubin is being educated by experience, but unlike the others, he gains no wisdom and earns no "redemption," which is perhaps why this book, ostensibly the least Jewish of all Malamud's novels, may well be the most Jewish by interior design. For it is the most thoroughly devoted to the actualities of common experience, rather than to the mythic or moral patterns that might be extracted from it.

Malamud allows Dubin and Fanny to have an affair and to enjoy their share of sensual delight. Dubin has been taking instruction in sexual freedom from Lawrence, and though the choice of Lawrence—sexologue, primitivist, anti-Semite—may seem paradoxical for so cautious a man of modest appetites, it conforms to a deeper logic. Lawrence is the shadow self, and thus a voice for repressed urges that have long been clamoring for release. He is midwife to this other Dubin, whose emergence into the first one's life produces the sorts of difficulties that come of mixing two literary worlds, or two regions of the mind. Dubin tries to become a Lawrencian hero in a Malamudian world, that is, a phallic narcissist in a life of modest designs and severe consequences. But then, too, as Dubin knows, Lawrence himself was not exactly *Lawrence*; his sexual manifestoes were not affirmations easily come by but protests against his own strict superego and unpredictable body. He was impotent at 42. If there is a touch of Lawrence in Dubin, there was apparently a touch of Dubin in Lawrence.

Thus the second and more interesting half of *Dubin's Lives* begins when Dubin and Fanny consummate the long flirtation and embark on a hazardous affair, thereby raising the level of complication. On the one hand, the affair represents a genuine release into the erotic. Dubin and Fanny (what's in a name?) take full pleasure in each other, and Malamud indulges himself, by indulging them, in genuine sensuality. But not too much of it. Even in this relationship, sensuality takes a back seat to the familiar commotions of conscience. Fanny may garland Dubin's penis with flowers, but she also wreathes his life with difficulties. It is symptomatic of Malamud's version of the bower of bliss that Fanny's apartment on New York's West 83rd Street should overlook an orthodox synagogue in which Dubin can see "a small candlelit room where a black-bearded black-hatted Jew, his white shawl glowing on his shoulders, bent back and forth in prayer." As a reminder that all is not lost to blood consciousness, here are the fathers perched at the very window, like so many Jewbirds of disapproval, reminding Dubin of the old ethics and forsaken duties. Such reminders can lead him in only one direction: home.

Just as nothing succeeds like failure in earlier Malamud books, nothing fails like success in this one. Dubin's marriage, difficult enough before Fanny, becomes increasingly dismal as he withdraws from Kitty. Indeed, it is not in the affair with Fanny that we find the heart of this book but in the portrait of a marriage which, for all its gloom, its bitter asperities, its bleak climate of empty habit and dessicated affection, is a vivid depiction of a real relationship, a marriage in progress.

Against temptations to resolve Dubin's impasse and heal the split between his lives, Malamud holds fast until the very last page, where he violates the logic of the entire book by having Dubin leap out of Fanny's bed with an erection (she now owns a house up the road from the Dubins) and rush home to make love to his wife before the erection droops. The reader is advised to skip that page. Like Levenspiel's appeal for mercy in *The Tenants*, this ending simply contradicts everything that has come before, and tries to rescue the book by magic from its own harsh conclusions. Up until that point, though, Malamud is fairly steadfast, and pursues the desperate situation relentlessly and imaginatively through page after page of bitterness, mutual recrimination and mutual withdrawal, as both Dubin and Kitty slowly retreat from each other into private enclaves of fantasy. Dubin armors himself against his wife, and she responds with bewilderment, then rage, then analysis and finally the inevitable affair of her own, in this case with her analyst.

That Dubin's crisis is no simple outcome of his secret life may be guessed from the alienation of his two children: Gerald and Maud. The former has deserted from the Army to Sweden (the year is roughly 1974), where he remains incommunicado and, indeed, will not even speak with his father when the latter tracks him down at his Swedish rooming house. At the end, he defects to the Soviet Union, so deep is his alienation. Maud has gone away to college at Berkeley, but has quit school after an unhappy love affair and joined a Zen Buddhist monastery, only to abandon it and return home for a few dismal days to announce that she is pregnant. (*Of course*, the father is black.) Neither Gerald nor Maud shares any particular warmth with Dad, who has never given much and is now totally encased in his own troubles. The affair with Fanny, rather than opening him up, has shut him down entirely, and when he is not with Fanny, he is holed up in his study in the barn with his manuscript and his miseries. For a man so vulnerable, Dubin appears to his family to be impregnably self-sufficient.

So, *Dubin's Lives* is the old Malamud after all, to the extent that Dubin's pleasure does not add up to satisfaction. Quite the opposite; it turns out to be just another road to disaster. Through the gradual dissolution of his marriage, the alienation of his children, impotence with his wife, writer's block, and a failing memory, Dubin pays richly for his victories over middle age, as his misery increases in geometric ratio to his pleasures. (That some of these punishments precede the crime is not to the point, since it is Malamud's mind we're talking about.) Sexual liberation means no less trial than renunciation; the Malamud hero suffers either way.

Where this novel succeeds and is, in my estimation, the richest of all Malamud's novels, is not in the conclusion, which is false, nor in Malamud's judgments, which are more ambivalent than ever, nor in the tortuous vision of transgression and retribution—by now old hat and hardly in need of restatement. It lies in Malamud's command of the idiom of domestic warfare, the day-to-day details of a marriage in decline. Here as nowhere else Malamud pursues his favorite myth of moral exigency without resort to folklore or to the easy affirmations of packaged morality and the equally easy negations of psychic disarray. Malamud has been more considerate of his turmoil this time around, and produced a novel whose cries of conscience, erotic remissions and ultimate vote for sanity are worked out with patience and therefore with credibility.

After *Dubin's Lives* it will be hard to treat Malamud as either a placid moralist or an ethnic hors d'oeuvre: that is, as either an expert in timeless wisdom and contemporary ethics or an exotic miniature to be savored before the main course of American literature. Either view makes him sound like a children's classic, or at least something suitable for high school seniors. For once, he has joined his private sexual obsessions to plausible contemporary circumstances in a thoroughly convincing manner, and in the process secured a place for himself in the front ranks of contemporary fiction writers. That does not mean, finally, that the Jewish element in Malamud's work is any less important but only that it is something different from what we used to think it was.

ROBERT ALTER

A Theological Fantasy

Bernard Malamud is a writer who early on established an emphatic paradigm for his fictional world and who ever since has been struggling in a variety of ways to escape its confines. His latest novel [*God's Grace*] is his most strenuous strategem of escape, moving beyond the urban horizon of his formative work into an entirely new mode of postapocalyptic fantasy—with intriguing though somewhat problematic results.

When I say "paradigm," I am not referring to the explicit Jewish themes or to the morally floundering Jewish protagonists that have been trademarks of Malamud's fiction, with the exception of his first novel, *The Natural*. In fact, *God's Grace* is the most self-consciously Jewish of all his books. Its hero, Calvin (née Seymour) Cohn, the son of a rabbi and himself a former rabbinic student, carries his dog-eared copy of the Pentateuch into the strange new world in which he finds himself, tries to transfer its ethical teaching to the new reality, conducts inward arguments with God, sometimes even alluding to rabbinic texts, and, above all, broods over the awesome story of the Binding of Isaac and wonders what it might suggest about God's real intentions toward humanity. What I mean by "paradigm" is, in essence, the phenomenological substructure of Malamud's fictional world—its constant tilting of its protagonists into narrow enclosures, preferably cluttered and dirty, and ultimately with no real exits. The novelist has repeatedly sought to give his own claustrophobic sensibility a moral as well as thematic justification by intimating that these sundry traps, prisons, and living graves in which he places his protagonists (Morris Bober's grocery

From *The New Republic* 12–13, vol. 187 (September 20, 27, 1982). Copyright © 1982 by The New Republic, Inc.

store, Yakov Bok's cell, Harry Lesser's condemned tenement) are the harsh limits within which a true moral life of commitment is realized. But, as I have had occasion to argue elsewhere, this is precisely the least convincing aspect of Malamud's work.

God's Grace, as a future fiction, sets to one side—without, however, entirely suppressing—the Malamudian vision of cluttered incarceration by sweeping the global slate clean. Calvin Cohn, a gentle-souled, rabbinically learned oceanographer, happens to be in a bathysphere at the bottom of the Pacific when a nuclear war is launched that in a few minutes destroys all animal life on earth, down to the last creeping things and the last fish swarming in the sea. By an absurd oversight of God—or is it, Cohn wonders, a new twist of His inscrutable design?—Cohn alone of all humanity is saved in the insulated roundness of his deep-sea submersible. Up to this point, the plot follows a familiar enough route of reasonably plausible science fiction, but by rapid stages, uninhibited fantasy takes over. Summary is bound to be a little unfair to the novel because Malamud makes it far more engaging than will be suggested by the bare fictional data.

Cohn discovers that another living creature has somehow survived with him on the oceanographic vessel, a young male chimpanzee named Buz, who has been extraordinarily trained by his late scientist-owner: as the story emerges, Buz has been given both the capacity for perfectly articulate speech and a stubborn adherence to the tenets of Christianity. Cohn assumes toward the chimp a benign Crusoe-to-Friday relationship of mentor and friend, though this eventually turns into something utterly different from what first appears. Meanwhile, once Cohn and Buz have established themselves on a blessedly fruit-bearing tropical island, other simian survivors of the devastation enter the scene: a huge melancholy gorilla who reveals a fondness for cantorial singing, a small group of chimps who under Cohn's tutelage prove as wonderfully educable as Buz, and a family of luckless baboons.

Cohn's island might of course be construed as another version of the Malamudian prison, but it has a spaciousness, a paradisiacal sense of benign nature, absent from the characteristic roach-ridden cells, literal and figurative, of Malamud's previous fiction. Even the Crusoesque cave that Cohn makes into his home, complete with rough-hewn furniture, shelves, and a rolling wooden barrier at the mouth, is more cosy womb than tomb. This mode of fantasy, moreover, releases an element of exuberance in Malamud's writing that was exhibited in some of his most attractive early stories, like "Angel Levine" and "Idiots First." The opening chapter, in which Cohn, in his dripping wet suit, discovers that, despite the promise recorded in Genesis, the Flood has come again, and then finds himself addressed from above by an impatient Lord of Hosts, is a bravura performance. Many of the pages that follow are informed by a winning zaniness of invention. Modulations of tone are always essential when Malamud's writing is working well, and the quality of wry bemusement, hovering between sad reflection and self-ironic laughter, lends a certain emotional authority to the fantasy. "Maybe this island was Paradise," Cohn wonders,

> although where was everybody who had been rumored to be rentless in eternity? No visible living creature moved through the outsize vegetation, only a lone Jewish gentleman and a defenseless orphaned chimp, befriended on a doomed oceanography vessel.

The muted comic effect of such writing seems just right avoiding mawkishness or the melodrama that Cohn's post-diluvian plight might invite through quietly witty formulations like the characterization of the blessed as "rentless in eternity" or the image of "a lone Jewish gentleman" (only five foot six) peering into the outsize vegetation.

Malamud has described his own novel as "a visionary tale with a prophetic warning." Some of his efforts, I fear, to convey a visionary argument through the story betray an underlying weakness, and the prophetic warning at the end, though it may seem to the author to serve a moral purpose, is a painful illustration of how Malamud's materials can go wildly out of control. Let me first address the visionary argument. Given the calamitous state to which humankind has brought the world, and, if you are a believer, to which God has permitted humankind to bring the world, Malamud not only questions human nature but also the nature of the God who allows His own handiwork such a cruel genius for self-annihilation. This theological inquiry is focused chiefly through a confrontation between Jewish and Christian views (in the persons of Cohn and Buz) of the story of the Binding of Isaac, the compelling and baffling parable of how God might seem to require the slaughter of His human sons. Christian tradition calls the story the Sacrifice of Isaac because it is taken as the typological intimation of the Crucifixion; Judaism calls it the Binding because the actual denouement of the story is stressed, in which the angel's voice stays the sacrificial knife just before it plunges. Cohn is led to speculate, considering what has happened to his own century from the Holocaust through Hiroshima to the ultimate devastation, that the Lord who oversees this world might in fact want an actual immolation of humanity.

Struggling to perpetuate a humane Jewish ethics, Cohn promulgates to his fellow primates what he calls the Seven Admonitions (in deference to his Mosaic predecessor, he avoids the term commandment), which reflect a cautiously hopeful, pragmatic view of the necessity for altruism and of man's small but real potential for good. The Second Admonition reads: "Note: God is not love. God is God. Remember Him." This Jewish theological emphasis, it might be observed, reverses certain subterranean Christian motifs that can be detected in the earlier Malamud. (The most opposite contrast is the story "The Magic Barrel" where the rabbinic student Finkle is led by the plot, according to sound Pauline doctrine, to turn away from the law, to which he has been devoted, for the sake of love.) Late in the book, at a point when Cohn's hoped-for new covenant is manifestly disintegrating, Buz, who has played a shadowy role in the process of disintegration, makes bold to erase the word "not" from the Second Admonition. The theological assertion, thus Christianized, that God is love, might seem benign enough, but in view of what is afterward perpetrated by the hand that has revised the Admonition, an anti-Christian polemic is clearly implied. Those who make such an ideal claim about God, we may infer, are the most likely to slip into the abyss of the anti-ideal; or, alternately, a God who is supposed to be love in a world where so little of it is in evidence may also enact the outrageous paradox of sacrificing mankind, His only-begotten beloved son, in the most ghastly way to demonstrate that He is love.

Malamud's theological argument, unlike the tonality and humor of his fantasy, is not misrepresented by summary. It is, in other words, schematic, sketchy, lacking weight of experience and density of intellectual texture. One symptom of his lack of anchorage is that Cohn's abundant references to Jewish tradition are patently secondhand and in some instances misinformed. More serious is the fact that this polemic with Christianity in the end contradictorily reimagines a doctrine of Original Sin, the plot concluding with an irresistible assertion of the Old Adam. There is an ambiguity here that is confused rather than fruitful: a reader, contemplating the conclusion, could easily turn the whole book around, something I doubt the author intends, and claim that Cohn's guarded Jewish optimism about humanity was all along a superficial view and, worse, an abysmal delusion.

The denouement involves a horrific orgy of infanticide and cannibalism and then dire consequences of a rather strained symbolic character for Cohn himself. Malamud wants this to be taken as prophetic warning, but it seems far more like sheer punishment inflicted by the author on his protagonist and thus implicitly on the reader as well. Punishing his incarcerated characters has been a temptation to which Malamud has of course succumbed again and again. The feel of the ending here is unfortunately very like that of the ghastly ending of *The Tenants*, when Harry Lesser sinks an ax into the skull of Willie Spearmint at the exact moment his black rival lashes off his testicles with a razor-sharp knife. Even without pursuing psychoanalytic conjecture, we may note that there is a palpable gap between such unleashing of aggression against characters and readers, and the moral claims made for the fictional expression of all that rage.

In just this regard, Gore Vidal's *Kaki* (1978) provides an instructive contrast to *God's Grace*. It is also a postapocalyptic fantasy, though the bulk of the novel is devoted to a brilliantly suspenseful account of the plot to bring about the apocalypse. Here, too, the relentless egoism of some of the survivors ends by subverting the possibility of survival. There is, however, a kind of purity of witty misanthropy in Vidal's treatment of this whole subject. No "prophetic" or moralistic claims are made for the story; it is an end-of-the world thriller that reveals the essential nastiness of the ingenious human animal, something about which the author has never been seriously in doubt. This is probably too glib and too limited a view of mankind to generate anything like major fiction, but it does give the work in question a certain consistency, even a kind of circumscribed integrity. *God's Grace*, by contrast, invites us to take it as an impassioned plea for kindness and pity for all living creatures in the face of man's enormous capacity for murderous destruction. The moral message is unexceptionable, but the vehemence with which the brutish counterforce to kindness and pity is imagined at the end is disquieting. Instead of holding a prophetic mirror to the contorted face of mankind, the novelist—at least so it seems to this reader—has once again taken his lovingly fashioned creatures, bound them hand and foot, and begun to play with axes, knives, tearing incisors, and other instruments of dismemberment.

ALVIN B. KERNAN

"The Tenants":
"Battering the Object"

The literary work of art now stands alone in its perfection as it does in the "art-for-art's-sake" movement and the cult of *"Le Mot Juste,"* it is idealized as symbolism and surrealism, it is stripped of its historical provenance and separated from its creator and its audience in the type of criticism now becoming generally known as "formalism," and it is hypothesized as the true or absolute text which editors and bibliographers spend infinite pains to disentangle from the complex process of transmission and restore down to the last comma as it was realized in pure form by the creator. No matter how the literary work is defined, whether as large as "the mythopoeic world of Balzac" or as small as the quick flash of being created by the Imagists, the literary work of art is an intensely real world, a harmonious and ordered microcosm, complete unto itself. "What I should like to write," said Flaubert, summarizing this belief in the absolute reality of the work itself,

> is a book about nothing, a book dependent on nothing external, which would be held together by the strength of its style, just as the earth, suspended in the void, depends on nothing external for its support; a book which would have almost no subject, or at least in which the subject would be almost invisible, if such a thing is possible. The finest works are those that contain the least matter; the closer expression comes to thought, the closer language comes to coinciding and merging with it, the finer the result.

From *The Imaginary Library: An Essay on Literature and Society.* Copyright © 1982 by Princeton University Press.

Joyce's *Finnegans Wake* probably comes as close as any work of literature to realizing Flaubert's dream.

For some critics in this tradition, literature remained close to craft, still dependent, as for William Morris, on good workmanship, functionalism, and honest materials. But for others in the line of Flaubert, Joyce, James, and Mann, style and writing became a religion which burned everything else away and left only the text behind. Wordsworth goes to the Lake Country, Flaubert to Croisset, Proust to his cork-lined room, and Joyce into European exile, to escape a no-longer relevant world and create the texts, those great testimonies of reality, in the silence of the imagination. For Faulkner, even the great figure of the romantic artist disappears while the books alone remain:

> I will protest to the last: no photographs, no recorded documents. It is my ambition to be, as a private individual, abolished and voided from history, leaving it markless, no refuse save the printed books; I wish I had had enough sense to see ahead thirty years ago and, like some of the Elizabethans, not signed them. It is my aim, and every effort bent, that the sum and history of my life, which in the same sentence is my obit and epitaph too, shall be them both: He made the books and he died.
> (Letter to Malcolm Cowley, 11 Feb., 1949)

Literature paradoxically achieved absolute reality for its texts by cutting them off from the world and the print in which they had found their necessary objectivity, but there have been persistent severe doubts about the absolute value of beauty, style, and the isolated work of literary art. Realists like Dostoevsky deliberately sought an anti-style. Freud, who defined literature as the expression of various psychic energies and struggles, saw style as only "aesthetic foreplay" or a disguise needed to smuggle illicit impulses past the censor. For the many Marxists who want to define literature as an outmoded bourgeois expression of economic interests, style is only a decadent aesthetic overlay for the class apologetics beneath it. Even within the literary establishment doubts have arisen, and in recent years a number of writers have increasingly begun to question openly whether cutting literary art off so severely from the world and emphasizing its independence through style are any longer possible, or make much sense for either art or the society of which it is inescapably a part. Hermann Broch, that follower of Joyce, and writer of two- and three-page sentences, reveals in *The Death of Vergil* the kind of uneasiness the pure stylist is beginning to feel. In Broch's book the poet who has been the model for the craft tradition agrees in a deathbed conversation with Augustus Caesar not to burn *The Aeneid,* not because it is artistically perfect, and not because of the emperor's social argument that the world needs a record of Roman achievements, but because the poem no longer matters very much, since it fails to foresee the new Christian era coming into being. These kinds of doubts about the importance of style and workmanship in literature appear even more definitely in Camus' *The Plague*, written just after the Second World War. Here the writer, Grand, is tested along with other types, the doctor, the journalist, the gangster, the priest, the administrator, by a mysterious and terrible plague in an African city, an image of the recent German occupation of France and all the mysterious disasters which man must simply endure. Despite his name, Grand is only a petty clerk, but he longs to be a great writer in the tradition of Flaubert and Proust, and he has spent years trying to perfect a single sentence: "One fine morning in the month of May an elegant young horsewoman might have been seen riding a handsome sorrel mare along the flowery avenues of the Bois de Boulogne." Entire days are spent on each detail of this trite sentence trying to give "the words . . . the exact *tempo* of this ride—the horse is trotting, one-two-three, one-two-three." But despite changes of "elegant" to "slim," then eliminating sibilants, then making the sorrel a black horse, the sentence is never finished. When Grand, seemingly dying of the plague, makes the required Vergilian gesture of asking the doctor to burn his imperfect manuscript, the doctor discovers that its fifty pages are covered only with different versions of the same sentence. Camus has created an utterly savage image of the meaninglessness of the aesthetic tradition in the face of suffering and death. Insofar as Grand is useful in the plague, it is not by his utterly irrelevant art but by his simple work in caring for the sick and the dying, in sharing in the great human effort of trying to find a way of dealing with life's great antagonist, death.

The very practical concerns of such writers as Broch and Camus about the value of thinking of literature as an independent artifice, a verbal icon or well-wrought urn, have been reflected, as social concerns about literature usually are, in recent criticism which has turned away from formalism and its "coldly spatialized objective mediations into which Platonists and New Critics, formalists all, would harden poems." This anti-formalistic critical movement, whose major activity Wimsatt aptly summarizes as "Battering the Object," operates today under many different names such as phenomenology, structuralism, deconstruction, and reader response, but, as Wimsatt very clearly saw, all have as their end the breaking down of the traditionally firm outlines of the literary text in a much vaster, even an infinite, context of other texts, of language, of the psychology of readers, and of the structure-building tendency of the mind. All these critical movements are an assault on the integrity and reality of the literary text, and therefore ultimately on the fact of literature itself as it has been understood since the eighteenth century. . . . Texts are the central fact of literature, and their importance has increased steadily from the late nineteenth century onward—particularly in the period of modernism—when the claims of the romantic artist and the creative imagination have been partly abandoned in favor of an emphasis on the texts, the library, the long line of monuments which are the objective reality of literature. "To divert interest from the poet to the poetry is," says Eliot modestly, "a laudable aim." Any attack on the texts—from literal book-pulping to deconstructive criticism—contains potentially the most dangerous consequences for literature as a whole, and literature seems to have made itself vulnerable to such attacks by a kind of institutional overdetermination. As a new institution, literature needed objective form to become real and meaningful in the world, and this objectification was in part the gift of the printing press. But the potential of the press for objectification, in number of books and in their fixed form, was almost unlimited, and in conjunction with the romantic desire to claim complete independence for literature from a disliked society, and absolute priority for the literary art, it led to claims for the perfection of the text which have proven impossible to sustain. It was inevitable that these claims would be challenged by critics who confronted the texts with uncomfortable facts about their dependence on other texts, about the nature of writing, and about the peculiarities of readers. It was equally inevitable—as the decline of the power of and interest in literature at the present makes us know—that society would challenge the texts' claim to absolute reality as they drifted farther away from and squared less and less with social realities and with what was believed by the majority of men to be true and knowable. This confrontation of text and society is the subject of Bernard Malamud's *The Tenants* (1971), which portrays very clearly the nature of traditional romantic beliefs about the reality of the literary text and the breakdown of these beliefs when they are confronted by social realities which directly contradict and confront them with an aggressive urgency and power born out of suffering and a need for help from all institutions, including art. I would not argue that *The Tenants* is one of the greatest of modern novels, but it is extraordinarily powerful and compelling in its realization of the view that is central to the conception of literature as a social institution: that literature and the arts are inescapably a part of society, and that the central literary values, though they are not totally socially determined, do respond in a dialectical manner to what takes place and is believed in that society.

Bernard Malamud, a writer with a strong investment in the craft tradition and the literary work as object, has dramatized the deconstruction of the literary text in a way which makes clear why it is becoming impossible for the writer any longer to believe that literature can remain independent of the world. Malamud begins with an image of what he considers the present situation of the writer. The Imaginary Library built by print, the House of Fiction built by Flaubert and Henry James, has degenerated in *The Tenants* into a squalid New York City tenement inhabited as the story begins by a solitary writer. Once there had been a small garden on the roof where the writer often sat after a day's work, looked at the sky and the clouds, "and thought of Wm. Wordsworth." But those recollections in tranquility have passed, along with Wordsworth's belief that poets make the world in their poetry, and now the garden is sterile, and unvisited. Below the garden, the building is untenanted except for a solitary person, the latter-day writer Harry Lesser, who lives, with many locks on his door, as high up in the building as he can, but without a view. The landlord Levenspiel has found the old-style tenement unprofitable and, in order to tear the building down and replace it with a more economical structure of modest size with stores on the bottom floor, has evicted all the tenants except Lesser, who refuses to go. But he is prevented from carrying out his practical plans by Lesser's refusal, protected by various laws on tenants' rights, to vacate. The House of Fiction has been invaded by the world and has degenerated into a fearsome place of decay and terror. Windows are smashed and doors broken down by vandals, the plumbing and lighting fixtures ripped out and sold by scavengers; the floors and walls are sour-smelling, covered with stains, debris, and mold. Stray animals and homeless men creep through the empty hallways to shelter in the icy rooms at night, leaving behind them odd garbage, the sticks of small fires, and piles of ordure on the floor or in the remaining tubs and toilets. In one room night-visitors have drawn a remarkable mural on the walls: "huge mysterious trees, white-trunked rising from thick folds, . . . dense ferny underbrush, grasses sharp as razor blades, giant hairy thistles, dwarf palms with saw-toothed rotting leaves, dry thick-corded vines entangling thorny gigantic cactus exuding pus; eye-blinding orchidaceous flowers—plum, red, gold—eating alive a bewildered goat as a gorilla with hand-held penis erectus, and two interested snakes, look on." On the wall of another room there is "a crayon cartoon of A. Hitler wearing two sets of sexual organs, male-female." The apartments had once been homes lived in by neat and kindly people with such warming names as Holzheimer, but now the only light in the empty building comes from a few dim bulbs, regularly smashed, on the stairs; the water runs in thin brown trickles from the few working taps; and the ancient furnace sends up only the faintest trace of heat. Rats scurry through the dark damp cellars, the wind howls over the frozen black snow outside where battered ashcans are filled with rotting garbage.

The Tenants is a carefully constructed parable in which every detail has meaning on at least two levels, and the tenement is not only a realistic depiction of the desperate state of much of New York City, particularly such areas as the South Bronx, but of the wasteland of modern western society and the incursion of this reality into literature toward the end of a terrifying century. The battered fragments of an older, better-ordered society, it is now foul, barely functioning, its corridors filled with darkness and terror, the temporary shelter of wounded, homeless, indistinguishable men and animals, haunted by nightmare visions such as the hermaphroditic Hitler and the scapegoat-eating flower. Responsibility for this invasion is divided between the profit-seeking capitalist landlord with his dream of wealth and the artist who by refusing to leave when the capitalist landlord tries to empty the old building for the wrecker, keeps it standing and therefore subject to the forces which reduce it to a grotesque chamber of horrors. Perhaps, The Tenants suggests, it might be better for the artist to move on and let the old culture and the old art end rather than to try to keep them standing in a world in which art has no function and against which it therefore no longer has any real defenses. Levenspiel's new world, his building in which the apartments above rest on the shops below, both architecturally and economically, might be preferable to the monstrosity that has resulted from the artist's stubbornly trying to work amid the ruins.

The artist, however, supported by the tangled laws of the old liberal society which ignore economic realities to protect the tenant from the owner, keeps the old building standing, trying to maintain the old literary values in the midst of the wasteland world. Lesser the novelist "squats"— Malamud's world is an intensified realistic version of Eliot's wasteland and frequently refers to it—in a few gray and cold rooms on the top floor which contain the minimal necessary furnishings of the old culture, the bookshelves with the patiently assembled library of cherished books, the hi-fi equipment and a few jazz and classical records, the desk, the typewriter, and the notes and files. The arrangements for eating, sleeping, and washing are rudimentary, but these matters of the flesh are not of much concern to the artist Lesser. He goes seldom outside, running quickly through the dangerous halls of his building to buy a few groceries or to telephone the rent control board to complain about the lack of heat. Occasionally troubled by rustlings or ominous sounds outside his door, he presses an eye to the keyhole, or, arming himself, opens the door briefly to stare into the darkness beyond. Behind the many locks on his door, he lives out the ultimacies of the totally dedicated romantic artist in a hostile world, a parody of Flaubert at Croisset or Proust in his cork-lined room of silence exploring his memories, of Joyce in his exile of silence and cunning creating a great work in the smithy of his soul.

Lesser reasons that he must stay on in the old building, despite the dangers and discomforts, because it is here that he began the book he is presently working on, and it is therefore here that he must finish it, if it is to be finished at all. He has written two earlier books, the first a *succès d'estime* which pleased him despite its small sales, and the second, in his opinion a poor book which nevertheless did well and was bought by the movies, providing him with enough money to live, very frugally, for a number of years while working on his third novel. (The movies are as regularly the *deus ex machina* which keeps authors alive in the modern *Künstlerroman* as Wordsworth is the progenitor poet.) Lesser is now deep into this third book which will, he hopes, prove to himself and to the world that he is a true writer; but he has been at it, like the Greeks before Troy, for over nine years, and the book is in deep trouble, for he cannot find the necessary ending for the already-written beginning and middle. Levenspiel cannot understand, of course, either why the book should take so long— "What are you writing, the Holy Bible?" which is what a craftsman-artist like Lesser thinks he is writing—or why it cannot be written in another, more comfortable place just as well. But Lesser knows that it must be finished here where it was begun because, on the surface level, only here can he find that complete isolation needed for the intense effort of completing the book. On the allegorical level the meaning would seem to be that only in this particular romantic stance of isolation from and antagonism towards a broken and ugly world is the concentrated, introspective, priestly work of the Dedalian artificer possible. His art is not possible in a setting, or condition of being, other than that which the scene of *The Tenants* realizes, for another setting would necessitate a different kind of art. He needs the ugliness of the world as a foil against which to create the beauty of the perfectly articulated work.

For Lesser art is "glory," a "sacred cathedral . . . with lilting bonging iron bell," and he is its high priest or rabbi, whose service is a willing servitude. He is a professional writer, a workman who lives for his work. He rises in the morning eager to begin writing, and he falls asleep each night planning the work of the next day. When he leaves the building he rushes back in order to get on with his work, and he is miserable and mentally upset when he leaves it for a time or when the work is not going well. Each day's production is put in a safety deposit box in the vault of a bank, as other men safeguard their jewels and money. "I've got to do the kind of job I have to as an artist," he says, and he does the job like the careful workman he is, "a man of habit, order, steady disciplined work. Habit and order fill the pages one by one. Inspiration is habit, order; ideas growing, formulated, formed." The ashcans outside the tenement are filled with thousands of crumpled pages of yellow paper covered with words which did not meet the standards of this exacting stylist.

Lesser not only has the compulsive work-ethic his art requires, but he has the technical skills and tools of the verbal craftsman as well. Words, language, grammar, rhetoric are his tools, and he can "no longer see or feel except in language." A thing can be true, real, convincing, alive for him only if it takes shape in the right words. He prefers a sharp, precise, sparse, clear style, the exact style of Flaubert, le mot juste, and he finds that writing flawed which contains irrelevancies, repetitions, or underdeveloped possibilities. He avoids the blurred image or the "shifting effect," and finds meaning in sharp focus, careful arrangement of the parts, in proportion and orderly development. He describes his method of writing as "moving along his lonely sentences," "stalking an idea that had appeared like a crack in night pouring out daylight."

For Lesser, art is finally "a matter of stating the truth in unimpeachable form," but the truth is always determined by language and form, not by any reference to the world. His key critical passage comes from Coleridge, "Nothing can permanently please which does not contain in itself the reason why it is so and not otherwise." Thus Lesser turns inward away from the world, living his solipsistic priestly life, ignoring the devastation around him, and trying to meet the merciless formal demands of a book which asks him by its own structure to "say more than he knew." "Form sometimes offers so many possibilities it takes a while before you can determine which it's insisting on," and so the writing goes on for nine long years. But then Coleridge had said that he "should not think of devoting less than twenty years to an Epic Poem," and though Lesser does not exactly think of himself as an epic poet, or Moses, he does see himself as "King David with his six-string harp, except the notes are words and the psalms fiction . . . writing a small masterpiece though not too small."

The Tenants opens with Lesser waking to work on his book and "catching sight of himself in his lonely glass," and the book he is writing is another mirror, for its subject is a writer created in almost the exact image of Harry Lesser, who is in turn writing a novel about love, hoping that the book will create the love he cannot find in or feel for people. Art seems to stretch out to infinity, pre-empting reality by simply duplicating itself, a perfect realization of the claim of the romantic literary text to depend on nothing but itself. Malamud's novel about a writer trying to write a novel about a writer trying to write a novel is a wilderness of mirrors, a completely enclosed and infinite world of formalistic art. The title of Lesser's novel, *The Promised End,* seems to praise this triumph of isolated formal perfection, but the words taken from *King Lear* also remind us of the remainder of Shakespeare's line, "Or image of that horror?" and of its context, the death of love in the person of Cordelia, which makes life seem an unbearable mockery to the survivors.

The title of Malamud's novel, *The Tenants,* suggests that Lesser is but a temporary resident in, not the owner of, the House of Fiction, and reminds us as well that there is more than one resident. The other tenant is a new arrival, the Black, Willie Spearmint—an obvious and not very happy reference to Shakespeare—who represents in the novel a view of writing which is the antithesis of Lesser's formalistic tradition of art for art's sake. Willie's life recapitulates the primitive phases of the development of the poet as romanticism hypothesizes it. His "election" takes place in prison where, suffering primal fear and bewilderment, he first begins to sing the blues and then finds in the song both comfort and his own identity as lyric singer: "he listens and hears, 'Willie Spearmint sings this song.' " He then begins to read and gradually begins to feel that he too can write. At first the writing is mere imitation of other writers he has read, but then he begins to record his own experiences, and then to create fictitious characters and scenes, and in doing so he finds freedom and escape from prison, "I am out of it as much as I am in. I am in my imagination." Once out of prison Willie continues to write, and his stories, in contrast to Lesser's involuted and isolated self-reflecting novel about a writer trying to write a novel, are almost unbearably painful reflections of the most terribly immediate aspects of life in Harlem, of wretched jobs and beaten children, of drugs and whores, of men cornered and shot in alleys and women who in despair drink lye and hurl themselves off buildings, and above all of the hatred and violence between black and white, a violence which culminates in the story "No Heart," in which a Black

> has a hunger to murder a white and taste a piece of his heart. It is simply a strong thirst or hunger. He tricks a drunken white down into a tenement cellar and kills him. He cuts into the dead man but can't find the heart. He cuts into his stomach, bowel, and scrotum, and is still cutting when the story ends.

Willie writes directly out of his own experience and himself: "You want to know what's really art? *I am art. Willie Spearmint, black man.* My form is *myself.*" His writings directly reflect his own feelings, his self-disgust, his hatred for whites, his fears and furies; and their ends are as primal as their origins, self-expression, advancing the cause of black revolution, and a desire to make a lot of money and use it to enjoy a lot of sex.

But Willie Spearmint's writing is in trouble too, for all the power that drives it. He cannot find the form which adequately expresses his experiences and feelings, and so he too comes to the isolated tenement to find the distance from himself and the world his writing also requires. If Lesser's work lacks reality and energy, Willie's suffers from the absence of what Lesser has too much of, art and form. Willie's manuscript is a conglomerate of several chapters of autobiography and several short stories, that minimal fictional form, but the autobiography is fiction and the stories are autobiographical, and taken together they are, despite their power, finally ineffective because they are not well enough written to express the meaning latent in them.

In Malamud's romantic view, art is the work of the outsider, in this case the Jewish writer and the black writer, and these marginal men need one another, for each has what the other lacks. At first, despite fear and suspicion on both sides, there is some feeling of brotherhood, both as men and as writers, and Lesser helps Willie to set up shop in the building, recognizing a fellow man and a fellow writer; Willie on his side invites Lesser to his parties, introduces him to his life, and saves him from a beating when he sleeps with a black woman. If Willie introduces Lesser to some of the vitality and passion his life and work lack, Lesser in turn introduces Willie to the concept of literary craft, reads and criticizes his manuscript, gives him a dictionary and a handbook of grammar. Perhaps his most effective lesson is delivered through his own books, which Willie gets from the library and reads with admiration, though as a "natural" writer he is able to distinguish the superiority of the first over the second. At first the results of the relationship seem ideal, for Willie begins his story again as a novel, moves into the tenement, and sweats the necessary long hard hours over his writing. But the attempt to become a craftsman destroys his writing, for he begins to overwrite in a florid, rhetorical style, employing a pressured stream-of-consciousness technique with elaborate mechanical connections between its various parts. This grotesque "arty" style conflicts directly with the "tensile spareness" of Willie's "sensibility" and the raw facts of a tale of a black mother trying to kill her son with a breadknife before drinking lye and "throwing herself out of the bedroom window, screaming in pain, rage, futility." Under the weight of Willie's rhetoric, the characters turn into zombies, and the language becomes "a compound of ashes and glue." When Lesser is forced by his own honesty and craft responsibility to tell Willie these truths about his work, Willie is nearly destroyed and vows to quit writing forever, turning to direct action to relieve his frustrated feelings and further his revolutionary cause.

Without art or self-conscious literary technique, *The Tenants* shows, literature lacks meaning and effect, remaining only a crude unmediated egoistic cry of rage and the satisfaction of hatreds, but craft, when applied, seems to desiccate all that it touches, destroying the artist and making it impossible for him to complete the work.

In Malamud's view, Flaubert is wrong: a book cannot be written "about nothing," form cannot complete itself, for writing is in the long run dependent upon the world in which it exists. Western poetry has traditionally expressed this interaction of life and art by marrying the craft of the poet to the love story, for love expresses in physical terms the beauty, completeness, and harmony of being which the craft of the poet also creates in his art. The physical loveliness of the beloved directly expresses those qualities the artist takes to be the essence of the beautiful, and the act of loving seeks in action that union of opposites and harmony of being, on the levels of both body and soul, which have been the central qualities of our conception of artistic beauty. The love story the poet tells, and the skill he uses to tell it have traditionally been but two aspects of the same desire for the beautiful which art seeks to create as an ideal in an ugly and fragmented world.

But earthly physical beauty, which Irene Bell (née Belinsky), represents in name and person, and the beauty of artistic form, which Lesser pursues, are separated in the grotesque world of *The Tenants*. At the beginning of the novel, Lesser lives a loveless existence, unmarried, without family relations. Seizing rare opportunities for occasional, and usually unsatisfactory, sex, he pursues an abstract Flaubertian beauty exclusively. Irene Bell belongs to Willie Spearmint, who frees her from her middle-class life and teaches her the power and pleasure of sexual love. But he finds that he cannot write near Irene, near the actuality of beauty, and so in order to complete his story he begins to work in the House of Fiction. At first he spends only weekdays there, but as his involvement with his craft becomes more intense he moves out of Irene's apartment and spends longer and longer periods in the tenement, forgoing all the physical pleasures of life, food, warmth, and love. But the farther he drifts away from physical love and its embodiment of beauty, the more difficult and less effective his writing becomes. At the same time, Lesser, who has gotten to know Irene through Willie, begins to love her and find comfort with her, and as he does so, his writing improves and moves easily and powerfully towards the promised end.

The point could not be made more clearly: the beauty of art depends upon the real beauty of flesh and the world, even as art rests inevitably upon an experienced reality. To write about nothing is not only cruel indifference but an impossibility. The "knot intrinsicate" of the form of art and the act of human love is drawn even tighter by the involvement of the two writers who need one another. Willie Spearmint has all the primal energy, the ego, the moral passion, and the deep involvement with the world which Lesser's writing lacks; Lesser has all the dedication, concentration, and formal skills Willie's writing lacks. They need each other as writers, even as in their circumstances as Black and Jew they need each other as men. But despite early uneasy movements toward brotherhood, to the apparent benefit of both men and both books, the relationship breaks down because of an insurmountable antagonism. Lesser steals Irene from Willie, who has already more or less abandoned her, and Lesser's attempts to improve Willie's writing destroy it. In fury at the knowledge that he has been cheated in both senses, Willie tries to kill Lesser, beats Irene, and in a culminating act which explains all the others, he breaks into Lesser's apartment and burns all his manuscripts. Since Lesser, close to the promised end, has removed the copy of his book from the safe deposit box for corrections, this means that his book is destroyed, even as Willie's has been, and both writers must either abandon their work or start over again. The mixture of art and life is, apparently, an ideal no longer available to the modern writer as it was to his predecessors. Art and life have become separate and the literary text cannot be written any longer, or if it is it is destroyed. Abandoning art and returning to the world seems to be the only answer, and Willie storms off proclaiming "Revolution is the Real Art," while Lesser considers marrying Irene and going with her to San Francisco to begin a new life. But the power of writing over the writer is absolute, and both men drift back to the tenement. Lesser returns first, in even more straitened circumstances, burying himself even more deeply in the attempt to reconstruct his novel. He works even harder and longer and begins to feel that he is improving on the earlier lost work, but he also drifts away from Irene, and she disappears, scarcely mourned, and barely sorrowing, into a world with no forwarding address. Inevitably, Lesser's shadow, his *doppelgänger*, Willie, finds his way back to the tenement as well, and the ghostly sound of his typewriter can again be heard in the corridors at night.

The writers seldom meet, but each avidly reads the scraps of writing the other discards in the ashcans, each hoping that the other will both fail and succeed. But the writing of both degenerates in hatred of the other. Having rejected form, at least outwardly—though he still endlessly rewrites and constantly changes subjects—Willie's writing grows more incoherent, and its formlessness is reflected in its themes, self-loathing and obsessed hatred of all whites, particularly all Jews. He writes of cannibal feasts in dark cellars where Blacks eat their Jewish landlord, and he creates fictional pogroms, lovingly dwelling on the horrifying details and describing again and again the destruction of the entire Jewish race. In the end, his writing, unable to become anything more than his own raw feelings and his own actual experiences, reduces itself to pages of paper which begin with two opposing words, BLACK-WHITE, and gradually eliminates WHITE, letter by letter, until only the single word BLACK appears over and over again. As Willie's writing realizes the tendency of a number of modern writings, such as Beckett's plays, to disappear into the vortex of a single word endlessly repeated, Lesser's skill gradually dies and he, the man of words, becomes "nauseated when he wrote, by the words, by the thought of them." He is still capable of dreaming of a promised end to both his life and his book in which he is married to a beautiful black girl by an African chief, while Willie is married to Irene Bell by a rabbi. But in reality, as their books are drawn down into silence, Lesser and Willie are consumed by their hatred for each other. Overcome by fury for his lost manuscript, Lesser takes an axe to Willie's typewriter. The two then meet in an apocalyptic scene, part dream, part reality, in the hallway where each attacks the other at his most vulnerable point: Willie castrates Lesser, and Lesser sinks his axe deep into Willie's brain.

Levenspiel, the owner of the house, is the appropriate person to put the question that society from Plato to the present has asked of poetry: "What's a make-believe novel, Lesser, against all the woes and miseries that I have explained to you?" To which the craftsman-artist had once answered proudly with Nietzsche, "No artist tolerates reality," or had pointed to Joyce's "luminous silent stasis of aesthetic pleasure" as the true reality redeeming a fallen world. But Malamud speaks for a later generation of authors. Art depends upon the world, and its values must be lived out in the world. It cannot generate its own conclusion but must find that conclusion in actual experience; that experience, however, is not satisfactory by itself, and if it is to live and have meaning it must take the shape and form that only art can give, transforming particular facts into believable and effective truths. Malamud cannot find any way of bringing these seeming opposites together to a promised end. Instead, art and experience seek their extremes, and in this extremity love dies and the art which seeks love's end through skill and form expires into silence or a single obsessive word sounded over and over again. Having failed to reconcile its artist protagonists, Malamud's own novel cannot reach the promised end but dies away with another word repeated hopelessly, "Mercy, mercy, mercy." Art no longer has the power to bind together a world of racial and class hatred, of decayed cities, individual isolation, of endless war and the broken forms of a former civilization. Nor can it any longer create, as the romantics believed they could, an abstract image of perfect beauty in words which will outlast the world. As its texts lose their power, unable to overcome any longer the destructive forces represented by the tenement and the racial hatred it contains, they lose their reality and become only unfinished manuscripts, a single word endlessly repeated, scraps of yellow paper in the garbage can.

SAM B. GIRGUS

In Search of the Real America

$$\text{B}$$y maintaining their commitment to
the American idea, Jewish writers follow in the path of earlier American
"Jeremiahs." As Sacvan Bercovitch says, "What distinguishes the American
writer—and the American Jeremiah from the late seventeenth century on—
is his *refusal* to abandon the national covenant." The commitment of Jewish
writers and thinkers to the national covenant grew out of and reflected the
interest of the larger Jewish culture in achieving a secure place within the
national consensus. Some established leaders of the dominant Protestant
culture like Howells, Mark Twain, and Hutchins Hapgood encouraged
Jewish participation in the cultural process of renewing the myth and ideology of America. For example, Hapgood believed that Jews in America
could teach the rest of the culture a great deal about achieving a harmony
between religious and material concerns. In his classic study of the Jewish
ghetto, he wrote, "What we need at the present time more than anything
else is a spiritual unity such as, perhaps, will only be the distant result of
our present special activities. We need something similar to the spirit
underlying the national and religious unity of the orthodox Jewish culture."
However, other leading figures in America saw in the Jews as a people an
unwanted challenge to their own class and cultural hegemony. In this sense,
the anti-Semitism of such figures as Henry Adams and Frederick Jackson
Turner provides a negative form of documentation of Jewish interest in the
myth and symbol of America. Thus, Henry Adams wrote about himself:
"His world was dead. Not a Polish Jew fresh from Warsaw or Cracow—
not a furtive Yacoob or Ysaac still reeking of the Ghetto, snarling a weird

Yiddish to the officers of the customs—but had a keener instinct, an intenser energy, and a freer hand than he—American of Americans with Heaven knew how many Puritans and Patriots behind him, and an education that had cost a civil war." As E. Digby Baltzell indicates, Adams, in his reaction to the Jews, not only "increasingly blamed the Jews for all he disliked about his age" but revealed something deep within himself. "The Adams family," Baltzell says, "had always taken a leading part in the destiny of America, and Henry's anti-Semitism was indeed a kind of self-hate born of his abhorrence of the path now taken by 'His America.' In fact, the more one contemplates the mind of Henry Adams, the more one sees it as a symbol *par excellence* of the powerless brahmin who is finally forced to embrace the idea of caste after losing faith in aristocracy."

Frederick Jackson Turner had somewhat similar feelings and problems. Daniel Aaron quotes Turner's description in 1887 of his discomfort upon being lost in the Jewish ghetto of Boston. " 'I was in Jewry,' " he wrote, " 'the street consecrated to "old clothers," pawnbrokers, and similar followers of Abraham.' " He describes the streets as " 'filled with big Jewmen—long bearded and carrying a staff as you see in a picture,—and with Jew youths and maidens—some of the latter pretty—as you sometimes see a lilly in the green muddy slime.' " He notes further with relief that he finally was able to extricate himself " 'after much elbowing' " from " 'this mass of oriental noise and squalor.' " More than three decades later the descendants of many of those Jews were crowding into Harvard, and Turner expressed his concern about the ultimate issue of reconciling " 'New English ideals of liberalism' " with the fear of the growing influence and power of the immigrants. He confessed that " 'I don't like the prospects of Harvard a New Jerusalem and Boston already a new Cork. Bad old world and the times out of joint.' "

Turner's point of view may be based in part upon his understanding of the frontier as the source of America's strength. He developed and took for granted the thesis that the greatest qualities of American character derived from the frontier experience. In his famous address before the American Historical Association in Chicago in 1893, Turner further suggested that with the frontier closed American culture itself would be forced to endure a distressing change. Clearly, the immigrants arriving in America indicated the wave of the future that seemed to Turner to counter the heart of what he considered to be most American. Ironically, the very qualities of national character that Turner calls the "traits of the frontier" could be cited with validity to describe the character of new immigrants. Thus, Turner attributes to the frontier character "that coarseness and strength combined with acuteness and acquisitiveness; that practical, inventive turn of mind, quick to find expedients; that masterful grasp of material things, lacking in the artistic but powerful to effect great ends; that restless, nervous energy; that dominant individualism, working for good and for evil, and withal that buoyancy and exuberance which comes with freedom." To modern immigrants America still seemed to offer what Turner thought was possible only from the conditions of an open frontier—"a new field of opportunity, a gate of escape from the bondage of the past; and freshness, and confidence, and scorn of older society, impatience of its restraints and its ideas, and indifference to its lessons." In a way, these immigrants did more than challenge Turner's sense of America. Even more galling for a historian, in effect they proved his thesis to be part of a larger myth rather than an analytical fact.

Accordingly, the myth of America could not be relegated exclusively to the myth of regeneration on the frontier for it to be relevant to the experience of the new immigrants. In the modern immigrant experience, the frontier was closed, but the belief in America as "promised land" and as an ideal remained. At the same time, the myth of the frontier and the West with its suggestion of freedom and renewal could titillate and captivate the imagination of Jews as much as gentiles. For example, Alfred Kazin reports his lasting disappointment with his father for failing to remain in the West where he could have settled permanently on a homestead. Kazin writes, "*Omaha* was the most beautiful word I have ever heard, *homestead* almost as beautiful; but I could never forgive him for not having accepted that homestead." However, while many Jews dreamed about finding their freedom and acceptance in the West, the actual experience often proved quite different from their expectations. For such Jews the encounter with the West inspired a reaction that included irony and sometimes suspicion and fear.

One of the most interesting autobiographical accounts of the West as a place for rebirth as an American can be found in Marcus Ravage's *An American in the Making*. In the book, Ravage seems to become a confirmed adherent to the myth of the regeneration and rebirth of the individual in the West. However, beneath the surface of his affirmation one senses layers of doubt and insecurity about the permanence and reality of his transmogrification into a "real American." Ravage's account describes the typical immigrant's journey from Rumania to New York. After years of labor, education, and struggle, he decides to go to college in what he and his friends consider to be a portion of the wild West—the University of Missouri. "I was going," he writes, "to the land of the 'real Americans.' " He spent a bitterly long and frustrating first year feeling like an alien and outsider among his college mates. With some justification he decides that "unpalatable as the truth was, there was no evading the patent fact that if I was not taken in among the Missourians the fault was with me and not with them." By the end of the autobiography, Ravage has become convinced that "the loneliness I had endured, the snubbing, the ridicule, the inner struggles—all the dreariness and the sadness of my life in exile" had been worthwhile when compared with the "idealized vision of the clean manhood, the large human dignity, the wholesome, bracing atmosphere" that had opened itself to him in the West. He comes to feel that his manhood and freedom depend upon his completion of the break with the East that would enable him to continue the process of Americanization in the West. His new sense of alienation from his past becomes distressingly apparent during a return visit to New York when he feels uncomfortable among his old friends. Changed by his vision of the real America, he hears old radical arguments in New York that now seem based on a misunderstanding of the true nature of the American system. "I listened to it all with an alien ear," he writes. "Soon I caught myself defending the enemy out there. What did these folks know of Americans, anyhow?" Finally, he makes an emotional appeal to his best friend to follow him to Missouri to find her salvation as an American. " 'Save yourself, my dear,' " he says. " 'Run as fast as you can. You will find a bigger and freer world than this. Promise me that you will follow me to the West this fall. You will thank me for it. Those big, genuine people out in Missouri are the salt of the earth. Whatever they may think about the problem of universal brotherhood, they have already solved it for their next-door neighbors. There is no need of the social revolution in Missouri; they have a generous slice of the kingdom of heaven.' "

While Ravage admits to the likelihood of exaggeration on his part, his statement and feeling about the West indicate a deeper level of insecurity and defensiveness. He seems to be caught in a classic bind between wanting to escape a minority culture in order to achieve dominant-culture acceptance while also feeling the equally powerful need to defend and justify his own culture. The ambiguity and conflict in Ravage's position lead him in his autobiography to see in the West, and in Missouri especially, qualities that not only were superhuman but super-American as well.

In other works by Jews about the encounter with the West, the same set of conflicts and ambiguities occur and lead to a process of irony and demythologization. Thus, David Levinsky [in *The Rise of David Levinsky* by Abraham Cahan], like Ravage, equates "the real America" with the

West. "The road," Cahan writes, "was a great school of business and life to me. . . . I saw much of the United States. Every time I returned home I felt as though, in comparison with the places I had just visited, New York was not an American city at all, and as though my last trip had greatly added to the 'real American' quality in me." In contrast to Ravage, however, Cahan views this feeling with irony because he understands about the guilt and insecurity involved in this process of self-transformation. This real America turns out to be one of manners and gestures that will never give Levinsky any sense of peace or place. Rather than a new sense of self, Levinsky only finds himself caught in a drive toward conformity. He grows embarrassed by "my Talmudic gesticulations, a habit that worried me like a physical defect. It was so distressingly un-American." For other Jewish writers as well, the myth of the West became filled with irony. Perhaps it achieves its most bitter treatment in Nathanael West's *The Day of the Locust* in which the West in the form of California becomes the exact opposite of the place for renewal. California is the end of the road where Americans go to die. It is a burial ground rather than a garden.

However, a more explicit treatment of the theme of the encounter of the city Jew with the myth of the West can be found in Bernard Malamud's *A New Life*. As the title suggests, the novel is literally about the myth. The hero, Sy Levin, a former alcoholic who has already been a failure in what could not be described even charitably as an academic career, moves from New York to a small college in the Pacific Northwest in a modern version of the traditional frontier pursuit of "a new life." "One always hopes," he says, "that a new place will inspire change—in one's life." Moreover, he has bought the myth that such a change can occur most readily in the West, which, theoretically, has been the scene of regeneration for millions of Americans. "My God, the West, Levin thought," writes Malamud. "He imagined the pioneers in covered wagons entering this valley for the first time, and found it a moving thought. Although he had lived little in nature Levin had always loved it, and the sense of having done the right thing in leaving New York was renewed in him. He shuddered at his good fortune." His gratitude for being part of this experience in the West is both naive and honest. "He was himself a stranger in the West but that didn't matter," Levin intimates to his students. "By some miracle of movement and change, standing before them as their English instructor by virtue of his appointment, Levin welcomed them from wherever they came: the Northwest states, California, and a few from beyond the Rockies, a thrilling representation to a man who had in all his life never been west of Jersey City." His naiveté allows him to believe that he approaches a successful metamorphosis. With his students in mind, he thinks, "In his heart he thanked them, sensing he had created their welcome of him. They represented the America he had so often heard of, the fabulous friendly West."

Of course, Levin must come to realize that there is no "new life" in a myth that takes him outside of his essential self. He is the classic *schlemiel*-victim figure in Jewish writing and humor who cannot escape his past. Malamud writes, "His escape to the West had thus far come to nothing, space corrupted by time, the past-contaminated self. . . . A white-eyed hound bayed at him from the window—his classic fear, failure after grimy years to master himself. He lay in silence, solitude and darkness. More than once he experienced crawling self-hatred. It left him frightened because he thought he had outdistanced it by three thousand miles. The future as new life was no longer predictable. That caused the floor to move under his bed."

Malamud intends in the novel for Levin to succeed through failure by seeing through himself and the society around him. In the reverse of the usual interpretation of David Levinsky's career, Sy Levin fails in the professional world in order to rise in the moral sphere. By finally accepting this failure he transcends and overcomes the false world and values of the new world in which he wanted so desperately to succeed. It is this aspect of the novel that so annoys Leslie Fiedler. In a typically brilliant and devastating article about the novel, Fiedler complains that the book fails to fulfill its potential of "becoming the first real Jewish anti-Western." Fiedler maintains that Malamud either "out of lack of nerve or excess of ambition" attempts to turn Levin into "a heroic defender of the Liberal Tradition, which is to say an insufferable prig like Stephen Dedalus rather than an unloved, loveable victim like Leopold Bloom."

It seems to me, however, that Levin's strength ultimately derives not from false heroics or brave deeds that are inconsistent with his character but from the very elements that comprise and govern his sense of self. In other words, a major force behind his qualities as a schlemiel-victim is the intensity of his beliefs and his unswerving sincerity. He is a victim and a schlemiel because he cares. In this sense, he accepts responsibility for his character. Those around him, like the Missourians who so intrigued Ravage, would be more than happy to have him act like one of them. Levin's charm, however, is a product of his inability to go along in spite of his desire to be part of the group. He finds that he cannot do the easy thing. In one of his conversations with a colleague, Levin reveals these aspects of himself.

"The way the world is now," Levin said, "I sometimes feel I'm engaged in a great irrelevancy, teaching people how to write who don't know what to write. I can give them subjects but not subject matter. I worry I'm not teaching how to keep civilization from destroying itself." The instructor laughed embarrassedly. "Imagine that, Bucket, I know it sounds ridiculous, pretentious. I'm not particularly gifted—ordinary if the truth be told— with a not very talented intellect, and how much good would I do, if any? Still, I have the strongest urge to say they must understand what humanism means or they won't know when freedom no longer exists. And that they must either be the best—masters of ideas and of them-selves—or choose the best to lead them; in either case democracy wins. I have the strongest compulsion to be involved with such thoughts in the classroom, if you know what I mean."

In one sense, this speech sounds like Malamud's voice in almost a How-ellsian form of address to the audience announcing moral priorities and principles. However, it clearly also is designed for comic effect portraying for sophisticated readers Sy Levin as a kind of Miss Lonelyhearts of the humanities and academic freedom. At the same time, the speech opens an important window to Levin's consciousness and adds depth to his qualities as a character. The result is not an epic clash between Sy Levin, the Matthew Arnold of Cascadia, and the forces of darkness and evil in the form of the corrupt and cowardly department administration. Rather, we get a realistic encounter between a born loser and defender of lost causes who fumbles his way to a self-determined defeat that leaves him carrying the moral baggage for others. Certainly, any sense of victory or triumph for Levin occurs with enough ambiguity, irony, and loss to maintain con-sistency with the central qualities of his character. Although he proves capable of getting the woman to leave with him, his initial status as a surrogate lover for her and her dubious distinctions and qualities tend to mitigate the value of his triumph. Furthermore, any moral victory he achieves goes unrecognized while his slight impact on improving the de-partment meets with deep silence from his colleagues. He leaves as a failure again but seems able to face his new problems and his "new life."

However, while Sy Levin functions as a realistic modern hero in the manner of the victim and the schlemiel figure, the novel itself belongs in the tradition of the American jeremiad. Through the character of a lonely "pariah" figure, who is not that much unlike classic American loners and nonconformists, Malamud attacks and criticizes his society and culture for failing to live up to its ideal vision of itself. Moreover, he does this by debunking one myth of America—the myth of regeneration in the West—

while revivifying a modern version of America as an ideal consistent with
the rhetoric of the jeremiad. Clearly, Malamud sees Levin as a fragile
guardian of the values and ideas of the myth of America just as Yakov Bok
in *The Fixer* must tragically assume the burden of being Jewish in a way
that makes him appear to be both the archetypal victim and the hero. In
addition, in *A New Life*, Malamud leaves intact the narrative structure of
the myth of America as it has emerged out of the Jewish urban experience.
The one important variation in this book is the Northwest setting, but
Malamud in effect simply has moved the city novel in the form of Sy Levin's
consciousness into the country. The *shikse* in the novel ties many of these
themes together by indicating that she had literally "called" Levin in the
mythic sense to perform his mission in the Northwest because of his Jewish
looks. Because of her role in the selection process for the job, she was
instrumental in hiring Levin. She says, " 'Your picture reminded me of a
Jewish boy I knew in college who was very kind to me during a trying time
in my life.' " " 'So I was chosen,' Levin said."

In the light of the rhetorical aspects of this novel, it is significant
that the hero of Malamud's recent novel *Dubin's Lives* has studied and
written biographies about some of America's most important nineteenth-
century Jeremiahs—Lincoln, Thoreau, Whitman, Twain. It is also interesting that *The Tenants*, another Malamud novel written after *A New Life*,
concerns a conflict between a Jewish writer and a black writer. In their
competition and hostility they live what they write so that fantasy, fiction,
and reality all intermingle. The novel suggests that the outcome of their
struggle will help determine who will write the future story of America.
" 'No Jew can treat me like a man—male or female,' " the black writer
says to the Jew. " 'You think you are the Chosen People. Well, you are
wrong on that. *We* are the Chosen People from as of now on. You gonna
find that out soon enough, you gonna lose your fuckn pride.' " The novel
ends with no false resolution of the conflict or bright promise for the future.
It does, however, perform the vital function of dramatizing the central
challenge facing the myth of America today. Can the myth work as a means
of consensus and unity for blacks and other minorities?

In 1883, a Jewish poet, Emma Lazarus, who saw herself as a disciple
of Ralph Waldo Emerson, metaphorically extended the myth of America
to new immigrants through her poem "The New Colossus," which transformed the meaning of the Statue of Liberty into a symbol of asylum. More
recently some black leaders also saw the destiny of blacks in terms of joining
the myth of American destiny and national consensus. As Bercovitch has
noted, Martin Luther King, Jr., attacked segregation "as a violation of the

American dream." Similar rhetoric has been adopted by leaders of other ethnic and minority groups such as Cesar Chavez, the Mexican American leader.

At the same time, the question of the viability of the myth in our own day remains. Strident voices often call for a kind of separatism reminiscent of the antijeremiad tradition. Among other things, such radicals fear destruction through absorption into the national consensus. Moreover, some of our best students of American pluralism and consensus question whether any meaningful consensus can exist today. Thus, John Higham believes that contemporary concerns with power and status among ethnic groups have superseded the earlier quest for "an inclusive community" that makes pluralism possible. "Apparently," Higham writes, "a decent multiethnic society must rest on a unifying ideology, faith, or myth. One of our tasks today is to learn how to revitalize a common faith amid multiplying claims for status and power."

The response of Jews to this challenge is interesting. For one thing, for some Jews the myth of America itself may serve as a conservative influence. The so-called new conservatism of some Jewish intellectuals perhaps can be explained as a natural outgrowth of those values associated with their original allegiance to the myth of America. Unfortunately, such conservative positions may cast some Jews in the role once played by Adams and Turner. A failure to incorporate new people and groups into the myth and national consensus can lead to a kind of caste system and cultural isolationism that at one time assured the political impotence and the downfall of established Protestants who were so afraid that the New Jerusalem of America would become a home for too many Jews. It would be a mistake for the Jews to imitate the "real Americans" in this regard. As Thomas Sowell says, "In a sense, Jews are the classic American success story—from rags to riches against all opposition. Moreover, like other groups that have found in the United States opportunities denied them in their homelands, Jews have been proud and patriotic Americans. Yet the history of Jews is longer and larger than the history of the United States. At other times and other places, Jews have risen to heights of prosperity and influence, only to have it all destroyed in unpredictable outbursts of anti-Semitic fury. Jews could not readily become complacent members of the establishment, however much they might possess all of its visible signs." Rather than complacency or fear, the times obviously demand the kind of cultural and political invention that has characterized the contribution of modern Jews to American life and the American ideology.

Chronology

1914	Bernard Malamud is born April 26 to Russian-Jewish immigrant parents, Bertha (Fidelman) and Max Malamud, a storekeeper in a relatively non-Jewish neighborhood in the Gravesend area of Brooklyn.
1928–32	Attends Erasmus Hall High School.
1932–36	Attends City College of New York, receiving his B.A. in 1936.
1936–38	Attends Columbia University, receiving his M.A. in 1942. Writes thesis on Thomas Hardy.
1940	Works as a clerk in the Bureau of the Census, Washington, D. C.
1940–48	Teaches evening classes in high schools, largely to immigrants in Brooklyn.
1941	Begins to write short stories.
1945	Marries Anne de Chiara and settles in Greenwich Village.
1947	His son Paul is born.
1948–49	Teaches evening classes at Harlem Evening High School.
1949	Joins faculty at Oregon State College, Corvallis, Oregon. Assigned sections of English Composition (departmental policy stated that only faculty members with Ph.D.'s were to teach literature classes).
1950	Stories published in *Harper's Bazaar, Partisan Review, Commentary*.
1952	*The Natural* published. His daughter Janna born.
1956	Lives in Rome and travels in Europe.
1957	*The Assistant* published.
1958	*The Magic Barrel*, a collection of short stories, is published. Malamud receives Rosenthal Award of the National Institute of Arts and Letters and the Daroff Memorial Award.
1959	*The Magic Barrel* is awarded the National Book Award.
1959–61	Malamud made Ford Fellow of the humanities and arts program.
1961	*A New Life* published; Malamud leaves Oregon State College and accepts a position on the faculty of Bennington College.

1963	*Idiots First*, a collection of short stories, is published. Malamud travels in England and Italy.
1965	Malamud visits the Soviet Union, France and Spain.
1966	*The Fixer* published; awarded National Book Award and Pulitzer Prize.
1966–68	Visiting lecturer at Harvard.
1969	*Pictures of Fidelman* published.
1971	*The Tenants* published.
1973	*Rembrandt's Hat,* a collection of short stories, is published.
1976	Malamud receives Jewish Heritage Award of the B'nai B'rith.
1979	Receives the Governor's Award of the Vermont Council on the Arts. *Dubin's Lives* published.
1981	Receives Creative Arts award for fiction, Brandeis University.
1982	*God's Grace* published.
1983	Receives Gold Medal for fiction from the Academic Institute.

Contributors

HAROLD BLOOM, Sterling Professor of the Humanities at Yale University, is the author of *The Anxiety of Influence, Poetry and Repression* and many other volumes of literary criticism. His forthcoming study, *Freud: Transference and Authority*, attempts a full-scale reading of all of Freud's major writings. A MacArthur Prize Fellow, he is the general editor of *The Chelsea House Library of Literary Criticism*.

IHAB HASSAN has taught at the Rensselaer Polytechnic Institute and Wesleyan University and is currently Vilas Research Professor of English and Comparative Literature at the University of Wisconsin. His books include *Radical Innocence, The Literature of Silence: Henry Miller and Samuel Beckett, Paracriticisms* and *The Right Promethean Fire*.

JOHN HOLLANDER is a Professor of English at Yale University whose critical works include *The Untuning of the Sky* and *The Figure of Echo*. A recent recipient of the Bollingen Prize, he is the author of many volumes of poetry, including *The Head of the Bed, Spectral Emanations, Blue Wine* and *Powers of Thirteen*.

ALFRED KAZIN, Distinguished Professor of English at Hunter College, CUNY, is the author of such books as *On Native Grounds, Contemporaries, Bright Book of Life, New York Jew* and *An American Procession*.

JONATHAN BAUMBACH is Professor of English at Brooklyn College, CUNY where he has directed the M.F.A. program in creative writing since 1974. His books include *The Landscape of Nightmare, Reruns, Babble, The Return of Service* and *My Father More or Less*.

HERBERT LEIBOWITZ, Professor of English at the College of Staten Island, CUNY, is the author of *Hart Crane: An Introduction to the Poetry*.

F. W. DUPEE was Professor of English at Columbia University and the author of *Henry James* and *"The King of the Cats," and other Remarks on Writers and Writing*.

EARL R. WASSERMAN was the author of *The Subtler Language: Critical Readings of Neoclassic and Romantic Poems* and *Shelley: A Critical Reading*. He was Professor of English at The Johns Hopkins University.

V. S. PRITCHETT has enjoyed a prolific career as author and free-lance journalist. Among his more recent books are *The Myth Makers*, *On the Edge of the Cliff*, *The Tale Bearers*, *Collected Stories*, *More Collected Stories* and *The Turn of the Year*.

SIDNEY RICHMAN, author of *Bernard Malamud*, is Professor of English at California State University.

JAMES M. MELLARD is in the Department of English at Northern Illinois University.

ALAN WARREN FRIEDMAN is Professor of English at the University of Texas at Austin and the author of *Lawrence Durrell and the Alexandria Quartet* and *Multivalence: The Moral Quality of Form in the Modern Novel*.

TONY TANNER's books include *The Reign of Wonder: Naivety and Reality in American Literature*, *Saul Bellow* and *Adultery in the Novel*. He is a Fellow of King's College, Cambridge.

ALLEN GUTTMANN is Professor of English and American studies at Amherst College and the author of *The Conservative Tradition in America*, *The Jewish Writer in America* and *From Ritual to Record: The Nature of Modern Sports*.

RUTH R. WISSE, a regular contributor to *Commentary* magazine, is the author of *The Schlemiel as Modern Hero*.

ROBERT DUCHARME, author of *Art and Idea in the Novels of Bernard Malamud*, teaches English at Mount St. Mary's College in Maryland.

MARK SHECHNER teaches English at the State University of New York at Buffalo.

ROBERT ALTER, Professor of Hebrew and Comparative Literature at the University of California at Berkeley, is the author of *Rogue's Progress: Studies in the Picaresque Novel*, *Fielding and the Nature of the Novel*, *After Tradition*, *Partial Magic: The Novel as Self-Conscious Genre*, *Defenses of the Imagination*, *A Lion for Love* and *The Art of Biblical Narrative*.

ALVIN B. KERNAN is Andrew Mellon Professor of the humanities at Princeton University and the author of *The Cankered Muse*, *The Plot of Satire*, *The Playwright as Magician* and *The Imaginary Library*.

SAM B. GIRGUS is Professor of American studies and American literature at the University of New Mexico. He is the author of *The Law of the Heart*, *The American Self* and *The New Covenant: Jewish Writers and the American Idea*.

Bibliography

Alter, Robert. "Bernard Malamud: Jewishness as Metaphor." In *After the Tradition: Essays on Modern Jewish Writing.* New York: Dutton, 1969.

Astro, Richard, and Benson, Jackson J., eds. *The Fiction of Bernard Malamud.* American Authors Series. Corvallis: Oregon State University Press, 1977.

Benedict, Helen. "Bernard Malamud: Morals and Surprises." *The Antioch Review* 1, vol. 41 (Winter 1983): 28–36.

Bluefarb, Sam. "Bernard Malamud: The Scope of Caricature." *English Journal* 23 (July 1964): 319–26.

Cadle, Dean. "Bernard Malamud." *Wilson Library Bulletin* 32 (December 1958): 266.

Cohen, Sandy. *Bernard Malamud and the Trial by Love.* Amsterdam: Rodopi, 1974.

Ducharme, Robert. *Art and Idea in the Novels of Bernard Malamud.* The Hague: Mouton & Co., 1974.

Epstein, Joseph. "Malamud in Decline." *Commentary* 4, vol. 74 (October 1982): 49–53.

Fiedler, Leslie A. "Malamud: The Commonplace as Absurd." In *No! In Thunder.* Boston: Beacon Press, 1960.

Field, Leslie A., and Joyce W., eds. *Bernard Malamud and the Critics.* New York: New York University Press, 1970.

————, eds. *Bernard Malamud: A Collection of Critical Essays.* Twentieth Century Views. Englewood Cliffs, N.J.: Prentice-Hall, 1975.

Freedman, William. "From Bernard Malamud, with Discipline and Love." In *The Fifties: Fiction, Poetry, Drama.* Edited by Warren French. Deland, Fla.: Everett-Edwards, 1971.

Gollin, Rita K. "Malamud's Dubin and the Morality of Desire." *Papers on Language and Literature* 2, vol. 18 (Spring 1982): 198–207.

Goodheart, Eugene. "Fantasy and Reality." *Midstream* 7 (Autumn 1961): 102–05.

Grebstein, Sheldon N. "Bernard Malamud and the Jewish Movement." In *Contemporary American-Jewish Literature.* Edited by Irving Malin. Bloomington: Indiana University Press, 1973.

Guttmann, Allen. *The Jewish Writer in America: Assimilation and the Crisis of Identity.* New York: Oxford University Press, 1971.

Hicks, Granville. "Bernard Malamud." In *Literary Horizons: A Quarter Century of American Fiction.* New York: New York University Press, 1970.

Hoyt, Charles A. "Bernard Malamud and the New Romanticism." In *Contemporary American Novelists.* Edited by Harry Thornton Moore. Carbondale: Southern Illinois University Press, 1964.

Kennedy, J. Gerald. "Parody as Exorcism: 'The Raven' and 'The Jewbird'." *Genre* 2, vol. 13 (Summer 1980): 161–69.

Kermode, Frank. "Bernard Malamud." *The New Statesman* (March 30, 1962): 452–53.

Klein, Marcus. "Bernard Malamud: The Sadness of Goodness." In *After Alienation.* Cleveland, Ohio: World Publishing Co., 1964.

Leer, Norman. "Three American Novels and Contemporary Society: A Search for Commitment." *Wisconsin Studies in Contemporary Literature* 3 (Fall 1962): 67–85.

Locke, Richard. "Malamud's Reach." *Saturday Review* 6, vol. 6 (March 17, 1979): 67–69.

Malin, Irving. "Portrait of the Artist in Slapstick: Malamud's *Pictures of Fidelman.*" *The Literary Review* 1, vol. 24 (Fall 1980): 121–38.

Meeter, Glenn. *Bernard Malamud and Philip Roth: A Critical Essay.* Contemporary Writers in Christian Perspective Series. Grand Rapids, Mich.: William B. Eerdmans, 1968.

Mesher, David R. "Malamud's Jewish Metaphors." *Judaism* 1, vol. 26 (Winter 1977): 18–26.

Pinsker, Sanford. "The Schlemiel as Moral Bungler: Bernard Malamud's Ironic Heroes." In *The Schlemiel as Metaphor: Studies in the Yiddish and American Jewish Novel.* Carbondale: Southern Illinois University Press, 1971.

Podhoretz, Norman. "Achilles in Left Field." *Commentary* 3, vol. 15 (March 1953): 321-26.

———. "The New Nihilism in the American Novel." *Partisan Review* 25 (Fall 1958): 589–90.

Popkin, Henry. "Jewish Stories." *Kenyon Review* 20 (Autumn 1958): 637–41.

Rahv, Philip. Introduction to *A Malamud Reader.* Edited by Philip Rahv. New York: Farrar, Straus & Giroux, 1967.

Ratner, Marc L. "Style and Humanity in Malamud's Fiction." *Massachusetts Review* 5 (Summer 1964): 663–83.

Richman, Sidney. *Bernard Malamud.* U.S. Authors Series. New York: Twayne Publishers, 1966.

Roth, Philip. "Writing American Fiction." In *The American Novel Since World War II.* Edited by Marcus Klein. Greenwich, Conn.: Fawcett Publications, 1969.

———. "Imagining Jews." *The New York Review of Books* 15, vol. 21 (October 3, 1974): 22–28.

Rovit, Earl. "Bernard Malamud and the Jewish Literary Tradition." *Critique* 2, vol. 3 (Winter–Spring 1960): 3–10.

Schultz, Max F. "Bernard Malamud's Mythic Proletarians." In *Radical Sophistication: Studies in Contemporary Jewish-American Novelists.* Athens, Ohio: Ohio University Press, 1969.

Shear, Walter. "Culture Conflict in *The Assistant.*" *Midwest Quarterly* (Summer 1966): 367–80.

Siegel, Ben. "Victims in Motion: Bernard Malamud's Sad and Bitter Clowns." *Northwest Review* (Spring 1962): 69–80.

Solotaroff, Theodore. "Bernard Malamud's Fiction: The Old Life and the New." In *The Red Hot Vacuum and Other Pieces on the Writing of the Sixties*. New York: Atheneum, 1970.

Weinberg, Helen. *The New Novel in America: The Kafkan Mode in Contemporary Fiction*. Ithaca: Cornell University Press, 1970.

Acknowledgments

"The Qualified Encounter" by Ihab Hassan from *Radical Innocence: Studies in the Contemporary Novel* by Ihab Hassan, copyright © 1961 by Princeton University Press. Reprinted by permission.

"To Find the Westward Path" by John Hollander from *Partisan Review* 1, vol. 29, copyright © 1961 by *Partisan Review*. Reprinted by permission.

"The Magic and the Dread" by Alfred Kazin from *Contemporaries* by Alfred Kazin, copyright © 1962 by Atlantic-Little, Brown and Company, Inc. Reprinted by permission.

"The Economy of Love" by Jonathan Baumbach from *The Kenyon Review* 3, vol. 25, copyright © 1963 by Kenyon College. Reprinted by permission.

"Malamud and the Anthropomorphic Business" by Herbert Leibowitz from *The New Republic* 25, vol. 149, copyright © 1963 by Harrison-Blaine, Inc. Reprinted by permission.

"The Uses and Abuses of Commitment" by F. W. Dupee from *"The King of the Cats," and Other Remarks on Writers and Writing* by F. W. Dupee, copyright © 1984 by The University of Chicago Press. Reprinted by permission.

"*The Natural:* Malamud's World Ceres" by Earl R. Wasserman from *Centennial Review* 4, vol. 9, copyright © 1965 by *Centennial Review*. Reprinted by permission.

"A Pariah" by V. S. Pritchett from *New York Review of Books* 4, vol. 7, copyright © 1966 by *The New York Review*. Reprinted by permission.

"The Stories" by Sidney Richman from *Bernard Malamud* by Sidney Richman, copyright © 1966 by Twayne Publishers, Inc. Reprinted by permission.

"Four Versions of Pastoral" by James M. Mellard from *Critique* 2 vol. 9, copyright © 1967 by the Bolingbroke Society. Reprinted by permission.

"The Hero as Schnook" by Alan Warren Friedman from *Southern Review* 4, vol. 4, copyright © 1968 by Louisiana State University. Reprinted by permission.

226 • ACKNOWLEDGMENTS

"A New Life" by Tony Tanner from *City of Words: American Fiction 1950–1970* by Tony Tanner, copyright © 1971 by Tony Tanner. Reprinted by permission.

" 'All Men Are Jews' " by Allen Guttmann from *The Jewish Writer in America: Assimilation and the Crisis of Identity* by Allen Guttman, copyright © 1971 by Oxford University Press, Inc. Reprinted by permission.

"Requiem for the Schlemiel" by Ruth R. Wisse from *The Schlemiel as Modern Hero* by Ruth R. Wisse, copyright © 1971 by The University of Chicago Press. Reprinted by permission.

"The Artist in Hell" by Robert Ducharme from *Art and Idea in the Novels of Bernard Malamud* by Robert Ducharme, copyright © 1974 by Mouton & Company, Publishers. Reprinted by permission.

"The Return of the Repressed" by Mark Shechner from *The Nation* 10, vol. 228, copyright © 1979 by the Nation Associates, Inc. Reprinted by permission.

"A Theological Fantasy" by Robert Alter from *The New Republic* 12–13, vol. 187, copyright © 1982 by The New Republic, Inc. Reprinted by permission.

"*The Tenants:* 'Battering the Object' " by Alvin B. Kernan from *The Imaginary Library: An Essay on Literature and Society* by Alvin B. Kernan, copyright © 1982 by Princeton University Press. Reprinted by permission.

"In Search of the Real America" by Sam B. Girgus from *The New Covenant: Jewish Writers and the American Idea* by Sam B. Girgus, copyright © 1984 by The University of North Carolina Press. Reprinted by permission.

Index